Economics
DeMYSTiFieD®

Melanie Fox
Eric R. Dodge

New York   Chicago   San Francisco   Lisbon   London   Madrid   Mexico City
New Delhi   San Juan   Seoul   Singapore   Sydney   Toronto

1 2 3 4 5 6 7 8 9 0   DOC/DOC   1 8 7 6 5   4 3 2

ISBN: 978-0-07-178283-8
MHID: 0-07-178283-4

e-ISBN: 978-0-07-178284-5
e-MHID: 0-07-178284-2

This publication is designed to provide accurate and authoritative information in regard to the subject matter covered. It is sold with the understanding that neither the author nor the publisher is engaged in rendering legal, accounting, securities trading, or other professional services. If legal advice or other expert assistance is required, the services of a competent professional person should be sought.

> —*From a Declaration of Principles Jointly Adopted by a Committee of the American Bar Association and a Committee of Publishers and Associations*

Trademarks: McGraw-Hill, the McGraw-Hill Publishing logo, DeMYSTiFieD®, and related trade dress are trademarks or registered trademarks of The McGraw-Hill Companies and/or its affiliates in the United States and other countries and may not be used without written permission. All other trademarks are the property of their respective owners. The McGraw-Hill Companies is not associated with any product or vendor mentioned in this book.

McGraw-Hill books are available at special quantity discounts to use as premiums and sales promotions or for use in corporate training programs. To contact a representative, please e-mail us at bulksales@mcgraw-hill.com.

This book is printed on acid-free paper.

To our boys:

Eli & Alex and Max

About the Authors

Melanie Fox was born and raised in the Montrose area in Houston, Texas. She attended the University of Houston, where she studied Economics and Russian. After she received her bachelor's degree in Economics, she was awarded a Stella Earhardt Fellowship and continued at the University of Houston, where she received master's and doctoral degrees in Economics. More recently, she expanded her training to include a graduate certificate in Public Health. Since 2005, she has been teaching economics at Austin College, where she teaches introductory economics, health economics, development economics, monetary theory, labor economics, game theory, and research methods. In addition to receiving several awards for teaching, her publications have appeared in the *American Economic Review* and *Economics and Human Biology*. In 2006, she co-created the Economics Scholars Program with the Federal Reserve Bank of Dallas to motivate undergraduate research in economics. She has served as a faculty consultant for the Educational Testing Service, reading AP Economics free-response exams, since 2007. In her spare time, she enjoys cooking, baking, knitting, and running, and hopes to some day get back in the left seat of a cockpit again. She lives in Sherman, Texas, with her son, Max.

Eric Dodge was born and raised in Portland, Oregon, and received his BA in Business Administration from the University of Puget Sound and his MA and PhD in Economics from the University of Oregon. Since 1995, he has been teaching economics at Hanover College in Hanover, Indiana. He teaches a wide variety of courses, such as principles of microeconomics, principles of macroeconomics, intermediate microeconomics, environmental economics, labor economics, industrial organization, quantitative methods for economics and business, econometrics, and the benefits and costs of dams. He is the author of *5 Steps to a 5 in Microeconomics/Macroeconomics* and the Teacher's Resource Binder and Test Bank for the popular Advanced Placement textbook *Krugman's Economics for AP*. Since 2000, he has served as a consultant for the AP economics program and has been a reader of free-response questions, table leader, and question leader at the annual AP Economics Reading. When he is not teaching or writing about economics, he enjoys hiking, traveling, home brewing, and "playing" golf. Eric lives in Madison, Indiana, with his son, Eli.

Contents

Introduction

The book you are holding is a good start toward learning basic economic concepts. If you have bought (or are thinking about buying) this book, you are probably one of the following:

A college student who needs a supplement to a textbook in a course on principles of microeconomics, principles of macroeconomics, fundamentals of economics, or some other similar introductory course

A college student in an introductory course who needs some additional practice problems to prepare for an exam

A high school student taking Advanced Placement (AP) courses in microeconomics or macroeconomics for college credit

A student in an undergraduate or MBA program who needs a quick go-to guide for reference in intermediate or advanced economics courses

Someone who just wants to study up on economics on his own so that he can better understand news, business, and government actions

This book gives an overview of the topics that would typically be covered in an introductory course in economics. Typically, this is done in a two-semester sequence of microeconomics and macroeconomics. In these courses, you get the basic toolkit of skills and thinking style that are used in economic problem solving. Completion of these courses prepares students for more advanced analysis in intermediate microeconomics and intermediate macroeconomics, courses that typically expand the skills learned in principles courses by using more rigorous methods (that is to say, using more advanced math). Once students have a good grounding in the basic tools of economics, they are ready to apply them to some of the special topics you see outlined in the curriculum guide inside the back cover of this book.

We think you will find this book helpful and informative, as well as making a very "wonkish" topic approachable. That being said, there are a few things you should consider as you begin using this book. First, economics is not an easy subject, and it is not one that you can learn by just reading. In our many years of teaching introductory courses, we have seen that nearly every student who falters does so because she makes the same mistake—reading the material thoroughly and believing that this is sufficient. Unlike courses that you might take in humanities or even other social sciences, this is a necessary first step, but in order to understand economics, you really need to be *doing* economics.

Second, this is not a comprehensive resource on all things economics. In fact, it's a "bare-bones" approach to understanding the basic ideas. We try to provide illustrative examples of the concepts covered, but this book is not saturated with the examples, inset boxes of relevant news stories, and slick graphics that have come to characterize the modern introductory economics textbook.

How to Use This Book

This book assumes that you have no background in economics, but that you are able to do high school–level mathematics. It may have been a while since you have used the kind of math and graphs included in this book, so we have included an appendix to give you a quick review.

The most important thing to remember as you study each chapter is that virtually every concept in economics can be broken down into three parts: the math (a formula representing the concept), the graph (a picture illustrating the concept and the formula), and the story (the explanation and verbal analysis of the concept). This is one of the reasons that many people find economics so challenging—most people are good at one or two of these things, but not so great in at least one of them. The good news is that if you know two of the three parts well, you can use them to help you remember the third.

As each concept is introduced, we walk you through the math (if math is involved), the graph, and the story behind the concept. To get the most out of this book, you need to do this yourself. This means that you need to go through the steps of solving each equation that is presented. Students almost universally struggle with using graphs on exams because they waited until the exam to get comfortable with replicating and using graphs. When you see a graph, replicate it and consider how you might graph a different situation from the one the example presents. Finally, be able to translate any graph or any formula you see into words to get used to providing analysis.

To give you practice in applying these economic tools and practice in using economic reasoning, there is a quiz at the end of each chapter. The best way to use each chapter is to go through all of the material thoroughly, working through the examples on paper, then take the end-of-chapter quiz. We recommend that you treat this as you would a closed-book exam and answer all the questions in a single sitting before reviewing the answers. Should you respond incorrectly to a question, don't just reread that section of the chapter and note the correct answer. Instead, try to think about where you went wrong in either your reasoning or your analysis. Give yourself some time to let this sink in, then retake the exam, but this time justify to yourself why a particular answer is correct, rather than just putting down the appropriate letter. Once you can do this comfortably with at least 90 percent of the quiz, you are ready to move on.

At the end of the book, we have included a 100-question final exam to test your knowledge of the content.

Economics is typically broken down into macroeconomics and microeconomics, but we have compiled these subjects into one book. This means that you may be using this as a supplement to either a macroeconomics or microeconomics course and don't need the other material. If you are using this to supplement a microeconomics course, you should focus on Chapters 1 to 10 and 18 to 20, and if you are using this to supplement a macroeconomics course, you should focus on Chapters 1 to 6 and 11 to 20. The final exam includes questions from both microeconomics and macroeconomics, but if you are focusing on microeconomics, you can stick to questions 1–50 and 86–100, and if you are focusing on macroeconomics, you can do questions 1–30 and 51–100.

We think that an important point needs to be made about graphs in the quizzes and final exams. Standardized multiple-choice and true-false test formats such as these don't require you to create graphs, but we think you should try to graph the situation in the question if at all possible for a couple of reasons. First and foremost, a graph is a tool of analysis. We have found that students can sometimes reason themselves into a corner if they don't use some other type of analysis (such as math or graphing) to help them work through their reasoning. Second, even though these quizzes and the final exam aren't grading you on your ability to reason by creating graphs, we can virtually guarantee that any college course you take will grade you on your ability to create a graph. Therefore, you should take every opportunity you can to practice this important skill.

We hope you enjoy learning economics!

chapter **1**

Introduction to Economics

This chapter introduces what economics is and why people are sometimes confused by the subject. In addition to the jargon that economists use, economics requires a different way of thinking about problems from the way most people are used to. While economists disagree on many topics, there are some basic principles that they do agree on.

CHAPTER OBJECTIVES

After completing this chapter, the student should be able to:

1. Describe the reasons why many people struggle with economics.

2. Describe what is meant by economic resources.

3. Define opportunity costs and explain why opportunity costs are considered more important than explicit costs.

4. Describe what is meant when economists say that someone thinks "rationally."

5. Define microeconomics and macroeconomics and be able to describe the difference between them.

As two self-described "econ-nerds," your coauthors have each, more times than we care to admit, engaged in versions of the following conversation:

New person (NP): "So what do you do?"

EN (politely, but vaguely): "I'm a college professor."

NP (sensing a productive and perhaps interesting conversation): "Oh really? What do you teach?"

EN (sensing where this is heading): "Economics."

NP (awkward pause, followed by one of the following):

    a. "Wow! I hated that class in college!"

    b. "Really? Where do you think the stock market is headed?"

    c. "Now there's something that I'll *never* understand."

EN (a little sheepishly): "Yes, I hear that a lot. Did you try that cheese platter? It's amazing!"

So why do so many people we meet have such adverse reactions to the topic? And why are these people so ready to share with us the reasons why they hate economics? We think there are three main factors:

1. **Language barriers.** Economists have unintentionally made their social interactions more difficult because they use complicated language to communicate simple ideas. Economists have managed to make common sense as difficult as possible. People read the headlines on "double-dip recession" or "currency revaluation" and just don't want to read any further. And who can blame them? In the interest of demystifying economics for you, we define some of these key words and phrases in a way that we think translates the complex language of economists into something simpler and more understandable.

2. **Economists don't always agree.** People often hear two economists making very different predictions about the same topic. One economist says that universal health care will reduce the federal budget deficit, while another states, with equal confidence, that universal health care will add to the deficit. This is very frustrating to people who genuinely want to be informed about such things. This frustration causes many people to tune out the debate and conclude that economists really don't know what they're talking about.

How can it be that these two "experts" can make such conflicting predictions? The explanation lies in the way in which economists do their research. Economists use theoretical models, simplified versions of the complex world, to predict how changes in one thing will affect other things. Underlying these economic models are assumptions concerning the way the world works. For example, the first economist believes that even if it increases the size of government, universal health care will push the price of medical services downward, making it less expensive for even a larger government to insure people and thus reducing the deficit. The second economist believes that, while the first argument might have some merit, the increased size and cost of the government bureaucracy will outweigh the cost savings for medical services. For the most part, the public wants easy answers to policy questions like the impact of universal health care, but the world is a very complicated place. The economists try to inform these debates with their best economic models, and different assumptions will often produce different predictions. When we look at some of these models, we try to demystify how critical some of these assumptions can be.

3. **Math is involved** (and graphs, but those are really just math in picture form). The state of Kentucky, like many states faced with a budget deficit, recently increased the tax on tobacco products. Most people understand that a higher tax on tobacco will increase the price of cigarettes to the consumer, and that fewer cartons of cigarettes will be purchased at the higher price. But economists ask a very important question that can be answered only with a little bit of math: "If the price of cigarettes is rising and fewer cigarettes are being bought, will the government actually receive more or less tax revenue from cigarette sales?" While much of the economic research out there involves some high-level math, we believe that most of economics can be demystified with just a few simple mathematical techniques and graphical analysis. The appendix to this chapter provides a little review if you think it's necessary.

Before we get into the real guts of the economic language, models, and graphical analysis, let's cover just a few of the basics that all economists can agree upon, starting with how economics is divided. When the focus is on the decisions made by individuals, households, firms, or industries, we are referring to the subfield of *microeconomics*. When the focus is on the decisions made by nations, we are referring to *macroeconomics*.

Scarcity

There is no fundamental economic concept that enjoys as much universal support from economists as does the concept of *scarcity*. Scarcity is the unfortunate imbalance between our limitless wants and needs and the limited resources that are available to satisfy those wants and needs. Scarcity is really very simple, but it drives all of our decision making and our behavior, and it forces us to choose some goods at the expense of other goods. For example, if a consumer chooses to purchase a $4 gallon of gasoline with her limited income, she cannot use that $4 to consume something else. If a nation chooses to spend $4 billion to improve the highway system, that $4 billion cannot be spent on education. The field of economics studies how society, whether it is the single consumer or a nation, can best make those decisions when confronted with scarcity.

Four Economic Resources

A key component of the notion of scarcity is the fact that society's enjoyment of goods and services is limited by the resources available to us. Economists typically recognize four categories of resources that are available to produce the items that we want.

1. **Labor** (usually abbreviated as L). The collective size and effort of a nation's workforce.
2. **Capital** (K). The manufactured productive assets (buildings, tools, and machinery) in the nation.
3. **Land** (or natural resources, l). The nation's stock of minerals, timber, fisheries, water, and so on.
4. **Entrepreneurship** (or technology, A). The nation's ability to creatively combine the labor, capital, and land to produce goods and services.

Still Struggling

Some students may be confused by the fact that the one "resource" they think is most associated with economics is not here: money. That is because money is not a resource. In economics, a resource is something that is used to create other things of value. For instance, a house is made by combining labor for the construction workers, capital in the form of equipment used to build the house, land in the form of the lumber and energy used, and entrepreneurship in the form of the "know-how" required to put the house together. Money isn't actually used to build the house; it just facilitates the exchange of all these things.

When you hear nerdy economists talk about resources, they are referring to those listed earlier. However, we often hear noneconomists talk about a firm that needs to "find additional resources" or "raise more capital." We believe that these statements are inaccurate, because the people making them are usually referring to the firm's need for more cash or other forms of money. Cash and other forms of money are not resources. They simply make it easier to obtain the needed resources. For example, suppose an entrepreneur wants to produce tables and sell those tables at his furniture store. He will certainly need cash to begin this company, but the cash is simply used to purchase the economic resources (labor, capital, and natural resources) that will actually be involved in the production of tables.

Opportunity Cost

Scarcity requires us to make choices. A consumer who chooses to purchase gasoline rather than a new pair of running shoes has given up the enjoyment that she would have received from the new shoes. Economists refer to this sacrifice as the *opportunity cost*. The opportunity cost of a choice, like the gasoline, is measured as the value of the next best thing the consumer has given up. How do we place a value on the enjoyment that the running shoes would have provided to our consumer? Economists believe that the price of a product, in this case the shoes, provides a pretty good idea of how much value consumers place upon it. After all, if people are paying $100 for a pair of running shoes, they must believe that they will receive at least $100 worth of enjoyment from them.

Here is where economists tend to think a little differently from "normal people." To an economist, the opportunity cost is more important than the cost measured in dollar terms. Why? Well, opportunity costs reflect what the true cost of something is. Consider the dollar price of something (also called an *explicit price*) like a concert ticket. If it is for an extremely popular band, chances are that you are going to have to wait in line to ensure that you get a ticket. So even if the face value of the ticket is only $80, the other costs involved may be substantial and may even outweigh the dollar price of the ticket. The true cost of the ticket was all the other things you could have purchased with the $80 plus the opportunity cost of the time involved in purchasing the ticket.

Rational Decision Making

Let's return to the example of the consumer who buys gasoline instead of running shoes. Why did she do this? An economist believes that she has examined her choices and, within the limits of her budget, has made a *rational decision* to forgo the shoes and purchase the gasoline because doing so makes her better off. Specifically, we assume that the rational consumer goes through life making decisions that will maximize her *utility* (the word that economists use to describe happiness, usefulness, or economic benefit). Rational consumers seek those things that make them the most happy (provide the most benefit) and avoid those things that make them unhappy (incur lots of cost). In other words, we all attempt to seek economic benefit and attempt to avoid economic cost. We will develop the model of consumer choice in Chapter 2.

Does that mean that consumers always make the best decisions? Not necessarily. All agents make decisions based on the information that they have available. If that information is incomplete or flawed, they might make a decision that they *think* will make them better off but that in fact does not. A classic example of this is a purchase that generates pollution. When gasoline, a polluting substance, is fairly cheap, people might end up consuming "too much" because they aren't aware of the pollution that it causes. We talk about this later in Chapter 18. What rationality does mean, however, is that decision makers do not knowingly make themselves worse off.

Marginal Analysis

If we accept the premise that consumers seek economic benefit and avoid economic cost, then we must assume that people try to maximize the difference, or *net benefit*, between the economic benefits they enjoy and the economic costs they incur through their decisions.

People often make decisions to consume or do something on an incremental basis, and at each step of these incremental decisions, they must reevaluate the benefits that they receive and the costs that they incur. Economists refer to the additional benefit received from the next unit of a good as the *marginal benefit* and the additional cost incurred from the next unit as the *marginal cost*.

For example, if I believe that I will enjoy $6 of economic benefit from my first cup of coffee, and that cup of coffee comes at a cost of $2, I am receiving $4 of net benefit from the coffee and it would be rational for me to purchase it. Suppose the second cup of coffee would provide me with only $4 of marginal benefit. Should I purchase the second cup? Yes, because I will still enjoy $2 of net benefit ($4 of enjoyment minus $2 of marginal cost) from the coffee. Maybe the third cup of coffee provides me with only $2 of marginal benefit. Should I buy it? Yes, because there is a perfect trade-off between $2 of marginal benefit and $2 of marginal cost. However, suppose the fourth cup of coffee makes me extremely jittery and won't give me any marginal benefit. As a rational consumer, I will not buy the fourth cup of coffee because the marginal cost is greater than the marginal benefit. In fact, the fifth cup kind of makes me nauseous and imposes negative $2 of marginal benefit, so I clearly won't purchase *that* one either.

The marginal benefits and costs from my coffee consumption are described in Table 1-1.

TABLE 1-1 Marginal Benefits and Marginal Costs of Coffee Consumption				
Cups of Coffee	**Marginal Benefit**	**Marginal Cost**	**Net Benefit**	**Should I Buy It?**
1	$6	$2	$4	Yes
2	$4	$2	$2	Yes
3	$2	$2	$0	Yes
4	$0	$2	−$2	No
5	−$2	$2	−$4	No

So long as the marginal benefit of the next unit of something is at least as great as the marginal cost of that unit, the consumer should always purchase the next unit. By consuming three cups of coffee, I receive a total benefit of $6 ($4 + $2 + $0), and thus by making my decisions "at the margin," I have picked the quantity of coffee that maximizes my total net benefit. Had I irrationally consumed the fourth cup, my total net benefit from coffee would have fallen to $4, so I will not make this choice. We will show in several upcoming chapters the importance of *marginal analysis* in economic decision making.

A common approach that people use when they think about costs and benefits is to think about things "on average." This can lead to irrational behavior. For example, consider the previous example about coffee. If I had consumed five cups of coffee, I would have enjoyed total benefit of $10 ($6 + $4 + $2 + $0 − $2), and so, on average, each cup provided an average benefit of $2 per cup. Given this calculation, one might be tempted to say that each cup was "worth" the price of $2 per cup. Was it? No! Drinking that fifth cup would actually have made me worse off.

TIP   *Whenever you see the word* marginal *in economics, you should be thinking "the last one" or "the next one." Our example here involves buyers, but marginal analysis applies to both buyers and sellers.*

Economic Models

A paper airplane is not a real airplane, but it has some of the important features of the real thing. We know that a real airplane is much more complex, but a person can see a lot about the fundamentals of aerodynamics by watching the way a paper airplane glides through the air. In the same way, economic models attempt to depict the decisions that consumers, firms, and nations make in a very complex, dynamic world. If a simple economic model can distill these complexities into something that reasonably predicts the outcome of economic decisions, it can be a powerful tool for us.

One important feature of economic models is the need to make assumptions about behavior. For example, in the model of consumer behavior in Chapter 2, we assume that consumers seek to maximize their utility within the constraints of their budget. Later in the book, we assume that firms seek to maximize their profits. Given these assumptions of behavior, we can study how choices are made to pursue the goals of utility (or profit) maximization.

Economic models can be very useful when they can predict how the change in one variable affects the decisions that consumers and firms make. The problem is that, in the real world, there are many variables that are changing at the same time. This makes it very difficult to isolate the impact of a change in just one key variable. Therefore, a second important feature of economic models is the use of the *ceteris paribus*, or "all other factors held constant," condition.

For example, we might wish to study how consumers react to a higher tax on electricity. We realize that, in reality, there are many factors that affect a consumer's decision to buy a certain amount of electricity for his household. The economist's model will predict that an increased tax on electricity, holding all other factors (like consumer income, weather conditions, and so on) constant, should prompt consumers to purchase less electricity. In fact, it is the *ceteris paribus* assumption that allows us to study a fundamental economic model such as the model of demand and supply.

Summary

This chapter described some of the basic ideas of economics. Scarcity is the basis of economics, as we all have unlimited wants, but we are faced with limitations on how we can satisfy those wants. Opportunity costs are the most relevant costs to an economic thinker, because the value of the next best alternative to something is what you are really giving up to get that thing. We use resources to try to create things that will satisfy our wants, and resources can be broken down into four categories: land, labor, capital, and entrepreneurship. A major assumption that economists make about agents is that they will act rationally, meaning mainly that they tend to make decisions based on the marginal benefits and marginal costs of those decisions. The basic idea behind economics is that every agent tries to make herself as well off as possible, and economics just describes the way in which agents go about making that happen. In the next chapter, we turn our attention to exactly how one group of agents, buyers, tries to make itself as happy as possible.

Appendix
Math and Graph Review

There are two reasons that students tend to fear economics: math and graphs. The good news is that the math isn't really all that complicated; in fact, you have almost certainly seen math just like it before. The math that is used in most introductory economics courses is no more complicated than what you did your first or second year of high school. There is a (very) little bit of algebra, an even smaller amount of geometry, and a lot of graphical analysis.

To lessen your anxiety, this appendix will walk you through the graphing and math that you are likely to encounter in an introductory economics course. The most common math you will encounter in such a course can be broken down into four categories: graphing, simple calculations, calculating area, and solving a system of two equations. Here is a tip before we continue: every graph and every equation you see, you should also be *drawing* and *writing down*. The best way to get experience using these types of analysis is to take pen to paper and practice, practice, practice.

Graphs—Pictures of Equations

A graph is simply a pictorial representation of the relationship between two things. In previous math courses, you have probably seen graphs represented on the *Cartesian coordinate system*. In this system, the "two things" are x and y, which are represented on the two axes (or sides) of a graph, and any lines or points on the graph show the particular value of y that goes with a particular value of x. In the case of a line, there is usually an equation that describes the relationship between x and y mathematically, and the graph simply translates that equation into a picture. Each of the axes represents a number line, and the axes intersect each other at zero.

The Cartesian coordinate system can be broken down into four quarters, I, II, III and IV, as shown in Figure 1-1. Each point on the Cartesian plane is a representation of a combination of a particular value of x and a value y associated with that value of x. For instance, in Figure 1-1, point A represents $(x = 0, y = 4)$, and point E represents $(x = -4, y = 4)$.

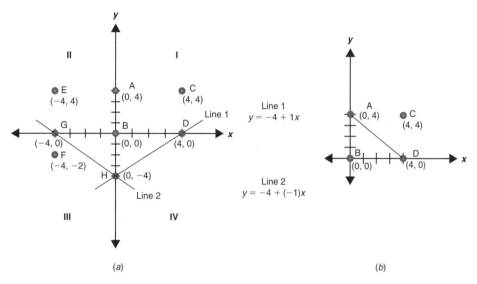

(a)   (b)

FIGURE 1-1 · (a) The Cartesian Coordinate System; (b) the Plane Typically Used in Economics. Each point represents a combination of coordinates (x, y). For the points in (a), the coordinates are A (0, 4), B (0, 0), C (4, 4), D (4, 0), E (−4, 4), F (−4, −2), G (−4, 0), and H (0, −4).

Line 1 in Figure 1-1a is a pictorial representation of the equation $y = -4 + (1) \times x$. Given the equation of this line, we can find the values of y that correspond to different values of x. For instance, point D on Figure 1-1a corresponds to the point $(4, 0)$. Plugging the value of x into the equation, we get $y = -4 + (1) \times 4 = 0$. Similarly, point H corresponds to the point $(0, -4)$, and if we plug the value of x ($x = 0$) into the equation, $y = -4 + 0 = -4$. The line is merely the description of all the possible values of y that will correspond to any given value of x.

There are two things to note about the relationship between the equation and the graph. First, -4 in the equation for line 1 is the point at which the line crosses the y axis. Second, the slope of this line is equal to $+1$, meaning that every time x increases by 1 unit, the corresponding value of y will also increase by 1 unit. In general, the equation of any line in the Cartesian plane can be expressed as $y = a + b \times x$, where a represents the y intercept and b is the slope of the line. In our example, $a = -4$ and $b = 1$. Any time that b is a positive number, the line slopes upward. On the other hand, consider line 2 in Figure 1-1a. The equation for this line is $y = -4 + (-1) \times x$. This equation is different from line 1 only in slope—the lines representing both equations cross the y axis at the same point, but line 2 is downward-sloping, so that every increase of 1 unit in x leads to a *decrease* of 1 unit in y.

Here is the good news about graphs in economics: we focus almost exclusively on quadrant I, which means that we get to simplify this even further. As practice, try recreating Figure 1-1a and then 1-1b, on graph paper if it helps, using the coordinates listed beneath each. Then, check your work against the graph. Next, try to figure out the equation of the line in Figure 1-1b using the $y = a + bx$ format. (We'll give you the answer at the end of the appendix.)

TIP   *When the value of b changes, the slope of the line ($y = a + b \times x$) changes. Positive values of b indicate a line that slopes upward, and negative values of b indicate a line that slopes downward. A line with a slope of zero is completely horizontal (meaning that y never changes, regardless of the value of x).*
When the value of a changes, the point at which the line intercepts the vertical axis (also known as the y-intercept) changes.

Where graphs in economics differ from the graphs you've seen before is that we are interested in the relationship between the things that x and y represent. Suppose we conducted a survey and asked four people what they had ordered for lunch at a fast food restaurant in terms of burgers and fries. We will let x indicate how many burgers each respondent ordered and y indicate how many fries each respondent ordered, and adapt Figure 1-1b to reflect this change, as shown in Figure 1-2. Each point now corresponds with the particular combination of hamburgers and fries that a particular person ordered. Thus, person A ordered no burgers and 4 orders of fries, person C ordered 4 burgers and 4 orders of fries, and so on.

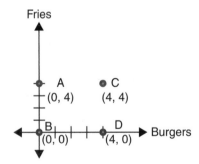

FIGURE 1-2 • Responses to a Survey on Fast Food Orders

Let's take another example and look at the relationship between the price of a good and how much of that good people are willing to buy. Suppose that we know for certain that nobody will ever buy a particular good, purpletts, if the price of it is greater than $20. In other words, if price is our y variable, then if $y > 20$, $x = 0$. We also know that once the price dips below $20, people *will* buy the good. In fact, for every $1 that the price drops, people will buy 1 more purplett. So if the price of purpletts is $19, people will buy a total of 1 purplett; if the price drops to $18, people will buy a total of 2 purpletts; and so on. We could figure this out for all possible quantities using the following equation:

$$20 = 20 - 1 \times x \rightarrow x = 0$$
$$19 = 20 - 1 \times x \rightarrow x = 1$$
$$18 = 20 - 1 \times x \rightarrow x = 2$$
$$17 = 20 - 1 \times x \rightarrow x = 3$$

and so on.

In equation form, we could represent the relationship between the price of purpletts and the amount of purpletts that people buy as $P = 20 - 1Q$, where 20 is the price axis intercept ($a = 20$) and the slope of the line is -1 ($b = -1$). Graphically, we show this in Figure 1-3. Try creating Figure 1-3 on your own, calculating the quantities that are bought at various prices and then plotting those combinations on your graph. As you recreate Figure 1-3 on your own, notice that each value of Q corresponds with a value of P according to the demand equation. For instance, when the price of purpletts is $10 each, people are willing and able to buy 10 purpletts, which corresponds to the point $(10, \$10)$ on the curve on the graph.

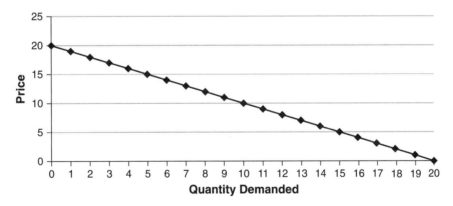

FIGURE 1-3 · Demand for Purpletts

In Chapter 3 we will learn that when any of the determinants of demand change, the demand curve shifts. A shift of a curve is a change of the intercept (a), not the slope. For instance, a shift of the demand curve $P = 20 - 1Q$ to the right would mean that for any given price, more Q is demanded. Such a shift is shown in Figure 1-4. Note that on the curve Demand 1, when $P = 10$, people

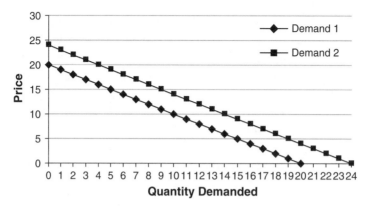

FIGURE 1-4 • Shifting Demand for Purpletts

were willing and able to buy 10 units of purpletts, and when $P = 20$, people were willing and able to buy 0 units of purpletts. Now that demand has shifted out to Demand 2, when $P = 10$, people are willing and able to buy 14 units of purpletts, and when $P = 20$, people are willing and able to buy 4 units of purpletts. This new demand curve is consistent with an equation $P = 24 - 1Q$.

TIP *A good application of graphs is to see the idea of* ceteris paribus *in action. Recall that* ceteris paribus *means "all else equal," meaning that nothing is changing except the particular problem that you are investigating. When we are looking at the different quantities that people buy when the price changes, the only thing that is changing is the price (and people are responding to that). In this case, we assume that other things are not changing in order to determine what people are willing to buy at various prices. Graphically, that means that the line representing this, and the equation of that line, are not changing; we are just plugging in various values. On the other hand, if something else had changed, like one of the determinants of demand, the entire curve and the equation would change as well.*

Of course, you can also have relationships that are nonlinear, that is, that are not straight lines. A common nonlinear function (that is, the equation that represents a curve) that you see in economics is *binomial*. These types of functions typically take the form $y = a + bx + cx^2$. These functions are often called *quadratic* functions and will have either a "U" shape or a "hill" shape.

For example, suppose that corn production (y) is a binomial function of rainfall (x) such that $y = 0 + 100x - \frac{1}{2}x^2$. (Note: We might model corn production this way because, in agriculture, there can be both insufficient rain and too much rain.) Figure 1-5 shows how this function would look in a graph. Notice that at first, more rain causes corn production to "grow," but the additional rain has a

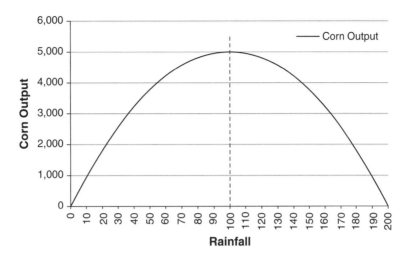

FIGURE 1-5 • Corn Output as a Function of Rainfall

smaller and smaller impact on the harvest. In fact, at $x = 100$, corn production is as great as it can be. If the crops get even more rain, output will actually begin to decline, and eventually the entire crop will be wiped out.

Unlike a straight line, which has a constant slope, these binomial functions have a slope that varies. The corn production function begins with a positive slope (more rain = more corn), but that slope begins to become less and less positive; the function is increasing at a decreasing rate. When we reach the maximum of the function, the slope is equal to zero. Beyond the maximum point, the function has a negative slope, and as rainfall increases, that slope becomes even more negative; the function is decreasing at an increasing rate.

Economists also study binomial functions that have a U shape (think of this as the hill shape, just upside down). Average total cost (ATC) curves are typically described this way. Let's suppose that average total cost (y) is a function of a firm's output (x) such that $y = 100 - 10x + \frac{1}{2}x^2$. This ATC function is shown in Figure 1-6. We see that, at first, additional output causes ATC to decline, but at 10 units of output, the ATC is minimized. Beyond 10 units of output, ATC is rising. We discuss cost curves in much more detail in Chapter 4 of the book.

Again, the slope of this function is not constant. At first the slope is negative and steep, but as output increases, the slope becomes less steep; the function is decreasing at a decreasing rate. The slope is zero at the minimum point, and from that point forward, the slope is positive and is becoming steeper; the function is increasing at an increasing rate.

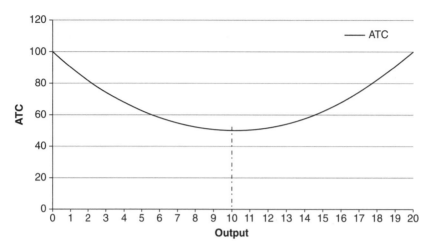

FIGURE 1-6 · Average Total Cost as a Function of Output

Simple Math: Calculating Percentages

Economists are frequently interested in the relative change in something rather than the actual amount of the change. For instance, suppose Eli gets an increase of $10 in his weekly allowance and Max gets an increase of $5 in his weekly allowance. Eli got the better increase . . . or did he? We actually can't tell who was made better off than he was previously without knowing what their allowances were before. Suppose that, prior to the increase, Eli got an allowance of $40 a week and Max got an allowance of $4. Max's allowance has more than doubled, meaning that Max can buy more than twice as much stuff as he could before, but Eli's didn't double, so he can't buy twice as much as he could before. Max's "raise" was clearly better in terms of the magnitude of the change.

An easy way to control for relative differences is to compute a percentage. Doing so is actually fairly simple and most easily illustrated with an example. Suppose you have a box of 50 chocolates, and 7 of them have nougat filling inside. You are interested in the percentage of nougat-filled chocolates in a box. To find this you divide the value of the part you are interested by the value of the whole and multiply that number by 100 to get the percentage. In this case:

$$(\text{Part/whole}) \times 100 = \text{percentage} \qquad (1.1)$$

$$(7/50) \times 100 = 0.14 \times 100 = 14\% \qquad (1.2)$$

Therefore, the box of chocolates is 14 percent nougat-filled. Note that we can rearrange this to get a different type of problem. Suppose we solved instead for "Part" by rearranging Eq. (1.1) to get:

$$\text{Part} = (\text{percentage}/100) \times \text{whole} \qquad (1.3)$$

We could use this to find what the actual number of something was, given the percentage and the whole. For instance, suppose we saw another box of chocolates that had 80 chocolates in it (the whole) and an advertisement saying that it had 15 percent nougat-filled chocolates inside. We could then determine the actual number of nougat-filled chocolates in this box by applying Eq. (1.3):

$$\text{Part} = (15\%/100) \times 80 = 0.15 \times 80 = 12 \qquad (1.4)$$

So the box of 80 chocolates that is 15 percent nougat-filled chocolates has 12 nougat-filled chocolates in it.

Another useful application is calculating percentage changes. Let's return to Max and Eli. We would like to know the exact percentage increase in the allowances that each of them received, so that we can compare their relative raises. To find the percentage change in a value, we calculate:

$$[(\text{New value} - \text{old value})/\text{old value}]$$
$$\times 100 = \% \text{ change from old to new} \qquad (1.5)$$

For instance, Max originally had an allowance of $4, and he gets a $5 raise, so that he now gets a $9 weekly allowance. The new value here is $9 and the old value is $4, so plugging these into Eq. (1.5) gives us:

$$[(\$9 - \$4)/\$4] \times 100 = (\$5/\$4) \times 100 = 125\% \qquad (1.6)$$

Therefore, Max's allowance went up 125 percent (note that an increase of 100 percent in something means that it doubles, so 125 percent would reflect an allowance that more than doubled). Let's now compare this to Eli. Before his raise, Eli got $40 per week (the old value), and after the $10 raise, he gets $50 per week (new value). Plugging this in, we get:

$$[(\$50 - \$40)/\$40] \times 100 = 0.25 \times 100 = 25\% \qquad (1.7)$$

Both Eli and Max are better off than they were before. In pure dollars, Eli got a higher raise. But individually, in terms of the allowance they now have relative to the allowance they used to get, Max is now relatively better off than Eli.

TIP *Percentage changes are calculated frequently in economics. Some common applications of percentage change that you see in an introductory economics course are in calculating elasticities and changes in economic output, growth, inflation, and unemployment.*

Simple Geometry: Areas

If you have memories (or even nightmares) of having to memorize endless formulas for endless shapes and other complicated elements of geometry, fear not. The geometry you are likely to encounter in an introductory economics course almost always involves only two things: the area of a rectangle and the area of a triangle. Luckily, these usually even have very intuitive interpretations.

Suppose you have an empty, rectangle-shaped bathroom that you want to put flooring into, and the bathroom is 12 feet long and 5 feet wide. Figure 1-7 shows the shape of such a bathroom. However, it is typical to express shapes in terms of their base and their height. Here, that would mean a base (length) of 12 feet and a height (width) of 5 feet.

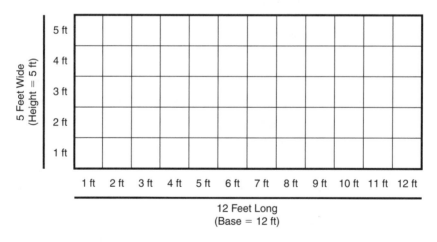

FIGURE 1-7 · Shape of a Bathroom

In order to find the appropriate amount of flooring to buy, we need to know the *area* of the bathroom. To find the area of a rectangle, we simply calculate the following:

$$\text{Area of a rectangle} = \text{base} \times \text{height} \tag{1.8}$$

For our bathroom, the length is 12 feet and the width is 5 feet, so the area is 12 ft × 5 ft = 60 ft². It would take 60 square feet of flooring in order to cover this area. Suppose the local hardware store sold square tiles that were 1 foot on each side (or the area of each tile was 1 ft × 1 ft = 1 ft²). It would therefore take 60 of these tiles to cover the floor.

Now let's consider an example that uses a graph. Suppose Margaret is selling pies for $6 each, so every time she sells a pie, she gets another $6. If she sells 5 pies, she makes a total of $30 (from 5 × $6). We could create a graph that shows how much money she earns (also called *revenue*). Figure 1-8 shows Margaret's earnings. Point A represents the quantity that Margaret sells (5) and the price that Margaret gets ($6), and point A also defines a rectangle with a base of 5 and a height of $6. When we find the area of that rectangle, we are finding the revenue that Margaret earns. Areas of rectangles can illustrate economic variables such as total earnings (or conversely, the total amount of spending), and also profit.

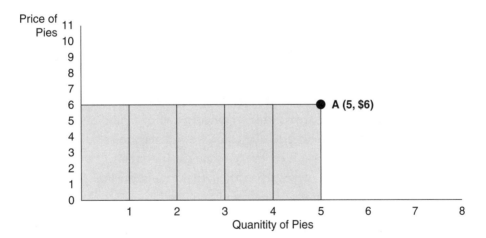

FIGURE 1-8 • Margaret's Revenue from Pies

The other common area you will need to calculate is the area of a triangle. Economists often use triangles to describe consumer and producer surplus. Suppose there is another room in your house that is 8 feet long and 15 feet wide, but you want to divide the room in half so that there are two triangles of different-colored flooring. Figure 1-9 shows just such a room.

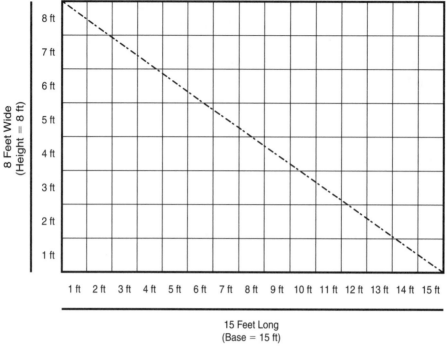

FIGURE 1-9 • Room with Two Flooring Colors

Note that if we were going to just tile the entire room the same color, we would need to find out the area of this rectangular room. Intuitively, if we want to tile only half of the room a particular color, we will need to calculate the area of half of the room. If you notice, every rectangle (or square) can be broken down into two triangles. It makes sense, then, that to find the area of a triangle, we find the area of the entire rectangle and divide by 2:

$$\text{Area of triangle} = \frac{1}{2} \times (\text{base} \times \text{height}) \qquad (1.9)$$

In our example, then, to tile half the room, we would need $\frac{1}{2} \times (8 \text{ ft} \times 15 \text{ ft})$ = 60 ft^2 of tile.

Occasionally, you will see more complicated shapes, such as the shaded trapezoid that appears in Figure 1-10. The good news is even complicated shapes such as this can be broken down into triangles and rectangles, and the area can easily be calculated. Try to figure out the area of the shaded trapezoid in Figure 1-10 (we'll give you the solution at the end of the appendix).

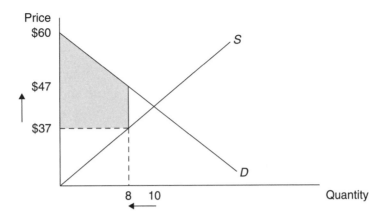

FIGURE 1-10 · A Market with a Price Floor

Solving Equations

Traditionally, a line represented on a graph is given as $y = f(x)$, where either y is known and you solve for x, or x is known and you solve for y. For instance, you could have the function:

$$y = f(x) = 3x + 2 \qquad (1.10)$$

If we are given that $x = 5$, we can solve this by substituting 5 for the x:

$$y = 3 \times 5 + 2 = 15 + 2 = 17 \qquad (1.11)$$

Conversely, if we are told that $y = 17$, we can solve to find the value of x that corresponds to $y = 17$:

$$17 = 3x + 2 \qquad (1.12)$$

First, isolate the term with x in it so that it is by itself on one side of the equation by subtracting 2 from each side:

$$15 = 3x \qquad (1.13)$$

Second, isolate x itself by dividing both sides by 3:

$$5 = x \qquad (1.14)$$

When you have a single equation with a single unknown, this is a fairly straightforward process. Note that this can be done no matter what way you express an equation. For instance, instead of $y = f(x)$, you could say that the quantity of a good that someone is willing to buy is a function of its price, $Q_d = f(P)$, or that the cost of producing a good is a function of the quantity produced, $Cost = f(q)$, and so on.

Also, we can solve such an equation only if we are given one of the unknown values. A function such as $y = 3x + 2$ has two unknowns, x and y. In fact, we can generalize this rule to describe what we need to do in order to solve any *system of equations* (that is, a set of one or more equations) to find the unknown values. The equation $17 = 3x + 2$ would be a system of one equation with one unknown value (x), so we can solve this system quickly. However, if we were given only $y = 3x + 2$, we could not solve this because it is a system of one equation with two unknown values. In general, in order to be able to solve for all of the unknown values in a system of equations, there must be at least as many equations as there are unknowns.

For example, suppose we are given the following system of equations:

$$y = 10x + 2$$
$$y = 2x + 18 \tag{1.15}$$

Here we have a system of two equations with two unknowns (x and y), so we can solve for both of the unknowns. To do so is fairly straightforward. First, we know that $y = y$, so we can set these two equations equal:

$$10x + 2 = 2x + 18 \tag{1.16}$$

Second, we want all of the x terms on one side of the equation, so we subtract $2x$ from each side:

$$8x + 2 = 18 \tag{1.17}$$

Next, we want to isolate the x terms, so we subtract 2 from each side:

$$8x = 16 \tag{1.18}$$

Finally, we solve for x by dividing both sides of the equation by 8:

$$x = 2 \tag{1.19}$$

To find the remaining unknown, we simply plug $x = 2$ into either of the original equations. It doesn't matter which one; we will get the same result:

$$y = 10 \times 2 + 2 = 20 + 2 = 22$$
$$y = 2 \times 2 + 18 = 4 + 18 = 22 \qquad (1.20)$$

Solving a system of two equations is particularly useful when we are talking about market equilibrium. Supply and demand are both equations in which the price and quantity are unknown values. In a market, we could express supply and demand as a system of two equations. For instance, suppose we knew that the market for a good was described by the following supply and demand functions:

$$\text{Supply: } P_s = 2Q_s + 2 \qquad (1.21)$$

$$\text{Demand: } P_d = 38 - Q_d \qquad (1.22)$$

At first this seems unsolvable: we have two equations (supply and demand), but four unknowns (P_s, P_d, Q_s, and Q_d). All is not lost, however. When we try to find equilibrium in a market, what we are really trying to do is to find a single price (that buyers will pay and sellers will get) that will make the quantity supplied and the quantity demanded the same. Translating that statement into an equation, we are assuming that:

There exists some P where $P_s = P_d$
There exists some Q where $Q_d = Q_s$

We can then substitute P and Q into the system of equations:

$$\text{Supply: } P = 2Q + 2 \qquad (1.23)$$

$$\text{Demand: } P = 38 - Q \qquad (1.24)$$

Now we have a solvable system! Go ahead and try to find the equilibrium price and quantity in this market (we will give you the answers at the end of the appendix).

Still Struggling

Math is like a language; the more you practice it, the better you get. If you are struggling with math, take your time, do extra practice, and know that you are not alone.

Answers and Explanations for Practice Problems

The first bit of practice we asked you to try was to find the equation of the line, in the form $y = a + bx$, in Figure 1-1b. This is a line that passes through two points: (0, 4) and (4, 0). We can do this a few different ways.

The first method is to examine the graph, get the y intercept from the graph, and use the line to calculate the slope. To find the y intercept, a in the equation, we find the value where the line crosses the y axis. In Figure 1-1b, the line crosses the y axis at 4, so $a = 4$. You might have once learned that the slope of a line is "rise over run." In other words, for every 1-unit change in the length of the curve, the slope tells us the change in the height of the curve. In this case, it is fairly simple: every time x decreases by 1 unit, y increases by 1 unit, so $b = -1$. This gives us the equation $y = 4 + (-1)x$.

The other way to solve this is to recognize that the equation $y = a + bx$ is an equation with four unknown values (a, b, x, and y). The points ($x = 0, y = 4$) and ($x = 4, y = 0$) each independently solve $y = a + bx$:

$$4 = a + b \times 0 \tag{1.25}$$

$$0 = a + b \times 4 \tag{1.26a}$$

We can now solve this system of two equations in two unknowns (a and b). First, isolate a in one of the equations. This is easy in this case, since $b \times 0 = 0$. Therefore, from the first point, $a = 4$. We can now plug this value of a into the second equation:

$$0 = 4 + b \times 4$$
$$-4 = b \times 4$$
$$-1 = b \tag{1.26a}$$

Next, we asked you to try to find the area of the trapezoid in Figure 1-10. If you draw a straight line across (as shown in Figure 1-11) from a price of $47, the shaded area is now made up of two shapes: a triangle with a height of $60 − $47 = $13 and a base of 8 units, and a rectangle with a height of $47 − $37 = $10 and a base of 8 units.

We now simply find the area of the triangle and the area of the rectangle and add these two areas together:

$$\text{Area of the triangle} = \frac{1}{2}(8) \times \$13 = \$52$$
$$\text{Area of the rectangle} = 8 \times \$10 = \$80$$
$$\text{Total area} = \$52 + \$80 = \$132 \tag{1.27}$$

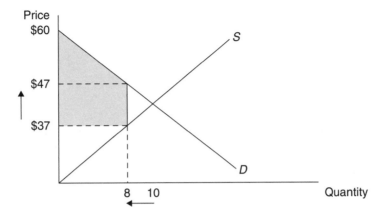

FIGURE 1-11 · A Market with a Price Floor

CAUTION *Notice that the area is expressed in dollars, so it is $132 and not 132. This is important: all measurements are expressed in some sort of unit of measure, such as dollars or square feet.*

Finally, we asked you to solve for a market equilibrium with a supply curve of $P = 2Q + 2$ and a demand curve of $P = 38 - Q$. Start by noting that $P = P$ and setting the two equations equal to each other:

$$2Q + 2 = 38 - Q \qquad (1.28)$$

Next, isolate the Q terms on one side of the equation, so add Q to both sides of the equation:

$$3Q + 2 = 38 \qquad (1.29)$$

Now isolate Q by subtracting 2 from each side:

$$3Q = 36 \qquad (1.30)$$

Finally, solve for Q by dividing each side by 3:

$$Q = 12 \qquad (1.31)$$

To find the equilibrium price, simply plug $Q = 12$ into either the supply or the demand function:

$$P = 2 \times 12 + 2 = 24 + 2 = 26 \qquad (1.32)$$

$$P = 38 - 12 = 26 \qquad (1.33)$$

Therefore, we find that the equilibrium in this market occurs when the price is $26, and at that price, 12 units will be sold.

QUIZ

Is each of the following statements *true* or *false*? Explain.

1. **Money is an economic resource.**

2. **Even if the monetary price of a Ferb is $100, this may not reflect its true cost.**

3. **The producer of a good who is thinking rationally will focus on the average cost of producing a good.**

4. **Decision making by households is in the realm of microeconomics, while decision making by large firms is in the realm of macroeconomics.**

5. **The price of a purplett is $9, the additional benefit from purchasing another purplett is $10, and the average benefit from purchasing another purplett is only $8. Given this, a buyer should not buy another purplett.**

For each of the following, choose the answer that best fits.

6. ***Ceteris paribus* means:**
   A. Nothing changes.
   B. All else equal.
   C. Rational thinking.
   D. Opportunity cost.

7. **Scharf sells T-shirts. When she sells 35 T-shirts, it costs her a total of $40, and when she sells 36 T-shirts, it costs her a total of $45. Based on this information, which of the following is definitely true?**
   A. It would be irrational for Scharf to sell any T-shirts for less than $40.
   B. It would be irrational for Scharf to sell the thirty-sixth T-shirt unless she received at least $45 for it.
   C. Scharf shouldn't sell T-shirts, as it will never be possible for her to make a profit.
   D. It would be irrational for Scharf to sell the thirty-sixth T-shirt unless she received at least $5 for it.

8. **Which of the following would be considered capital?**
   A. The money raised to start a business.
   B. A factory.
   C. A worker.
   D. Electricity.

9. **Ruby, as a rational consumer, does not:**
    A. Intentionally make herself worse off.
    B. Try to maximize her net benefit from consuming goods and services.
    C. Ever consume the wrong amount.
    D. Think marginally.

10. **Scarcity is defined as:**
     A. The sum total of all economic resources.
     B. The difference between the marginal costs and marginal benefits of an action.
     C. The difference between unlimited wants and limited resources.
     D. The difference between the price of a product and the cost of producing it.

chapter 2

Utility and Consumer Choice

Understanding what motivates choices is at the root of understanding how consumers make them. Economists assume that consumers *maximize utility*. Utility is a measure of the satisfaction that the consumer enjoys from the consumption of goods and services (you can think of it as "happiness"). And while consumers seek as much utility as possible, they are constrained by a limited budget, which forces them to make choices within that constraint.

In this chapter, we first discuss what are known as *utility functions*, and then move to *budget constraints*. We then combine these to get a rule for how consumers maximize utility across all items that they choose to purchase.

CHAPTER OBJECTIVES

After completing this chapter, the student should be able to:

1. Distinguish between the total utility received from the consumption of a good and the marginal utility received from the consumption of the next unit of that good.

2. Explain the concept of diminishing marginal utility and how it predicts when a person will stop consuming units of a good.

3. Draw a budget constraint to show the limits of a person's consumption possibilities.

4. Find the combination of two goods that maximizes a consumer's utility given a budget constraint.

Utility Functions and Preferences

Some people receive utility from watching college football on an autumn Saturday; other people would rather use their Saturdays to go to the movies or read a book. Every consumer has different *preferences* for goods and services, so it is impossible to measure one person's utility function against another person's utility function. At first, this might imply that it is impossible to study consumer behavior because each consumer has unique preferences. However, to understand how consumers behave, we don't need to know each person's preferences; we simply need to assume that, *given those preferences*, each person seeks as much utility as possible. In other words, each consumer is a total utility maximizer.

For example, suppose Lily enjoys exercising at her campus fitness center every week. In economics lingo, her utility is a function of how much weekly exercise she consumes. Economists use a fictional unit of measurement, the *util*, to measure how much total utility a person receives, and that total utility is represented by the second column in Table 2-1. The first two columns show the amount of total utility Lily gets from each unit of exercise. The third column in the table shows the *marginal utility* she enjoys with each additional hour of exercise. For example, when she exercises for one hour, she receives 17 utils, but when she exercises for two hours, she receives 32 utils. Therefore, the marginal utility of the second hour of exercise is 15 *additional*, or *marginal*, utils.

TIP *The idea of a util might seem strange to the uninitiated. How can you measure happiness? The point of the util isn't actually to measure happiness; it is to compare happiness. For instance, do we need to know how "happy" 32 utils is? No, we need to know only that 32 utils of happiness is better than 17 utils of happiness.*

Figure 2-1 shows a graph of Lily's total utility function, with utils on the vertical axis. We can see that Lily's total utility rises with more exercise, but

TABLE 2-1 Lily's Utility per Hour of Exercise		
Hours of Exercise	Total Utility (utils)	Marginal Utility per Hour (utils)
0	0	
1	17	17
2	32	15
3	45	13
4	56	11
5	65	9
6	72	7
7	77	5
8	80	3
9	81	1
10	80	−1

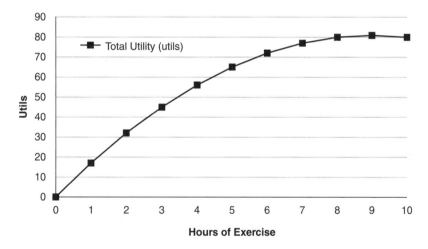

FIGURE 2-1 • Lily's Total Utility

peaks at nine hours of exercise and then begins to fall with the tenth hour. Why? Because it turns out that consuming more and more of something doesn't always make you happier and happier.

Principle of Diminishing Marginal Utility

When you're very thirsty, the first glass of water is incredible! The second glass is also pretty thirst-quenching, but the fourteenth glass of water might actually be enough to make you sick. In other words, the first glass provides a lot of marginal utility, the second provides a little less, and the fourteenth provides much less (so much less that drinking it makes you worse off). This illustrates a nearly universal truth that economists recognize as the *principle of diminishing marginal utility*: marginal utility declines as more units of a good are consumed.

We can see this both in Table 2-2 and in Figure 2-2, both of which show Lily's marginal utility. Each additional hour of exercise adds fewer utils to Lily's total utility than the hours that came before. In fact, at the tenth hour, she is actually losing utility, and we see this as marginal utility that dips below zero. Once the marginal utility becomes negative, you are actually making yourself worse off if you increase your consumption. To maximize her total utility, it is clear that Lily should continue to exercise until the ninth hour and should never consume the tenth hour. This is important because it tells us that, even when we don't have to pay to consume each unit, we will eventually stop consuming.

TABLE 2-2 Lily's Marginal Utility per Hour of Exercise	
Hours of Exercise	Marginal Utility per Hour (utils)
0	—
1	17
2	15
3	13
4	11
5	9
6	7
7	5
8	3
9	1
10	−1

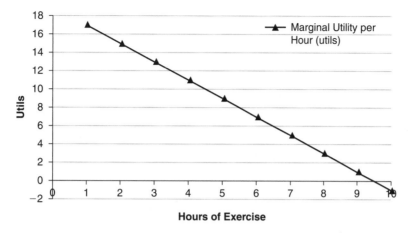

FIGURE 2-2 • Lily's Marginal Utility

 Still Struggling

When people first learn about marginal utility, a common mistake that they make is to assume that once marginal utility begins to diminish, a consumer should stop consuming units of that good. It is important to understand that marginal utility is the *additional* total utility received from the next unit of a good. If *total* utility will increase with the next unit of a good, the consumer is wise to consume that unit. So while marginal utility may be diminishing, so long as it is greater than zero, the next unit consumed will still increase the consumer's total utility.

Budget Constraints

We have seen that the principle of diminishing marginal utility predicts that a consumer will stop his consumption before the marginal utility becomes negative, even if a good is free. Most of the time, however, consumers must pay a monetary price to consume goods and services, and they must be mindful of how much money they have to spend on those items. We now introduce the concept of a *budget constraint* for a consumer. In the real world, there are many different goods at many different prices that we must choose among. To keep it simple, though, we will start with a consumer who chooses between only two items.

Suppose that our college student, Lily, had to pay $10 for each visit to the fitness center, that she also consumed meals at the campus center at $5 each, and that she had a weekly income of $50 to divide between these two things. Assuming that Lily cannot spend more than her income (she cannot borrow), we can create an equation for her budget constraint:

$$\text{Income} \geq \text{spending on exercise} + \text{spending on meals}$$

Her spending on exercise is simply the price of each visit ($10) multiplied by the number of times she goes to the fitness center (E). Likewise, her spending on meals is the price of each meal ($5) multiplied by how many meals (M) she buys. And recalling that she only has $50 of income, we can rewrite her budget constraint equation as:

$$\$50 = \$10 \times E + \$5 \times M$$

Still Struggling

Why did we switch from a "≥" sign to an "=" sign? Recall that Lily's objective is to maximize her utility. Since we have only two goods, it doesn't make sense for her not to spend all of her money (we assume that she cannot save, and that she doesn't get utility from money itself, but only from the goods that money buys). Therefore, if we assume that Lily is rational, she will always spend all of her money.

Table 2-3 shows six possible *consumption bundles* (labeled points A through F) for these two goods that would use exactly her income. Figure 2-3 shows these *consumption possibilities* in a graph in which the budget constraint is shown as a downward-sloping line that separates the bundles that are affordable from those that are unaffordable. Combinations that lie below the *budget line*, like

TABLE 2-3 Lily's Consumption Bundles for Meals and Exercise		
Quantity of Meals (*M*)	Quantity of Exercise (*E*)	Consumption Bundle Point
0	5	A
2	4	B
4	3	C
6	2	D
8	1	E
10	0	F

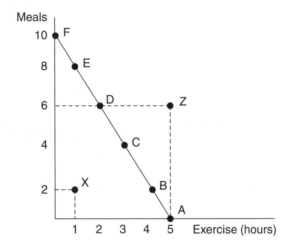

FIGURE 2-3 • Consumption Possibilities

point X, use less than $50 of her income. Assuming that Lily would be happier spending more of her income on these two goods, a point like X would not maximize her utility. Combinations that lie beyond the budget line, like point Z, would probably make Lily happier, but would require more than $50 to purchase.

TIP *The slope of the budget line is also informative. The slope of (−2) tells us that in order to buy one more hour of exercise at the fitness center, she must give up two meals. In other words, the slope of the budget constraint represents the opportunity cost of an hour of exercise.*

Constrained Utility Maximization

If Lily knows her budget constraint, which consumption bundle should she choose so that she achieves the maximum amount of utility that is possible within that constraint? To answer that, we need a little more information.

Table 2-4 shows how much utility Lily receives from the consumption of several different combinations of meals and exercise and what each of these would cost.

Note that some of these combinations (the ones that are crossed out) are unaffordable and therefore unattainable, so we shouldn't even consider them as options. Some combinations (the ones that are in italics) aren't spending all of her money, so we shouldn't consider those either. Instead, we need to focus only on the combinations that lie on the budget line. For example, suppose Lily chooses point B, where $M = 2$, $E = 4$, and she enjoys 330 utils. If she can reshuffle her consumption along the budget line and increase her utility, then she should do so. As we can see in Table 2-5, maximum utility of 390 utils is received when she buys four meals and exercises for three hours.

TABLE 2-4 Lily's Utility and Cost				
Hours of Exercise (E)	Utility from Exercise	Quantity of Meals (M)	Utility from Meals	Cost of This Combination (10 × E + $5 × M)
0	0	0	0	$ 0
1	80	2	70	$30
2	150	4	130	$60
3	210	6	180	$90
4	260	8	220	$80

TABLE 2-5 Lily's Maximum Utility			
Quantity of Meals	Hours of Exercise	Total Utility	Consumption Bundle Point
0	5	300	A
2	4	330	B
4	3	390	C
6	2	330	D
8	1	300	E
10	0	250	F

Spending the Marginal Dollar

Another way to think about Lily's problem is to think about her spending decision incrementally. We can ask the question: if Lily has $1 to spend, how should she best spend that dollar? She should probably spend it on the item that will increase her utility by the most utils. If she goes through life spending her next $1 on the thing that gives her the highest marginal utility for that dollar, she is bound to maximize her utility! We modify Table 2-4 to create marginal utility per dollar spent. Before we do that, let's introduce a very minor bit of math: marginal utility per dollar.

Marginal utility (MU) for some good X is defined as the change in total utility (ΔTU) divided by the change in the units of X consumed (ΔX). Mathematically, this creates the ratio

$$MU(X\text{th unit of consumption}) = \frac{\Delta TU}{\Delta X}$$

So, for example, when Lily goes from two meals to four meals, her total utility increases from 330 to 390:

$$MU(4) = \frac{\Delta TU}{\Delta X} = \frac{TU(4) - TU(3)}{4 - 2} = \frac{390 - 330}{4 - 2} = \frac{60}{2} = 30$$

and to get MU per dollar for that fourth meal (m), we just divide this by the price:

$$\frac{MU_m(4)}{P_m} = \frac{30}{5} = 6$$

This tells us that each dollar that Lily spends on the fourth meal gives her 6 additional utils. When we fill out the rest of the table in a similar fashion, we get Table 2-6.

We already know from trial and error that Lily maximizes her utility by consuming 4 meals and 3 hours of exercise. Going through the process of trial and error would be tedious, but luckily we can see in this table that this bundle has an interesting outcome: the marginal utility per dollar is equal for both goods. This condition is often described as the *utility maximization rule*. The consumer should spend all of her income on two goods, X and Y, such that:

$$\frac{MU_X}{P_X} = \frac{MU_Y}{P_Y}$$

TABLE 2-6 Lily's Marginal Utility per Dollar					
Quantity of Meals	Utility from Meals	MU/$ Spent on Meals	Hours of Exercise	Utility from Exercise	MU/$ Spent on Exercise
0	0		0	0	
2	70	35/$5 = 7	1	80	8
4	130	6	2	150	7
6	180	5	3	210	6
8	220	4	4	260	5
10	250	3	5	300	4

As long as one good provides more utility per dollar than another, the consumer will buy more of the first good; as more of the first product is bought, its marginal utility diminishes until the amount of utility per dollar just equals that of the other product.

Why is this a utility maximization rule? It makes sense on two levels. Mathematically, this turns out to be the combination that makes total utility the highest possible. Note from Tables 2-5 and 2-6 that any combination for which the utility maximization rule doesn't hold results in a lower level of utility.

Second, on an intuitive level, it makes sense that you spend your money in such a way that you are getting the same "bang for the buck" for everything you buy. If you are consuming at a point where you are getting a different bang for each good, you should reallocate your consumption. For example, what if the following were true?

$$\frac{MU_X}{P_X} < \frac{MU_Y}{P_Y}$$

In other words, you are getting more "bang for the buck" with good Y, so you should consume more of good Y! This requires that you decrease your consumption of X in order to stay within your budget constraint. For example, consider the consumption bundle of 6 meals and 2 units of exercise. From Table 2-6, we can calculate that the marginal utility of the sixth meal is 25 and the marginal utility of the second unit of exercise is 70, so

$$\frac{25}{5} < \frac{70}{10}$$

Since you are getting more bang for the buck from exercising, you should increase your consumption of exercise.

What happens to MU_Y when you consume more? The principle of diminishing marginal utility says that MU_Y falls. And as you consume fewer units of X, MU_X increases. The theory of consumer choice predicts that this kind of reshuffling will cease when the ratios are equal again, and the net result is that total "happiness" increases.

Utility maximization can tell us what a rational consumer will do in order to make herself as happy as possible. When consumers are faced with consumption decisions, they go through this process (although probably on a more intuitive level than sitting down and calculating it all). However, mapping it out in this manner turns out to be very useful for the economist. For instance, if we go through this process, we can figure out how much a consumer will change her consumption of a good in response to a change in the price of that good. This is something that we will see in the next chapter.

Still Struggling

Working with the utility maximization rule can be difficult at first. Some students find it easier to locate the correct bundle of goods X and Y by rearranging the rule in the following way:

$$\frac{MU_X}{MU_Y} = \frac{P_X}{P_Y}$$

This tells us that we need to limit our search to combinations of X and Y that produce a ratio of marginal utilities (MU_X/MU_Y) that is equal to the ratio of the prices. In the example we have been using, $P_X = \$10$ and $P_Y = \$5$, and so the ratio ($P_X/P_Y$) = 2. Any combination of X and Y that *does* provide a ratio of marginal utilities equal to 2 is a candidate for *the* combination that maximizes utility. Once you limit the search to only those combinations, find the one that uses up exactly the consumer's income and you've solved the problem.

Summary

This chapter describes how economists measure the "happiness" that consumers get from consumption as utility, and assumes that consumers seek to maximize their utility. The additional utility received from the consumption of the next unit of a good is known as marginal utility, and the law of diminishing marginal utility assumes that buyers receive less and less additional utility from each additional unit that they consume. A budget constraint shows how a consumer's income and the prices of two goods, X and Y, limits the combinations of X and Y that the consumer can afford. Consumers are believed to maximize their utility given the limits of the budget constraint. The utility maximization rule states that the best (utility-maximizing) combination of goods to consume will be the one where the marginal utility per dollar spent on each good will be the same for all goods. Mathematically, this rule is expressed as ($MU_X/P_X = MU_Y/P_Y$).

QUIZ

Is each of the following statements *true* or *false*? Explain.

1. **When you consume more of a good, both your total utility and your marginal utility will always increase.**

2. **Utility can be thought of as the dollar value of happiness.**

3. **If a consumer gets 80 marginal units of happiness from consuming Gams, which cost $4 each, and 100 marginal units of happiness from consuming Ferbs, which also cost $4 each, the consumer would be better off if he increased his consumption of Ferbs.**

4. **If the marginal utility of the next unit is less than zero, that unit should not be consumed.**

For each of the following, choose the answer that best fits.

TABLE 2-7	
Quantity of Chicken Livers	Total Utility
0	0
1	10
2	18
3	24
4	28
5	30
6	28

5. **The Table 2-7 shows Sissy's total utility from the consumption of fried chicken livers. Given the information in the table, the marginal utility of the fourth chicken liver is:**
   A. 28 utils.
   B. 7 utils.
   C. 4 utils.
   D. zero utils.

6. Table 2-7 shows Sissy's total utility from the consumption of fried chicken livers. Sissy also buys cans of soda and is receiving six utils per dollar from her soda consumption. Given the information in this table, if Sissy is maximizing her utility by consuming three chicken livers, the price of chicken livers must be:
   A. $1
   B. $2
   C. $6
   D. $5

7. Jamaal is currently spending all of his income on coffee and doughnuts. The price of coffee is $2 per cup, and the price of doughnuts is $3 each. Suppose that Jamaal's current marginal utility for a cup of coffee is 5 utils and his marginal utility for a doughnut is 9 utils. Is there a way for Jamaal to adjust his consumption to increase his utility?
   A. Yes. He should consume more doughnuts and less coffee.
   B. Yes. He should consume more coffee and less doughnuts.
   C. No. He has already maximized his utility.
   D. Yes. He should consume more coffee and more doughnuts.

8. A consumer has $100 of income to spend on goods X and Y. The price of good X is $4, and the price of good Y is $5. Which of the following combinations of X and Y lies on the consumer's budget line?
   A. 10X and 5Y.
   B. 25X and 20Y.
   C. 12X and 10Y.
   D. 10X and 12Y.

9. A consumer has $100 of income to spend on goods X and Y. The price of good X is $10, and the price of good Y is $2. Which of the following combinations of X and Y is currently unaffordable?
   A. 10X and 0Y.
   B. 6X and 25Y.
   C. 4X and 20Y.
   D. 5X and 25Y.

10. Grace really enjoys cupcakes. In fact, the graph of her total utility curve from eating cupcakes is a straight line that always rises by 5 utils for every cupcake she eats. This tells us that her marginal utility curve:
    A. Also rises 5 utils with every cupcake she eats.
    B. Begins at 5 utils for the first cupcake, but diminishes with more cupcakes.
    C. Is a horizontal line at 5 utils for all cupcakes eaten.
    D. Initially rises for the first cupcake, is highest at 5 utils, then diminishes with more cupcakes.

chapter **3**

Demand

The previous chapter showed that consumer behavior is motivated by utility maximization and that consumer choices are very much a function of income and prices. These principles of consumer behavior lay the foundation for one-half of the most widely used model in all of economics: supply and demand.

CHAPTER OBJECTIVES

After completing this chapter, the student should be able to:

1. Make the connection between utility-maximizing behavior, the law of demand, and the downward-sloping demand curve.

2. Understand how the determinants of demand shift demand curves outward or inward.

3. Compute and interpret the price elasticity of demand and relate this to the total revenue of a firm.

4. Compute and interpret the cross-price and income elasticities of demand and understand what these measures tell us.

We covered two important concepts in the previous chapter. First, the principle of diminishing marginal utility tells us that as more of a good is consumed, the marginal utility of each additional unit falls. Second, we developed something called the utility maximization rule, which says that a consumer has maximized her utility when she has spent her income in such a way that the marginal utility per dollar is equal for all goods. The motivation behind this is simple: when the price of something goes down, we are getting increased "bang for the buck" from it compared to that from our consumption of all other things, and if we want to make ourselves as happy as possible, we should rearrange our consumption by consuming more of this item. It is this movement along a downward-sloping marginal utility curve that gives us the foundation for the *law of demand*.

The Law of Demand

The *law of demand* says that if we hold all other factors constant (*ceteris paribus*), a decrease in the price of a good will cause consumers to increase their consumption of that good. For example, suppose Max is a consumer of chicken nuggets. Table 3-1 shows that at several different prices, Max will adjust his weekly consumption according to the law of demand. At higher prices, he will reduce the quantity that he demands, and at lower prices, he will increase the quantity that he demands. In other words, there is an inverse relationship between the price of nuggets and the quantity demanded.

TABLE 3-1 Max's Demand for Chicken Nuggets	
Price per Chicken Nugget	**Quantity Demanded (Weekly)**
1.00	0
$0.80	20
$0.60	40
$0.40	60
$0.20	80
$0	100

Although Max has a strong preference for chicken nuggets, he won't consume any nuggets if the price is $1 or higher. Why will Max consume only 100 nuggets if they are free? After all, if he doesn't have to pay for them, maybe he should consume an infinite number of nuggets. There is a limit to

Max's consumption of nuggets because of his diminishing marginal utility, which is the basis for the law of demand. Diminishing marginal utility tells him that consuming anything beyond 100 nuggets in a week would reduce his total utility from chicken nuggets, so he will stop consuming them.

Demand Curves

If we convert the data seen in Table 3-1 into a graph, we create a downward-sloping *demand curve*. Figure 3-1 illustrates Max's weekly demand for chicken nuggets, and again we see that when the price falls, his quantity of nuggets demanded rises along the demand curve.

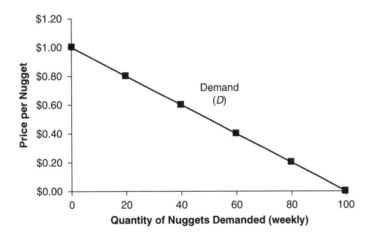

FIGURE 3-1 • Max's Demand for Chicken Nuggets

There are also many factors (or *determinants*) that affect Max's demand for nuggets, but for now we are holding all such determinants constant and focusing on the impact of price on his consumption. When we allow these determinants to change, we see changes in the location of the demand curve.

TIP *It is very important to distinguish between two concepts: demand and quantity demanded. Demand refers to a description of all of the possible quantities that a consumer would buy of a good at each possible price. Quantity demanded refers to the quantity of a good that a consumer will purchase at one specific price. This means that graphically, demand refers to the entire demand curve, while quantity demanded refers to a single point on a demand curve.*

Determinants of Demand

Economists recognize a handful of variables that can shift the demand curve to the right or to the left. A rightward shift like the one shown in Figure 3-2 (from D_0 to D_1) is called an *increase in demand*. This tells us that at any price, consumers like Max will want to consume more units of the good. A leftward shift, also shown in Figure 3-2 (from D_0 to D_2), is called a *decrease in demand*. Of course this means that at any price, consumers will want to consume fewer units of the good.

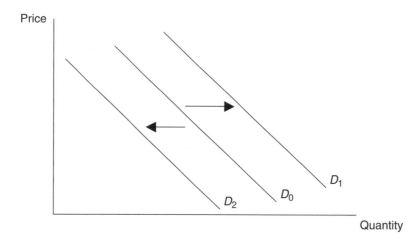

FIGURE 3-2 · Shifts in the Demand Curve

TIP   *It is a good idea to think of these shifts as being increases or decreases, rather than as "shifting up" or "shifting down." (We will see why when we talk about supply in Chapter 5).*

Let's briefly discuss each of the determinants of demand.

1. Income

A change in consumer income can affect the demand for goods in two different ways, depending upon how the good fits into consumer utility functions.

Normal goods are the most common. For these goods, more income leads to an increase in demand, and less income leads to a decrease in demand. Goods like steak, textbooks, running shoes, and iPods are all normal goods.

Inferior goods are those for which more income leads to a decrease in demand. City bus tickets, secondhand clothing, and store-brand food items are all examples of inferior goods.

2. Tastes

Sometimes consumers just have a stronger taste for a certain good or service, and sometimes these tastes change. A favorable change in tastes leads to an increase in demand, and an unfavorable change in tastes leads to a decrease in demand. For example, we usually see demand for a sports team's apparel increase when the team is winning. If a product, like asbestos insulation, is shown to be harmful to people's health, demand for it decreases.

3. Prices of Related Goods

Two goods can be either substitutes for each other or complementary with each other. *Substitute goods* are those that can be used in place of each other. If the price of one such good rises, the demand for its substitute will increase. For instance, if the price of fish sticks increases, Max's demand for chicken nuggets will increase. Recall that as the price of something increases, we consume less of this good. Therefore, if the price of fish sticks increases, Max's quantity demanded for fish sticks will decrease, but his demand for chicken nuggets will increase at any possible price for chicken nuggets. This is because no matter what the actual price of chicken nuggets might be, their price relative to that of fish sticks is now lower.

Complementary goods are those that are used together. When goods are complementary, there is an inverse relationship between the price of one and the demand for the other. If the price of tennis rackets rises, demand for tennis balls will shift to the left. Max likes to dip his nuggets in ketchup, so if the price of ketchup declines, his demand for nuggets will increase. In Figure 3-3, we can see the increase in the quantity of ketchup demanded at the lower price and the increase in the demand for nuggets because the goods are complementary.

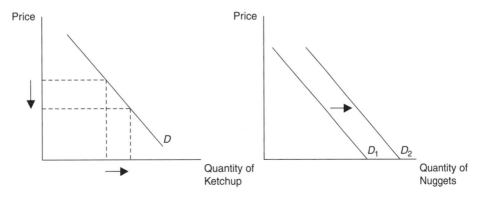

FIGURE 3-3 · Demand for Nuggets and Ketchup

4. Expectations

Consumers have expectations about future prices, product availability, and income, and these expectations can shift demand. If Max expects the price of nuggets to decrease next week, his demand for nuggets this week will decrease as he waits for the price to fall. If Max expects his income to increase next week, he might increase his demand for nuggets this week to stock up.

5. Number of Buyers

It is straightforward to assume that if there are more buyers of a product, this will lead to an increase in demand, and that fewer buyers will lead to a decrease in demand. For example, the demand for prescription drugs has increased as the population has grown older. The demand for diapers would decrease if families had fewer babies.

Still Struggling

If you feel overwhelmed by whether an event might shift a demand curve to the right or to the left, ask yourself: "Would this outside event cause consumers to increase their willingness and ability to purchase this good at any price?" For example, for the majority of goods, higher income does exactly this, and demand shifts to the right.

Price Elasticity of Demand

If we ask a typical consumer, "What happens to the quantity of milk demanded when the price rises?," we will surely receive a response like, "It will decrease." But the economist wants to know the answer to a more important question, "Yes, but by how much?" Will dairy farms go out of business? Will consumers completely stop drinking milk, eating yogurt, and ordering pizzas with extra cheese? Or will the change be negligible?

Most people who have any experience as consumers have an intuitive understanding of the law of demand, but the follow-up questions are both more interesting and more difficult to answer. When economists want to know how one variable might change in response to a change in another variable, they calculate something called *elasticity*. Elasticity refers to the responsiveness of a consumer's behavior to some sort of change. Think of a physical change like pulling. If we pull on each end of a rubber band, it responds by stretching because it is elastic. However, if we pull on each end of a kitchen table, it doesn't respond to this action because it is inelastic.

In terms of our original query, the question "how much?" is a question about the responsiveness of the quantity demanded to a change in the price. To measure this responsiveness, or sensitivity, to a price change, economists use the *price elasticity of demand*. Price elasticity of demand falls into two general categories:

1. If consumers are relatively responsive to price changes, demand is said to be elastic.
2. If consumers are relatively unresponsive to price changes, demand is said to be inelastic.

It is important to note that with both elastic and inelastic demand, consumers still behave in accordance with the law of demand. A precise definition of what we mean by "responsive" or "unresponsive" follows. (Note: if the reader feels the need to review how to work with percentages or with fractions, it might be wise to read the appendix to Chapter 1.)

Mathematically, the price elasticity of demand is defined as the percentage change in quantity demanded divided by the percentage change in the price, or

$$E_d = \frac{\%\Delta Q_d}{\%\Delta P}$$

The law of demand tells us that price and quantity demanded will always move in opposite directions, so the price elasticity of demand will always be a negative number. Knowing this, economists usually focus on the absolute value and ignore the negative sign. For example, if the price of laptop computers increases by 1 percent and quantity demanded falls by 2 percent, we would calculate

$$E_d = (2\%/1\%) = 2$$

Still Struggling

It may seem confusing that we ignore the sign of price elasticity of demand and not the sign of other elasticities (like income or cross-price). The reason is that in this instance, the sign doesn't given us any meaningful information but has the potential to confuse us. Consider two numbers, -2 and 1.5. If we are comparing numbers, 1.5 is the larger number. However, elasticities are really a magnitude of change: something that changes by 1.5 times doesn't change as much as something that changes by 2 times.

In the case of the laptop computer example, the percentage decrease in Q_d (the response) was twice as large as the percentage increase in P (the trigger). We would say that consumers have exhibited a sensitive, or elastic, response to a higher price. Suppose the price of milk increases by 10 percent and quantity demanded falls by 2 percent. We calculate

$$E_d = (2\%/10\%) = 0.20$$

In the case of the milk example, the percentage decrease in Q_d was only one-fifth the size of the percentage increase in P. In other words, consumers have exhibited an insensitive, or inelastic, response to a higher price.

TIP *In general, any elasticity greater than 1 describes an elastic response, and any elasticity less than 1 describes an inelastic response. If price elasticity happens to exactly equal 1, it is referred to as* unitary elastic. *The largest response to a price change is one that is infinitely large, or* perfectly elastic. *In this case, the demand curve is drawn as horizontal, as any price increase will instantly drive quantity demanded to zero units. The smallest response to a price change is no response at all, and in this case the price elasticity is equal to zero; this is known as* perfectly inelastic. *In this case, the demand curve is drawn as vertical. A handy way to remember these is using a number line, as shown in Figure 3-4.*

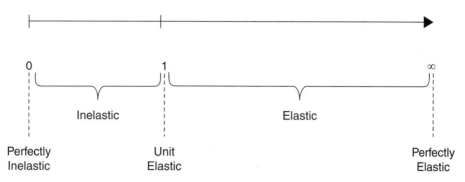

FIGURE 3-4 · Using the Number Line to Show Elasticity

Figure 3-5 shows two overlapping demand curves to show how different elasticities affect the shape of demand curves. The curve D_e is nearly horizontal, and the curve D_i is nearly vertical. Suppose that the price for both of these goods is initially at P_0 and consumers are buying the same quantity of each good, Q_0. If the price of both goods increases by 10 percent, the quantity demanded falls by many more units along demand curve D_e than it falls along demand curve D_i. These simple demand curves tell us that, all else equal, curves with steeper slopes will exhibit less elastic responses to a given price change.

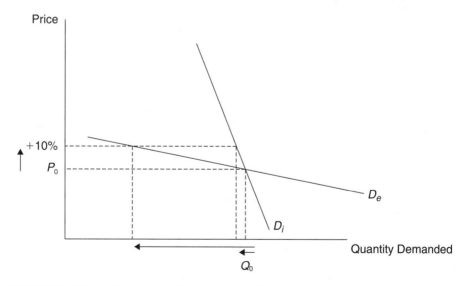

FIGURE 3-5 · Effect of Elasticity on Quantity Demanded

Another way to interpret the price elasticity of demand is to begin with a specific value. Suppose you were told that the price elasticity of demand for coffee is 0.9. What does this mean? Well, mathematically:

$$0.9 = \frac{\%\Delta Q_d}{\%\Delta P}$$

Rearranging this, we get

$$0.9 \times \%\Delta P = \%\Delta Q_d$$

So, for every 1 percent increase in price, there will be a 0.9 percent decrease in the quantity demanded of coffee.

An interesting (and sometimes confounding) thing about elasticity computations is that the numerical result changes if the new and old prices (or quantities) are reversed. For example, if a price rises from a value of 10 to a value of 11, this is a 10 percent increase. But if price were to fall from a value of 11 to a value of 10, this would be a 9.1 percent decrease. Because of this, the value of the price elasticity will change, depending upon whether the price is rising or falling and the actual point on the demand curve we are investigating. In order to account for this, economists sometimes use the average price and average quantity between two points on a demand curve. This method is called the *midpoint method*.

Suppose the price is changing between two points along a demand curve and, as a result, the quantity demanded is changing. To compute the price elasticity between these two points, let's designate the initial price as P_0, the new price as P_1, and the average of those two prices as $\bar{P}$. Likewise, we will designate the original quantity demanded as Q_0, the new quantity demanded as Q_1, and the average of those two quantities as $\bar{Q}$. Using this notation, the percentage change in quantity demanded is then computed as

$$\%\Delta Q_d = \frac{Q_1 - Q_0}{\bar{Q}}$$

Similarly, the percentage change in price is computed as

$$\%\Delta P = \frac{P_1 - P_0}{\bar{P}}$$

We can combine these two fractions to produce the price elasticity of demand between these two points on the demand curve by substitution into the original elasticity equation:

$$E_d = \frac{\%\Delta Q_d}{\%\Delta P} = \left(\frac{Q_1 - Q_0}{P_1 - P_0}\right) \times \left(\frac{\bar{P}}{\bar{Q}}\right)$$

We can see how this equation is used by giving an example. Suppose the price of a new truck in the local market falls from $20,000 to $18,000 over the course of a month. Truck dealerships discover that trucks sales rise from 100 to 140 in a month. We would compute the midpoint elasticity of demand between these two points on the demand curve as

$$E_d = \left(\frac{140 - 100}{18,000 - 20,000}\right) \times \left(\frac{19,000}{120}\right) = 3.17$$

Based on this result, we conclude that, at least between these two points on the demand curve, truck buyers are very sensitive to price changes.

Is this stuff at all useful? Most definitely! Elasticities are some of the most useful and practical tools in an economist's toolkit. In the case of price elasticity of demand, it is actually *very* useful to the sellers of these goods. Let's look at what happens to the *total revenue* received by the dealerships that were selling the trucks in the previous example. Total revenue is equal to the number of units sold multiplied by the price at which they were sold. Prior to the decrease in price, trucks were generating total revenues of $2,000,000 (100 units @ $20,000 each). After the price fell, trucks generated total revenues of $2,520,000 (140 units @ $18,000 each).

Let's briefly explore what is happening here. We know that when the price falls, the quantity demanded will rise. Because total revenue is the product of these two variables, a falling price and a rising quantity have competing influences on total revenue. Whether total revenue rises, falls, or stays the same depends upon which effect, the lower price or the higher quantity, is relatively stronger. These are described as the price effect and the quantity effect.

- **Price effect.** After a price decrease, each unit sold sells at a lower price, which tends to decrease revenue.
- **Quantity effect.** After a price decrease, more units are sold, which tends to increase revenue.

In the case of the truck example, the lower price produced a very elastic response, so the upward effect of a larger quantity demanded outweighed the downward effect of a lower price, and total revenue increased. Had there been an inelastic response to the lower price, the price effect would have been stronger and total revenue would have fallen. In general, this leads to something known as the *total revenue rule:* all else equal, in order to raise total revenue, lower the price of a good if the demand for the good is price-elastic and raise the price of a good if the demand for the good is price-inelastic.

So, sellers of all products have a very strong incentive to know, or have some estimate of, the price elasticity of demand for their products. But how can a seller have an estimate of the price elasticity for the product that it is selling? Even without mathematical analysis, we can look at some general tendencies that seem to predict whether products have elastic or inelastic demand:

1. **Substitutes for the product.** Generally, the more substitutes there are, the more elastic the demand.

   If there are many substitutes for a product and the price rises, consumers will have an elastic response because they can easily find alternative products. The converse is also true: the fewer substitutes there are for a good, the less elastic the demand.

2. **Whether the product is a luxury or a necessity.** Generally, the less necessary the item, the more elastic the demand. In the case of a luxury, if the price increases, consumers will just do without and have an elastic response. Intuitively, this follows from the first tendency. Things that are necessities tend to have fewer substitutes (for instance, water, food, and similar goods).

3. **Share of income spent on the good.** Generally, the larger the expenditure relative to one's budget, the more elastic the demand, because buyers will notice the change in price more.

4. **The amount of time involved.** Generally, the longer the time period involved after a price increase, the more elastic the demand becomes, as consumers discover new substitutes for the product or go without.

TIP *When discussing inelastic demand, some students make a mistake by thinking that consumers will not stop consuming a particular good if the price increases. Gasoline is a good example of this. When gasoline prices increase, since gasoline demand is certainly inelastic, many people say, "Well, people need gasoline, so there will be no decrease in the quantity of gallons consumed." Statements like this wrongly assume that the demand for gasoline, even in the short run, is vertical. And while the demand might be quite inelastic, there will still be a reduction in the quantity of gasoline demanded when the price rises.*

Cross-Price and Income Elasticities of Demand

Economists, governments, and firms are quite interested in how one variable responds to a change in another variable. For example, suppose the price of gasoline were to increase. The producers of large trucks and SUVs will be very interested in knowing how this might affect sales of these vehicles. A cross-price elasticity of demand would be used to measure this response.

Suppose the economy is suffering a recession and personal incomes are lower. The housing industry would be interested in knowing how this will affect the demand for new homes. An income elasticity of demand would be used in this case.

The cross-price elasticity of demand refers to the effect of a change in one product's price on the quantity demanded for another product.

Mathematically, the formula is shown for products X and Y:

$$E_{xy} = \frac{\%\Delta Q_{xd}}{\%\Delta P_y}$$

If the cross-price elasticity is positive, then X and Y are substitutes. For example, if the price of Nike shoes increases, the quantity demanded for Converse shoes should increase. Because both numerator and denominator are increasing, the cross-price elasticity will be a positive number.

If the cross-price elasticity is negative, then X and Y are complementary goods. Suppose the price of gasoline increases. We expect the quantity demanded for large SUVs to decrease. The numerator and denominator are moving in opposite directions, so the cross-price elasticity is negative.

If the cross-price elasticity is zero, then X and Y are unrelated, independent products. For example, if the price of aspirin rises, there is likely to be no impact on the quantity of cotton T-shirts demanded.

The income elasticity of demand refers to the percentage change in quantity demanded that results from some percentage change in consumer incomes.

The income elasticity formula is shown as

$$E_i = \frac{\%\Delta Q_{xd}}{\%\Delta I}$$

A positive income elasticity indicates that this is a normal good because for normal goods, higher incomes shift the demand curve to the right. Negative income elasticities indicate inferior goods; higher incomes shift the demand for inferior goods to the left.

An important difference to remember about the price elasticity and other elasticities is the role of the sign. The sign of the price elasticity of demand is not particularly useful. It will always be negative, no matter what type of good you are talking about (this is because of the law of demand). However, in cross-price and income elasticities of demand, the sign conveys important and useful information about the type of goods you are talking about.

Summary

This chapter connected utility maximization to the law of demand and downward-sloping demand curves. All else equal, when the price of a good increases, consumers decrease the quantity demanded of that good. There are several demand determinants that shift demand curves either to the right or to the left because they fundamentally affect consumers' willingness and ability to buy the good at any price. The price elasticity of demand measures how sensitive consumers are to a change in the price of the good. If the price elasticity is greater than 1 (elastic), a percentage change in the price will cause a larger, and opposite, percentage change in the quantity of the good demanded. If the price elasticity is less than 1 (inelastic), a given percentage change in price will cause a smaller percentage change in quantity demanded. The cross-price elasticity of demand tells us how sensitive the quantity demanded for one good is to a change in the price of a related good. The income elasticity tells us how sensitive quantity demanded is to a change in consumer income.

QUIZ

Is each of the following statements *true* or *false*? Explain.

1. **Diminishing marginal utility is the foundation for the law of demand and the downward-sloping demand curve.**

2. **A lower price of oranges will cause the demand for oranges to increase, shifting the demand curve to the right.**

3. **The income elasticity of demand for beef is positive, telling us that beef is an inferior good.**

4. **Pork and beans are complementary goods. If the price of pork increases, the demand for beans will decrease.**

For each of the following, choose the answer that best fits.

5. **How will the demand for cans of soda be affected by an increase in consumer income?**
   A. Demand increases if sodas are inferior goods.
   B. Demand decreases if sodas are normal goods.
   C. Demand increases if sodas are normal goods.
   D. Demand for sodas will be unaffected because income is not a determinant for this good.

6. **Table 3-2 shows Melanie's daily demand for cups of iced tea. If the price of tea falls from $3 to $1, how will Melanie adjust her consumption of tea?**

TABLE 3-2 Melanie's Demand for Iced Tea	
Price per Cup	**Quantity of Cups Demanded (Daily)**
$6	1
$5	2
$4	3
$3	4
$2	5
$1	6

A. Quantity demanded will rise from 4 to 6 cups per day.
B. Quantity demanded will rise from 4 to 5 cups per day.
C. Quantity demanded will fall from 6 to 4 cups per day.
D. Quantity demanded will remain constant at 4 cups per day.

7. Margaret enjoys riding lessons. When the price is $100 per lesson, she will purchase 10 lessons each year. If the price rises to $140, she will purchase only 6 lessons in a year. Using the midpoint formula, Margaret's price elasticity of demand for lessons is:
A. Inelastic and equal to $\frac{2}{3}$.
B. Elastic and equal to 2.0.
C. Elastic and equal to 1.5.
D. Inelastic and equal to 1.0.

8. Assuming that consumers like to consume tortillas and refried beans together, which of the following statements is accurate?
A. When the price of tortillas increases, the demand for refried beans increases.
B. When the price of tortillas decreases, the demand for refried beans decreases.
C. When the price of refried beans decreases, the demand for tortillas increases.
D. When the price of refried beans increases, the demand for tortillas increases.

9. Suppose that consumers consider wheat to be a normal good and that the response to a change in income is fairly inelastic. Given this, we would expect:
A. The income elasticity to be positive and less than 1.
B. The income elasticity to be positive and greater than 1.
C. The income elasticity to be negative.
D. The income elasticity to be equal to zero.

10. The price elasticity of demand for Pietro's Pizza is equal to 3. Mr. Pietro wants to increase total revenue, so he should:
A. Decrease the price because demand is inelastic.
B. Decrease the price because demand is elastic.
C. Increase the price because demand is elastic.
D. Increase the price because demand is inelastic.

chapter 4

Production and Cost

In the previous chapter, we covered the demand half of the model of demand and supply; now we turn to the supply half. As we saw in Chapter 3, demand is a result of a buyer's objective of maximizing utility. Similarly, supply is the result of a seller's objective of *maximizing profit*. Before we discuss things like the law of supply and supply curves, it's important to present the processes that go into supplying goods—production and cost. This leads us into the idea of profit maximization—if a seller knows what price a good will sell at, there is some quantity that will give the seller the highest amount of profit at that price (in fact, there is even a handy rule for knowing what that quantity will be).

CHAPTER OBJECTIVES

After completing this chapter, the student should be able to:

1. Understand the difference between inputs that are fixed and inputs that are variable in the production process.

2. Distinguish between the short-run and long-run production periods.

3. Compute the marginal and average products of labor from data on the total product of labor and graph these functions.

4. Understand the concept of diminishing marginal product and why it exists in the short run.

59

5. Make the connection between short-run production and short-run cost functions and how diminishing marginal product of labor implies an increasing marginal cost of production.

The Inputs Used in Production—Fixed and Variable

When we talked about demand in Chapter 3, it was intuitively easy to understand how demand decisions are made. After all, we have been consumers for many years. But when it's time to switch to the supply half, it can be more difficult. Let's try to think about production the way a cook thinks about a recipe. If Eli is going to bake some cakes (the output), he is going to need some production inputs. He will need raw materials (sugar, butter, flour, and chocolate), tools (pans, bowls, mixers, spoons, an oven, and his kitchen), his labor, and his talents (entrepreneurial ability) in bringing these things together to produce cakes. In Chapter 1 we introduced four economic resources. When discussing production, economists often refer to these resources as production inputs or *factors of production*.

If Eli wants to bake more cakes, he will need to acquire more production inputs for the task. He will need to increase his labor input by hiring some assistants in the kitchen. He will also need to increase his purchases of natural resources (the raw materials he uses). The quantities of labor and natural resource inputs are easy to increase if production must increase; because of this, they are often described as *variable inputs*. However, it will be more difficult to increase the size of Eli's kitchen to accommodate more ovens, mixers, and other tools of capital. Because he cannot easily change the quantity of the capital input, it is a *fixed input*. Could he increase the size of his kitchen? Yes, but it would take some time, and this leads us to the next distinction: short- and long-run decisions.

The Short Run and the Long Run

Economists define a time period as the *short run* if it is too brief to change the fixed inputs. If it would take Eli three months to expand the size of his kitchen, install new ovens, and acquire more mixers, then any period of time briefer than three months is his production short run. This allows us to define the *long run* as a period of time long enough for the quantity of fixed inputs, usually capital, to be changed. In Eli's case, the long run would be any period of time longer than three months. This distinction is important because there are limits to what can be produced, and how efficiently it can be produced, in the short run while capital is fixed.

CAUTION   *There is no defined period of time that makes something the long run or the short run. For instance, the short run may be 3 months, 3 years, or even 30 years. The real distinction between the short run and the long run is whether or not the fixed inputs can be changed.*

Short-Run Production

When firms produce output in the short run, they employ variable inputs and combine them with their fixed inputs. We follow the typical pattern by using labor as the variable input and capital as the fixed input to show a short-run production function. Table 4-1 shows how Eli's cake production is a function of how many assistants he employs. When labor is the only variable input with a fixed amount of capital, the output being produced is referred to as the *total product of labor* (TP_L). The *marginal product of labor* (MP_L) is the change in total product when an additional unit of labor is employed, how much more each additional worker produces, or how much the *last* worker produced. The *average product of labor* (AP_L) is the total product divided by the units of labor employed. If units of labor are workers, we can think of this as the average production per worker hired. The two formulas given here show how the marginal and average products of labor are both derived from the total product of labor:

$$MP_L = \left(\frac{\Delta TP_L}{\Delta L} \right)$$

and

$$AP_L = \frac{TP_L}{L}$$

We can then calculate the total, marginal, and average product based on the number of units of labor we use.

For instance, Table 4-1 shows us that when 4 workers are hired, on average, each of those 4 workers produces 8 cakes. The marginal product of the fourth worker shows us that output increases by 6 more cakes than when 3 workers are hired.

TABLE 4-1 Eli's Cake Production as a Function of Labor			
Units of Labor (L)	Total Product of Labor (TP$_L$)	Marginal Product of Labor (MP$_L$)	Average Product of Labor (AP$_L$)
0	0		
1	8	8	8
2	18	10	9
3	26	8	8.66667
4	32	6	8
5	36	4	7.2
6	38	2	6.33333
7	39	1	5.57143
8	38	−1	4.75

Still Struggling

Students sometimes have trouble understanding marginal product and average product intuitively. Here are some hints on how to do so:

- **Marginal product.** Remember to think "the last" or "the next" when you see the word *marginal*. Marginal product is how much production the last unit of input got you (or, conversely, how much additional product the next unit of input will get you).
- **Average product.** This is the production of a typical worker when you have a given number of workers. So if the average product of labor for 4 units of labor is 8, the 4 workers are producing an average of 8 cakes each.

When we convert the first two columns of data in Table 4-1 into the graph in Figure 4-1, we see the short-run production function, which for the most part rises as more units of labor are hired. The shape of this production function is critical to our understanding of how firms are able to supply their output and the topic of our next section.

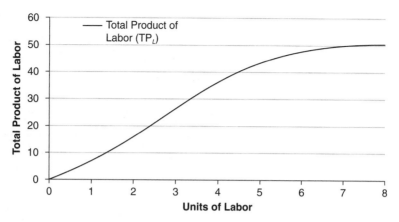

FIGURE 4-1 • Total Product of Labor (TP$_L$)

Diminishing Marginal Product

In Figure 4-1, up to a point, total product rises as more workers are employed. However, output doesn't rise at a steady rate; it rises more slowly up to the maximum output at 7 workers, then falls with the eighth worker. Referring back to Table 4-1, the data show us that after the second worker, the marginal product of labor declines, and eventually becomes negative as more workers are added. The marginal product of labor and average product of labor curves are shown in Figure 4-2.

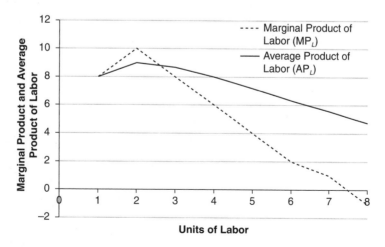

FIGURE 4-2 • Marginal and Average Product of Labor

This *diminishing marginal product* tells us that when you add more and more workers to a fixed quantity of capital, the next unit of labor is unable to contribute as much additional output as the unit of labor that came before. Why does this happen? Eli is hiring additional workers and asking them to work in a fixed space (the kitchen) and to work with a constant quantity of capital tools. As more and more workers are added to this fixed quantity of capital, it simply becomes more difficult for them to produce cakes effectively, and marginal product declines. Eventually it may even become negative as more workers start getting in each other's way.

TIP   *Each point on the marginal product of labor curve is simply the slope of the total product of labor function (the curve shown in Figure 4-1). If the total product curve is getting steeper, the slope is rising, and thus the marginal product of labor curve is rising. If TP_L is rising but getting flatter, the slope is falling, and so the MP_L curve is falling. And if the TP_L begins to fall, the slope is negative, and therefore MP_L has fallen below zero.*

Figure 4-2 also includes the average product of labor curve. Average product rises, reaches a maximum, and then declines as more units of labor are added. There is a close connection between marginal product and average product. If the marginal product of the next worker is greater than the current average product, the next worker will pull the average up. Thus, if marginal product is greater than average product, the average product curve will be rising. Likewise, if the marginal product of the next worker falls below the current average product, that next worker will be pulling down the average. In the graph, this means that if marginal product is below average product, the average product curve will be declining.

Costs in the Short Run

The previous section presented the production function and diminishing returns. We showed that in the short run, there are variable inputs and at least one fixed input. In order to employ these inputs, the firm must incur production costs (that is, pay for the inputs). These costs help to explain how and why firms can supply units of output to the market.

Total fixed costs (TFC) are costs that do not change when the firm wishes to increase or decrease output in the short run. These are the payments necessary to employ the fixed inputs in the production function. *Total variable costs* (TVC) are costs that rise and fall with short-run output. These are the payments necessary to employ the variable inputs in the short-run production function. It makes sense, then, that *total cost* (TC) is the sum of total fixed and total variable costs at each level of output. In an equation, we say that

$$TC = TFC + TVC$$

Suppose that Eli has determined that he has $200 of total fixed costs and that he must pay $50 to each assistant that he employs. Table 4-2 incorporates the short-run production data with these fixed and variable costs.

TABLE 4-2 Eli's Short-Run Costs

Units of Labor (L)	Total Output (Q)	Total Variable Cost	Total Fixed Cost	Total Cost
0	0	$ —	$200	$200
1	8	$ 50	$200	$250
2	18	$100	$200	$300
3	26	$150	$200	$350
4	32	$200	$200	$400
5	36	$250	$200	$450
6	38	$300	$200	$500
7	39	$350	$200	$550
8	38	$400	$200	$600

To see how these short-run total costs look in a graph, we plot them with total output on the horizontal axis in Figure 4-3. Total fixed cost appears as a horizontal line at $200 because it doesn't change when output rises or falls. Total variable cost begins at zero, but rises as more output is produced. In fact, it begins to rise more and more quickly at the highest levels of output. The total cost curve is simply the constant dollars of total fixed cost added to the total variable cost curve, so it has the same shape as the total variable cost curve. At any level of output, the vertical distance between total cost and total variable cost is the $200 of total fixed cost.

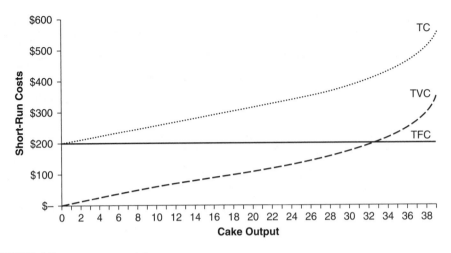

FIGURE 4-3 · Short-Run Total Costs

Increasing Marginal Cost

There are several important short-run cost functions, but for the moment we focus on *marginal cost*. Marginal cost (MC) is defined as the additional cost of producing the next unit of output, or, in the bakery, how much more it costs to produce one more cake. Mathematically,

$$MC = \left(\frac{\Delta TC}{\Delta Q} \right) = \left(\frac{\Delta TVC}{\Delta Q} \right)$$

The marginal cost of producing additional cakes is presented in Table 4-3. For example, the marginal cost of increasing output from 0 to 8 cakes is equal to ($50/8 cakes), or $6.25 per additional cake. Similar computations show that marginal cost briefly declines, but then increases rapidly as more cakes are produced. When marginal cost is graphed, as in Figure 4-4, we can see that once output exceeds 18 cakes, the marginal cost curve is upward-sloping and getting steeper. This increasing marginal cost curve is a direct result of the diminishing marginal returns that Eli experienced in his short-run production function.

Recall that each worker was producing fewer and fewer additional units, yet Eli is paying each worker $50 when he or she is employed. Because each worker produces fewer additional units, the additional *cost* of those units is rising.

TABLE 4-3 Eli's Marginal Cost		
Total Output (Q)	**Total Variable Cost (TVC)**	**Marginal Cost (MC)**
0	$ —	
8	$ 50	$ 6.25
18	$100	$ 5.00
26	$150	$ 6.25
32	$200	$ 8.33
36	$250	$12.50
38	$300	$25.00
39	$350	$50.00

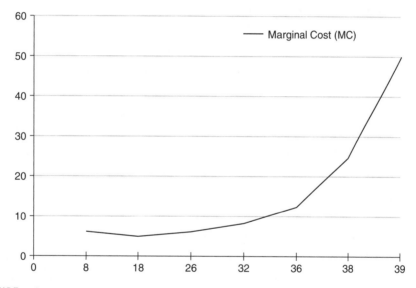

FIGURE 4-4 · Marginal Cost

There is some intuition about supply curves in this rising curve: because the marginal cost of each additional unit is rising, the only reason that Eli's firm will produce additional units is if he is able to sell them at higher and higher prices. This positive relationship between more output, higher marginal cost, and higher selling prices is the foundation for supply curves, the topic of our next chapter. Profit, and the firm's motivation to maximize profit, will be covered in much more detail in Chapter 7.

Still Struggling?

With a little bit of algebra, we can see the relationship shared by the marginal product of labor and the marginal cost of production. Suppose that a firm's only variable input is labor (L), and that it is paid a constant market wage (w). In this case, the total variable cost TVC is equal to $w \times L$. Marginal cost can be written as

$$MC = \frac{\Delta TVC}{\Delta Q} = \frac{\Delta(w \times L)}{\Delta Q}$$

And because the wage is constant, and because ($\Delta L/\Delta Q$) is the inverse of the marginal product of labor, we can make the following substitutions:

$$MC = \frac{\Delta TVC}{\Delta Q} = \frac{\Delta(w \times L)}{\Delta Q} = w \times \left(\frac{\Delta L}{\Delta Q}\right) = w \times \left(\frac{1}{MP_L}\right)$$

So marginal cost is simply the inverse of marginal product of labor, multiplied by the constant wage. This clearly shows us that if MP_L is falling, MC must be rising.

TIP *Calculating many of these quantities by hand is tedious and doesn't really help you develop your skills unless you need additional practice in basic math. A good alternative is to use a simple spreadsheet program (such as Microsoft Excel) to perform these calculations for you. This has the added benefit of making it easy to see how your conclusions might change if something changed, such as the cost of labor, without your having to go back and recalculate everything by hand.*

Summary

This chapter began by discussing how the hiring of some production inputs can be changed to produce more or less output, but that in the short run, some inputs must remain fixed in quantity. The short-run period of time is a period that is too brief to change these fixed inputs. If labor is the only variable input and labor is being hired to work with a fixed amount of capital, the marginal product of labor will eventually diminish. When inputs are hired, they must be paid, and so in the short run, there are some costs that are fixed and some that are variable. As more output is produced, the total variable cost of production rises more quickly; thus the marginal cost of producing the next unit also rises. The rising marginal cost of producing the next unit is a direct result of the diminishing returns from hiring the next unit of labor. When the marginal product of labor is falling, the marginal cost of production is rising.

QUIZ

Is each of the following statements *true* or *false*? Explain.

1. When the marginal product of labor is falling, the total product of labor is falling.

2. In the long run, all inputs are variable.

3. Diminishing marginal product is a short-run phenomenon.

4. The short-run total fixed cost curve rises at an increasing rate as more output is produced.

5. Diminishing returns to variable inputs implies rising marginal production costs.

For each of the following, choose the answer that best fits.

6. Which of the following statements is *false* about short-run production functions?
    A. As more labor is employed, the marginal product of labor eventually decreases.
    B. If the marginal product of labor exceeds the average product of labor, the average product is rising.
    C. If the total product of labor is rising, the marginal product of labor must be positive.
    D. If the marginal product of labor is rising, the total product of labor is falling.

Use Table 4-4 to answer questions 7 and 8.

TABLE 4-4	
Units of Labor (*L*)	Total Product of Labor (TP$_L$)
0	0
1	5
2	13
3	20
4	26
5	31
6	35
7	38
8	40
9	39

7. In Table 4-4, the first unit of labor to see diminishing marginal product is the _____ unit.
    A. third
    B. second
    C. fourth
    D. ninth

8. The average product of labor is equal to _____ units when 8 units of labor are hired.
    A. 40
    B. 2
    C. 5
    D. −1

9. When the marginal cost curve is rising, it must be the case that:
    A. The total cost curve is falling.
    B. The marginal product of labor curve is falling.
    C. The total variable cost curve is constant.
    D. The average product of labor is falling.

10. Haley operates a shop that will gift-wrap and ship presents to friends and family. Which of the following choices is most likely a short-run fixed cost for her small business?
    A. Wages paid to her part-time hourly employees
    B. The cost of stamps used to send the packages
    C. The cost of wrapping paper, ribbons, and bows for the packages
    D. The monthly rent she pays the owner of her building

chapter **5**

Supply

The previous chapter showed that firms experience diminishing marginal product in the short run. This diminishing marginal product implies that the marginal cost of producing additional units of output is rising. An upward-sloping marginal cost curve is an important concept because it allows us to understand something called the *law of supply*.

CHAPTER OBJECTIVES

After completing this chapter, the student should be able to:

1. Explain how the upward-sloping marginal cost curve serves as the basis for the upward-sloping supply curve.

2. Understand how several determinants of supply can shift the supply curve outward or inward.

3. Compute and interpret the price elasticity of supply.

The Marginal Cost Curve

You might recall from Chapters 1 and 2 that economists assume that consumers make choices at the margin. On the consumer's side, this means that if the marginal benefit of consuming the next unit is greater than or equal to the marginal cost of that unit, the person will consume it to increase his utility. The same kind of choice is available to the producer who is considering the production of the next unit. If the marginal benefit (for the supplier, that would be the price that it receives) of producing that unit is greater than or equal to the marginal cost of producing it, the firm will produce that unit, and the profits earned by the firm will rise.

Figure 5-1 shows an upward-sloping marginal cost curve for a firm. At the current price P_1, the firm has found it optimal to produce quantity Q_1 because that is where the price equals the marginal cost. However, suppose the price rises to P_2. The firm will then realize that, at the current production level Q_1, the price is now greater than the marginal cost. In fact, this is true for *all* additional units up to Q_2, so the firm will increase output upward along the marginal cost curve. Had the price fallen, the firm would have made the rational choice to produce fewer units by moving downward along the marginal cost curve. This behavior allows us to predict a positive relationship between the price of a product and the quantity of that product produced by firms.

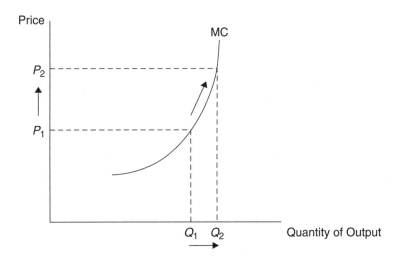

FIGURE 5-1 • Upward-Sloping Supply Curve

TIP   *Here is another way to think about it. Suppose the price is P_1. It would not make sense for the producer to produce Q_2 units when the price is P_1 because the marginal cost of Q_2 is higher at P_2. At a price of P_1, producing Q_2 units would be producing at a point where MC > MB.*

The Law of Supply

The *law of supply* says that if we hold all other factors constant (*ceteris paribus*), an increase in the price of a good will cause suppliers to increase their production of that good. Suppose that Margaret is a supplier of chicken nuggets who can produce boxes of nuggets that contain 12 nuggets in each box. Table 5-1 shows the quantity of nuggets that she will supply at a variety of prices. The law of supply is seen in the table because she chooses to increase her quantity supplied only at higher prices, and at lower prices she will reduce the quantity she supplies.

| **TABLE 5-1** Margaret's Supply of Chicken Nuggets ||
Price per Box of a Dozen Chicken Nuggets	**Quantity Supplied (Boxes per Week)**
$0	0
$1.00	20
$2.00	40
$3.00	60
$4.00	80
$5.00	100

Supply Curves

When we convert the data seen in Table 5-1 into a graph, we create an upward-sloping *supply curve*. Figure 5-2 illustrates Margaret's weekly supply of chicken nuggets, and again we see that when the price rises, her quantity of nuggets supplied rises along the supply curve.

There are many factors (or *determinants*) that might affect Margaret's supply of nuggets. The law of supply holds all other determinants constant and focuses on the impact of price on her production. When we allow the determinants to change, we see changes in the location of the supply curve.

CAUTION *There is an important distinction between a change in quantity supplied and a change in supply. When the price of chicken nuggets rises, there is an increase in the quantity supplied of nuggets. This is seen on a graph as an upward movement along the fixed supply curve. But if one of the determinants*

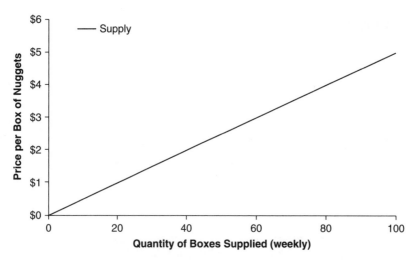

FIGURE 5-2 • Margaret's Supply of Chicken Nuggets

described in the next section changes, the entire supply curve will move to the right or to the left. It seems like an unimportant nuance, but using very precise language allows us to clearly differentiate these two very different changes.

Determinants of Supply

In Chapter 3 we discussed how demand curves can shift rightward or leftward in a graph when certain demand determinants change. Supply curves can also shift to the right (an increase in supply) or to the left (a decrease in supply) as a result of a change in a small number of supply determinants. Figure 5-3 shows an increase in supply as a shift from curve S_0 to S_1. When this occurs, suppliers like Margaret will be willing to supply more units to the market at any price. A decrease in supply is shown as a shift from curve S_0 to S_2. In this case, the quantity that producers are willing to supply has fallen at all potential prices.

Economists usually describe the following as determinants of supply:

1. Input Prices

Producers must employ inputs (or factors of production) to supply their final products. When an input becomes more expensive to employ, it becomes more costly to produce each unit, and the supply curve will shift to the left, or decrease. If the price of an input decreases, the supply curve will shift to the

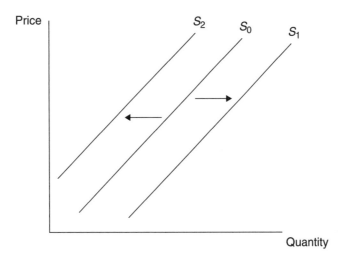

FIGURE 5-3 · Shifts in the Supply Curve

right, or supply will increase. For example, if the price of chicken increased, Margaret's supply curve would shift to the left because it would now be more costly to produce chicken nuggets.

2. Production Technology

Producers all use some level of technology to produce their goods and services. It may be rather simple, like that used to wash windows, or it may be quite complex technology, like that used in the development of Microsoft's Windows software. If available production technology improves, perhaps through faster machinery or better communications, it makes it easier for firms to supply goods and services, and we will see supply curves shift to the right. For example, if Margaret had faster machines that could package more nuggets in a day, she would be able to supply more boxes at any price, and her supply curve would shift to the right.

3. Prices of Related Goods and Services

Firms can often produce several different products for sale to consumers, and they will alter their production plans if one of these products becomes less lucrative than the others. For example, suppose that Margaret, in addition to chicken nuggets, can also produce fish sticks. If the price of fish sticks is rising, Margaret will earn more money if she decreases the supply of chicken nuggets and increases the quantity of fish sticks that she will supply. Graphically, the supply curve for chicken nuggets is shifting to the left, but the supply curve for fish sticks is not shifting; there is simply an upward movement along the supply curve at the higher price of fish sticks.

4. Expectations

Producers, like consumers, respond to expectations of future prices. For example, the producers of lawn chairs know that demand for these items increases in the summer months. Consumers are willing to pay higher prices for lawn chairs in the summer, so producers decrease the supply of lawn chairs in the winter when demand, and price, is lower. If firms expect the future price of a product to be higher, they will decrease the supply of that product today.

5. Number of Producers

When more firms are engaged in the production of a particular good, the total supply of that good begins to increase. The supply of chicken nuggets will be greater if several firms enter the market to compete with Margaret's product. In this case, the market supply curve for chicken nuggets shifts to the right.

The Price Elasticity of Supply

The law of supply tells us that, all else held constant, when the price of a product rises, firms increase the quantity of that product that they supply. The *price elasticity of supply* gives us more information by telling us how responsive quantity supplied is to that change in the price.

Mathematically, the price elasticity of supply is defined as the percentage change in quantity supplied divided by the percentage change in the price, or

$$E_s = \frac{\%\Delta Q_s}{\%\Delta P}$$

For example, if the price of gasoline increases 10 percent and the quantity of gasoline supplied increases by 5 percent, the calculation is simply $E_s = (5\%/10\%) = 0.50$. In this example, supply is inelastic because the increase in the quantity supplied is smaller than the increase in the price. Any elasticity that is less than 1 is an inelastic supply response to a change in price. The least elastic, or perfectly inelastic, supply curve is a vertical supply curve. In this special case, a change in price would have no effect on the quantity supplied and the price elasticity of supply is equal to zero.

If the price of chicken nuggets increases by 10 percent and the quantity of nuggets supplied increases by 20 percent, the price elasticity of supply is equal to 2. Any elasticity greater than 1 describes an elastic supply response. The most elastic, or perfectly elastic, supply curve is one that is drawn as horizontal. In this special case, any small change in price would cause a huge response in supply, and the elasticity would be infinitely large.

As in the analysis in Chapter 3, we can use two overlapping supply curves to show how different elasticities affect the shape of supply curves. Figure 5-4 shows curve S_e as nearly horizontal and the curve S_i as nearly vertical. Suppose that the price for both of these goods is initially at P_0 and firms are producing the same quantity of each good, Q_0. If the price increases by 10 percent, the quantity supplied rises by many more units along supply curve S_e than it rises along supply curve S_i. We can see that, all else equal, steeper supply curves will exhibit less elastic responses to a given price change.

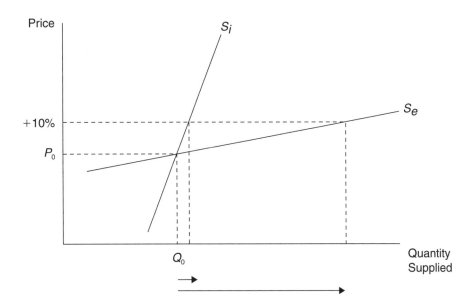

FIGURE 5-4 • Effect of Elasticity on Quantity Supplied

In Chapter 3 we introduced the price elasticity of demand and the midpoint method of computing the elasticity between two points on the demand curve. The same thing can be done for the price elasticity of supply between two points on the supply curve. Using similar notation to that presented in Chapter 3, the midpoint formula would look like

$$E_s = \frac{\%\Delta Q_s}{\%\Delta P} = \left(\frac{Q_1 - Q_0}{P_1 - P_0}\right) \times \frac{\bar{P}}{\bar{Q}}$$

Economists generally assume that price elasticity of supply is influenced by a couple of factors.

1. Availability of Inputs

A firm can increase output quickly in response to a higher price if more inputs can be quickly employed. For example, suppose that Margaret's chicken nuggets factory operates only one production shift, from 8 a.m. to 5 p.m. If the price of chicken nuggets begins to rise, Margaret doesn't need to build a new factory; she can simply employ more workers to work a night shift. If she can do this easily, her price elasticity of supply may be large. If a firm cannot find more inputs easily, or if those inputs are quite expensive to employ, the price elasticity may be smaller. The same would be true if there were no good ways to substitute machines for those workers. For example, suppose that it was impossible to find enough workers, but it was possible to find nugget-making machines that could do the same job as those workers. In this case, Margaret's elasticity of supply would be elastic and she could produce more nuggets at the higher price.

2. Time

The price elasticity of supply is typically larger when firms have more time to respond to changes in the price of the product. For this reason, supply curves will be more elastic in the long run than they are in the short run. Suppose that Margaret's chicken-nugget factory is already working 24 hours a day with three production shifts. If the price of nuggets continues to rise, she may be unable to increase the quantity supplied this week, so her short-run price elasticity of supply could be very low. A year from now, when she has built a new factory, she will be able to double her production and her price elasticity of supply will be much larger.

Still Struggling

It seems like there are many elasticities to remember, so it might be helpful to review Table 5-2, which provides a quick summary of what each elasticity tells us. Keep in mind one similarity among all elasticities: they all measure the sensitivity of one variable (like quantity demanded or quantity supplied) to a change in some other variable (like a price or income). If the response is relatively big, we say that it is an elastic response, and if it is relatively small, we say that it is an inelastic response.

TABLE 5-2 Summary of Elasticities

Elasticity	Formula	What Does It Measure?	Key Indicators
Price elasticity of demand	$E_d = \dfrac{\%\Delta Q_d}{\%\Delta P}$	The sensitivity of consumption of good X to a change in the price of good X.	$E_d > 1$: elastic $E_d = 1$: unit elastic $E_d < 1$: inelastic (Absolute value)
Income elasticity of demand	$E_i = \dfrac{\%\Delta Q_{xd}}{\%\Delta I}$	The sensitivity of consumption of good X to a change in consumer income.	$E_i > 0$: normal good $E_i < 0$: inferior good
Cross-price elasticity of demand	$E_{xy} = \dfrac{\%\Delta Q_{xd}}{\%\Delta P_y}$	The sensitivity of consumption of good X to a change in the price of good Y.	$E_{xy} > 0$: substitutes $E_{xy} < 0$: complements
Price elasticity of supply	$E_s = \dfrac{\%\Delta Q_s}{\%\Delta P}$	The sensitivity of production of good X to a change in the price of good X.	$E_s > 1$: elastic $E_s = 1$: unit elastic $E_s < 1$: inelastic

Summary

This chapter began by demonstrating the key relationship between the upward-sloping marginal cost curve from the previous chapter, the upward-sloping supply curve, and the law of supply. As the price of a good rises, firms will see that they can profit by increasing the quantity of the good that they supply to consumers. There are also several supply determinants that, when changed, can shift the supply curve either to the right or to the left. Finally, we revisit the concept of elasticity by introducing the price elasticity of supply. In the next chapter we combine demand with supply to build the model of a competitive market.

QUIZ

Is each of the following statements *true* or *false*? Explain.

1. The law of supply is really a result of diminishing marginal returns to production.

2. If the price of corn chips falls, suppliers will increase the quantity of corn chips supplied.

3. An outward shift in the supply curve for soybeans means that, at any price, firms will increases the quantity of soybeans supplied.

4. As more time passes after a change in the price, supply curves become less elastic.

Give a short answer to the following questions.

5. When the price of a pound of bacon is $3, suppose that a local farmer will supply 300 pounds of bacon. If the price falls to $2 per pound, the farmer will supply 200 pounds of bacon. Using the midpoint formula, calculate the price elasticity of supply.

6. Consider the supply of automobiles. What will happen to the supply of automobiles if steel, a key production input, becomes less expensive? In a graph, show any movements of the supply curve for automobiles.

For each of the following, choose the answer that best fits.

7. Consider the supply of televisions. If the price of televisions increased, we would expect:
   A. The supply of televisions to shift to the right.
   B. The supply of televisions to shift to the left.
   C. An increase in the quantity of televisions supplied along the fixed supply curve.
   D. No change in the supply of televisions.

8. Consider the supply of apple pies. If the price of a pound of apples rises, we would expect:
   A. The supply of apple pies to shift to the right.
   B. The supply of apple pies to shift to the left.
   C. A decrease in the quantity of apple pies supplied along the fixed supply curve.
   D. No change in the supply of apple pies.

9. Suppose the marginal cost of producing textbooks is constant and always equal to $80. This would imply that the supply of textbooks is:

   A. Horizontal at a price of $80.
   B. Downward-sloping between the prices of $80 and $0.
   C. Upward-sloping between the prices of $0 and $80.
   D. Vertical at a quantity of 80 textbooks.

10. Which of the following might cause the supply of chocolate chip cookies to be *less* elastic after an increase in the price of the cookies?

   A. Cookie producers are now operating in the long run.
   B. Cookie producers can ask their employees to work overtime at the bakeries.
   C. Chocolate chips are currently unavailable because of a shortage of cocoa beans.
   D. Sugar cane growers currently have had a huge crop, and there is a surplus of sugar.

Market Equilibrium

While the first few chapters of this book have mentioned a "market" for certain products, we have not yet formally defined a market. A *product market* is any mechanism through which buyers and sellers meet to exchange goods and services. There are also *factor markets*, like the labor market, where buyers and sellers exchange the factors of production. We address factor markets in Chapter 10, but our focus now is on product markets. We also show in this chapter how economists believe competitive markets come to an efficient equilibrium outcome and what happens to this outcome when the government intervenes in the market.

CHAPTER OBJECTIVES

After completing this chapter, the student should be able to:

1. Describe the characteristics of competitive markets.

2. Explain why the market equilibrium price exists only at the output level where quantity demanded equals quantity supplied.

3. Draw a graph that shows the market equilibrium and how the market adjusts to shifts in demand, supply, or both.

4. Show the areas of consumer and producer surplus in a graph of the market.

5. Understand why competitive markets produce the most efficient outcome and how policies like price controls and excise taxes create deadweight loss.

Competitive Markets

There are two halves to any market: buyers and sellers. We have shown that the behavior of the buyers is grounded in utility maximization and is embodied in the downward-sloping demand curve. The behavior of the sellers is grounded in profit maximization and is embodied in the upward-sloping supply curve. There is a special kind of market, known as a *perfectly competitive market*, that has certain characteristics that predict how these two groups will interact to produce an outcome that economists believe to be the most efficient. Before we get to this market outcome, however, let's quickly identify the characteristics of competitive markets. (We provide a more in-depth analysis of perfectly competitive producers in Chapter 7.)

So what makes a market competitive? Essentially, it's the combination of two assumptions: first, there are many buyers and sellers, and second, because there are many buyers and sellers, no single individual can affect the price through her individual actions. For example, if I decide to buy more gasoline today, my decision will not affect the market price of gasoline. If one corn farmer has a bountiful harvest and supplies more corn to the market, his actions will not affect the market price of corn. We see in later chapters that when there is only one seller (monopoly) or one buyer (monopsony), the market outcome is far different from the competitive outcome, and not in a good way. Under these two assumptions, the equilibrium market price is determined by the competitive interaction of buyers and sellers.

Equilibrium

When we combine the demand for a particular good with the supply of that good, we create a model for that product market. Our purpose now is to determine how the market manages to find the *equilibrium* price and quantity. Equilibrium refers to a state of rest or balance between opposing forces. In a market, it describes an outcome in which the price has no tendency to rise or to fall. It also describes an outcome in which the quantity of units demanded by consumers is exactly the quantity of units supplied by producers.

TIP *Mathematically speaking, when a market is in equilibrium, we say that there exists a price P* such that*

$$Q_d(P^*) = Q_s(P^*)$$

where $Q_d(P^*)$ is the quantity demanded when the price is P* and Q_s is the quantity supplied when the price is P*.

For example, suppose that the market for bicycles is competitive. Table 6-1 presents both the quantity of bicycles demanded and the quantity supplied at a variety of prices. As we can see, consumers respond to lower prices by increasing the quantity of bikes demanded. Suppliers are encouraged by higher prices to increase the quantity of bikes supplied. The only price where the quantity of bikes demanded is equal to the quantity of bikes supplied is the price of $300. This is the equilibrium price, and the equilibrium quantity of bikes exchanged in the market is 600.

TABLE 6-1 Supply and Demand for Bicycles

Price of Bicycles	Quantity Demanded	Quantity Supplied
$100	1,000	200
$150	900	300
$200	800	400
$250	700	500
$300	600	600
$350	500	700
$400	400	800
$450	300	900
$500	200	1,000

TIP *Mathematically speaking, the equations associated with the supply of bicycles curve and demand for bicycles curve are:*

Demand:

$$P_d = 600 - \frac{1}{2} Q_d$$

Supply:

$$P_s = \frac{1}{2} Q_s$$

The market for bikes is shown in Figure 6-1. The demand curve intersects the supply curve at the equilibrium price of $300 and equilibrium quantity of 600 bikes. This intersection point is the *equilibrium* in this market, that is, the point at which the quantity demanded is equal to the quantity supplied.

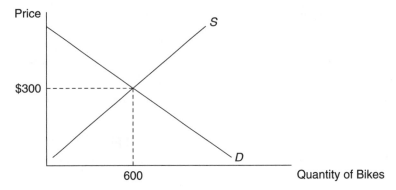

FIGURE 6-1 • Supply and Demand for Bicycles

TIP *The equilibrium price and quantity can also be found by solving the two equations for supply and demand for the two unknowns, P and Q*

Assume that there exists some equilibrium price $P^* = P_s = P_d$ where $Q^* = Q_d(P^*) = Q_s(P^*)$. In this case, our two equations become

$$P^* = 600 - \frac{1}{2} Q^*$$

and

$$P^* = \frac{1}{2} Q^*$$

We can now set these equal to solve for Q^*:

$$600 - \frac{1}{2} Q^* = \frac{1}{2} Q^*$$
$$600 = Q^*$$

We can then plug this into either the supply or the demand curve to get the equilibrium price:

$$P^* = 600 - \frac{1}{2} (600) = 600 - 300 = \$300$$

or

$$P* = \frac{1}{2}\,(600) = \$300$$

What would happen if the current price of bikes were something other than $300? Suppose that the current price of bikes is $400. We see from Table 6-1 that the quantity of bikes supplied would be 800, but the quantity of bikes demanded would be only 400. When the quantity supplied exceeds the quantity demanded, we say that there is *excess supply* or that a *surplus* of bikes exists. Specifically, there is a surplus of 400 bikes that are unsold at the price of $400, and that surplus can be seen in the graph in Figure 6-2 as the difference between the quantity supplied and the quantity demanded.

Why couldn't this be an equilibrium outcome? Because sellers are not going to sit and stare at 400 bikes going unsold; they will begin to lower the price. As the price falls, the quantity of bikes demanded begins to rise and the quantity of bikes supplied begins to fall. Refer back to Table 6-1 again. At a slightly lower price of $350, the surplus is smaller, only 200 bikes. Eventually the price will fall to $300 and fall no further because the surplus will have been cleared and the market will be back to where the supply curve intersects the demand curve.

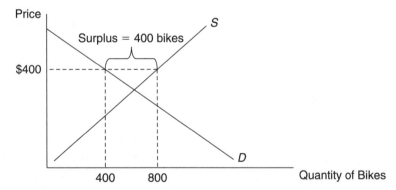

FIGURE 6-2 • Supply and Demand with a Surplus of Bicycles

Suppose instead that the current price of bikes is a very low $150. Table 6-1 tells us that the quantity of bikes demanded would be 900, but the quantity of bikes supplied would be only 300. When the quantity demanded exceeds the quantity supplied, we say that there is *excess demand* or that a *shortage* of bikes exists. In fact, there is a shortage of 600 bikes that are unavailable at a price of $150, and that shortage can be seen on the graph in Figure 6-3 as the difference between the quantity demanded and the quantity supplied.

Why couldn't this be an equilibrium outcome? When there are many buyers clamoring for low-priced bikes, but the sellers are unwilling to sell at that price, buyers will begin to offer higher prices. As the price rises, the quantity of bikes supplied begins to increase and the quantity of bikes demanded begins to fall. If the price were to rise to $250, the shortage would be only 200 bikes. Eventually the price will rise to $300, then rise no further because the shortage will have been cleared and the market will be back to where the supply curve intersects the demand curve. There is only one price, $300 in this example, that will clear a market of either a surplus or a shortage. In fact the equilibrium price is often called the *market-clearing price*.

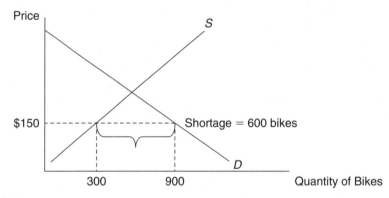

FIGURE 6-3 • Supply and Demand with a Shortage of Bicycles

Changes to Equilibrium

Once a market has reached equilibrium, it may not remain at that price for long. When the demand curve, the supply curve, or both curves shift, the market will adjust to a new equilibrium price and quantity. Using some of the determinants of demand (Chapter 3) and supply (Chapter 5), we take a look at some possible scenarios.

Shifts in Demand

Suppose that bikes are normal goods and consumer income rises. This causes the demand for bikes to increase (shift to the right or shift out) from the original demand curve D_0 to the new demand curve D_1 in Figure 6-4. The graph shows that at a price of $300, there are now twice as many bikes demanded (1,200) as there are supplied (600). This increase in demand has caused a shortage of bikes, but this shortage is only temporary, as there will be pressure on the price to increase to clear the shortage. In fact, the equilibrium price will rise from $300 to $400, and the equilibrium quantity will increase from 600 to 800 bikes.

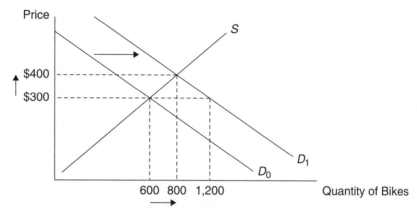

FIGURE 6-4 • Supply and Demand with an Increased Demand for Bicycles

Suppose that people who don't own cars can commute to work and to school either by city bus or by riding their bikes. If the price of riding the bus falls, this low-cost substitute will become more popular and the demand for bikes will decrease. This causes the demand for bikes to shift to the left, from the original demand curve D_0 to the new demand curve D_1. Figure 6-5 shows that after this shift, there are only half as many bikes demanded (300) at a price of $300 as there are supplied (600). Falling demand has caused a surplus of bikes, but this surplus is only temporary, as there will be pressure on the price to decrease until the surplus is cleared. In fact, the equilibrium price will fall from $300 to $200, and the equilibrium quantity will decrease from 600 to 400 bikes.

TIP *Notice that these two demand shifts demonstrate that the price and quantity change in the same direction as the demand shift itself. When demand increases, price and quantity both increase; when demand decreases, price and quantity both decrease.*

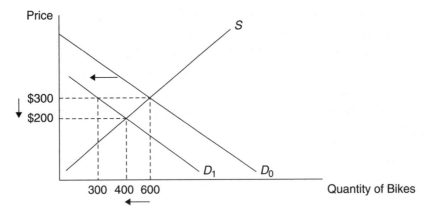

FIGURE 6-5 • Supply and Demand with a Decreased Demand for Bicycles

Shifts in Supply

Suppose that there are vast improvements in the technology used in producing bicycles. As a result, the supply increases, which shows up as a shift to the right of the supply curve from S_0 to S_1 in Figure 6-6. We see in the figure that at the original price of $300, the quantity supplied of 1,200 bikes exceeds the quantity demanded of 600. This surplus of bikes will not last because there will be pressure on the price to decrease. The new market-clearing price falls to $200, and 800 bikes is the new equilibrium quantity in the market.

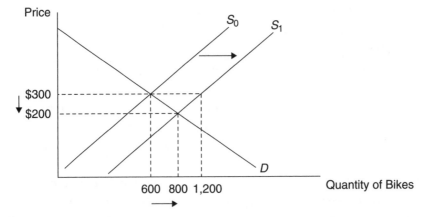

FIGURE 6-6 • Supply and Demand with an Increased Supply of Bicycles

Now suppose that the price of titanium, a key input in the construction of bicycles, increases. This causes the supply curve to shift to the left from S_0 to S_1 in Figure 6-7. We see in the figure that at the original price of $300, the quantity supplied of 300 bikes is less than the quantity demanded of 600. This shortage of bikes is temporary because there will be pressure on the price to increase. The new market-clearing price rises to $400, and the new equilibrium quantity in the market falls to 400 bikes.

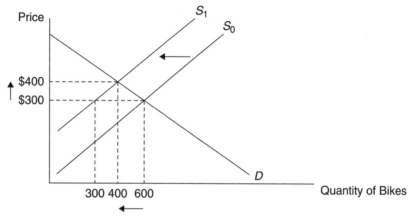

FIGURE 6-7 • Supply and Demand with a Decreased Supply of Bicycles

TIP *When supply shifts, the equilibrium quantity goes in the same direction, but the price goes in the opposite direction. When supply increases, quantity increases and price decreases; when supply decreases, quantity decreases and price increases.*

CAUTION *It is tempting to think of the shifts as "up" when demand or supply increases and as "down" when supply or demand decreases. Resist this urge—what looks like a shift up of a supply curve is really a decrease in the supply curve.*

Shifts in both Demand and Supply

Market equilibrium can be complicated when demand and supply *both* happen to shift. In these cases, predicting the ultimate impact on both price and quantity is less clear.

For example, suppose we combine a rightward shift of demand (caused by higher consumer income) with a rightward shift of supply (caused by better productive technology). These shifts are presented in Figure 6-8 without using specific numbers. The demand shift would cause both quantity and price to rise in the market for bikes. The supply shift would cause quantity to rise, but price to fall. When the two phenomena are combined, we can see that quantity will certainly rise, but that the change in price is ambiguous. If the demand shift is stronger than the supply shift, the price will rise. However, if the demand shift is weaker than the supply shift, the price will fall.

If we had shown both demand and supply shifting to the left, we would see a similar result. The demand shift would cause both quantity and price to fall, while the supply shift would cause quantity to fall and price to rise. Once again, the change in equilibrium quantity is clear; it would decrease. However, the change in equilibrium price would depend upon which shift, demand or supply, was stronger.

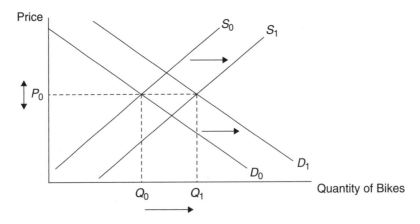

FIGURE 6-8 • Increases in both Supply of and Demand for Bicycles

CAUTION *When you see a graph like the one in Figure 6-8, it is tempting to say that the price "hasn't changed." Resist this urge. The fact is that without more information, we don't know whether the ultimate impact on price is that the price goes up, goes down, or stays the same. If you say that the price hasn't changed, you are asserting that this is the only possible outcome, and this is inaccurate.*

Suppose we combine a leftward shift in demand (caused by inexpensive bus tickets) with a rightward shift in supply (caused by improved bike-making technology). The impact of these shifts is shown in Figure 6-9. The demand shift will cause both quantity and price to fall in the market for bikes. The

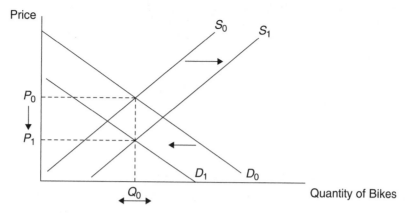

FIGURE 6-9 • Increased Supply of and Decreased Demand for Bicycles

supply shift will cause quantity to rise, but price to fall. When the two phenomena are combined, we can see that price will definitely fall, but that the change in quantity is ambiguous. If the demand shift is stronger than the supply shift, quantity will fall. If the demand shift is weaker than the supply shift, quantity will rise.

If demand had shifted to the right and supply had shifted to the left, we would see a similar result. The demand shift would cause both quantity and price to rise, while the supply shift would cause quantity to fall and price to rise. Once again, the change in equilibrium price is clear: it would increase. But the change in equilibrium quantity is ambiguous and would depend upon which shift, demand or supply, is stronger.

Still Struggling

Until you have had enough practice, all of these potential shifts can seem confusing. The best way to tackle an assignment or an exam is to draw the graphs and see what happens to the price and the quantity. Until you become more comfortable with shifting these graphs, Table 6-2 summarizes how shifts of demand, supply, or both curves cause changes in equilibrium market price and quantity.

TABLE 6-2 Effects of Supply and Demand Changes on Price and Quantity

Change in Demand	Change in Supply	Market Price	Market Quantity
Increases		Increases	Increases
Decreases		Decreases	Decreases
	Increases	Decreases	Increases
	Decreases	Increases	Decreases
Increases	Increases	Ambiguous	Increases
Decreases	Decreases	Ambiguous	Decreases
Increases	Decreases	Increases	Ambiguous
Decreases	Increases	Decreases	Ambiguous

TIP *Another way you can make a table of the changes, using shorthand, is shown in Table 6-3.*

TABLE 6-3 Shorthand for Effect of Supply and Demand Changes on Price and Quantity

Change	Effect on P^*	Effect on Q^*
$D\uparrow$	$P\uparrow$	$Q^*\uparrow$
$D\downarrow$	$P^*\downarrow$	$Q^*\downarrow$
$S\downarrow$	$P^*\uparrow$	$Q^*\downarrow$
$S\uparrow$	$P\downarrow$	$Q^*\uparrow$

It's not a problem that this table shows only one curve changing at a time. If you see arrows going in the same direction, you know for sure what is happening to price and quantity. If the arrows are going in opposite directions, then the effect is ambiguous. For instance, if demand and supply are both increasing at the same time, the quantity arrows are both pointing up, so we know for sure that quantity will increase. However, the arrows on price go in opposite directions.

Efficiency in Competitive Markets

The simplifying assumptions of competitive markets produce a nice result—they are efficient. This efficiency is why many economists promote competition in as many markets as possible. Efficiency means something very specific to economists. In the context of a market equilibrium price and quantity, an outcome is efficient if it maximizes *total surplus*, the sum of *consumer surplus* and *producer surplus* (the term *welfare* is frequently used instead of *surplus*, so you may sometimes see the terms *consumer welfare*, *producer welfare*, and *total welfare*). Consumer surplus is the difference between the highest price that a consumer *would have* paid for an item and the price she *actually* paid for that item. The highest price that a consumer would have paid for each unit of a good is found from the demand curve for that good, and the price a consumer actually pays is determined in the market, at the intersection of the market demand and market supply curves. So if Sally would have paid $20 (her marginal benefit) for a large pizza, but the market price for that pizza was only $15, Sally enjoyed $5 of consumer surplus. In a demand and supply graph, we see consumer surplus as the area under a demand curve and above the market price.

Producer surplus is the difference between the price that a seller *actually* received for a unit produced and the lowest price he *would have* accepted for that unit. Again, the price that a producer actually receives is determined in the market, at the intersection of the market demand and market supply curves. The lowest price that a producer would have accepted for each unit of a good is found from the supply curve for that good. So if Pedro would have accepted $5 (his marginal cost) to produce a large pizza, and the market price for that pizza was $15, Pedro enjoys $10 of producer surplus. In a demand and supply graph, we see producer surplus as the area below the market price and above the supply curve.

Let's consider all the buyers and sellers in this market, not just Sally and Pedro. Figure 6-10 shows both the consumer surplus (CS) and the producer surplus (PS) in the market for large pizzas. At the equilibrium price of $15, suppose 1,000 large pizzas are bought and sold each week. Note that this means that some people who would have been willing to pay more than $15 benefit from this price, and that some sellers who would have been willing to sell at a lower price also benefit.

This outcome is efficient because the sum total of consumer and producer surplus, total surplus, is as large as it can be. In other words, no other quantity of pizzas can produce a larger combined area of total surplus. How do we know that this is true?

Suppose that we were able to control this market and we decided that only 900 pizzas could be bought and sold at a price of $15 (a fixed quantity like this

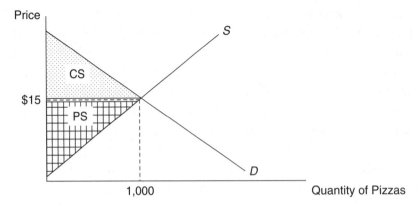

FIGURE 6-10 · Consumer and Producer Surplus

is known as a *quota*). In other words, we blocked the market's natural inclination to move to the equilibrium quantity of 1,000 pizzas. The impact on total surplus is seen in Figure 6-11. Much of the original consumer and producer surplus still exists, but there is a triangle of surplus between 900 and 1,000 pizzas that is not earned by consumers or producers. This lost surplus is called *deadweight loss* (DWL), and it represents the combined loss of consumer and producer surplus that goes unearned because there are 100 transactions (the pizzas) that go unmade. There are consumers who are willing to pay more than $15 for a pizza, and there are producers that would profit from selling those 100 pizzas. Mutually beneficial transactions are prevented from happening because we have blocked the market from operating freely, and thus we have lost our efficient outcome.

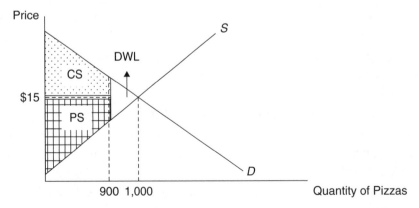

FIGURE 6-11 · Deadweight Loss from a Smaller than Equilibrium Amount

Suppose instead that we decided that the market should produce 1,100 pizzas at the price of $15. Isn't more pizza preferred to the market equilibrium of 1,000? Not really. Beyond 1,000 pizzas, the market supply curve rises above $15. This means that the marginal cost to producers is more than $15 to produce the pizza, yet they are receiving only $15 when they sell it. This is actually subtracting from their producer surplus. In addition, the demand curve is falling below $15 beyond 1,000 pizzas. This tells us that consumers are receiving marginal benefit of less than $15 for consuming the next pizza, yet they are paying $15 for it. This subtracts from consumer surplus. The deadweight loss associated with the reductions in producer and consumer surplus is seen in Figure 6-12 as the triangle between the supply and demand curves for pizzas 1,000 to 1,100.

These two examples illustrate that any quantity below or above 1,000 pizzas causes deadweight loss and a reduction in total surplus. Thus, the only level of output that maximizes total surplus is the output determined in the competitive market.

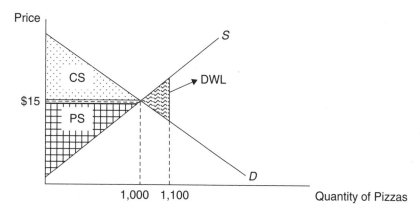

FIGURE 6-12 · Deadweight Loss from a Larger than Equilibrium Amount

Price Controls

The pizza example just given illustrated that if the government tried to control the level of output in the market, deadweight loss and inefficiency would result. Government can also, if it chooses, attempt to manipulate the market price through either *price floors* or *price ceilings*. We use the market for pizza again as an example of how these controls affect efficiency.

Once again consider the competitive pizza market where the equilibrium price is $15 for a large pizza and 1,000 pizzas are exchanged in a week.

Suppose that the government is convinced that pizza producers cannot be profitable at a price of $15. In an attempt to help the producers, the government sets a minimum price of $20 for each large pizza. This minimum price is called a *price floor* because the price is not allowed to fall below it. The impact of the price floor (Pf) is seen in Figure 6-13. At a price of $20, the quantity of pizzas supplied will be 1,200, but only 800 pizzas will be demanded. This surplus of 400 pizzas will go unsold, but the price cannot, by law, fall back to equilibrium. The impact of the price floor on total surplus can also be seen. Because the price is significantly higher than $15, the area of consumer surplus has shrunk, while the area of producer surplus has risen. However, the combined area of total surplus is smaller, and thus deadweight loss and inefficiency are created. While it is unlikely that government would ever set a price floor in the market for pizza, we are familiar with price floors in the form of minimum wages and crop supports. These real-life price floors create similar inefficiencies and thus are typically not endorsed by economists.

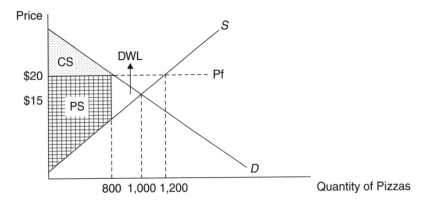

FIGURE 6-13 • The Effect of a Price Floor on Total Surplus

Now suppose that the government is convinced that pizza is too expensive for consumers at a price of $15. To provide relief to the consumers, the government sets a maximum price of $10 for each large pizza. This maximum price is called a *price ceiling* because the price is not allowed to rise above it. The impact of the price ceiling (Pc) is seen in Figure 6-14. At a price of $10, there are only 800 pizzas supplied, but 1,200 are demanded. The shortage of 400 pizzas would remain because the price cannot, by law, rise to equilibrium. We can also see the impact of the price ceiling on total surplus. Because the price is significantly lower than $15, the area of consumer surplus has grown, but the area of producer surplus has shrunk. The combined area of total surplus is ultimately smaller, and thus deadweight loss and inefficiency arise. We have seen real-life price ceilings in cities with rent control, and some governments have frozen wages and prices during wartime. Again, because they distort the market and promote inefficient outcomes, economists do not typically favor price ceilings any more than they promote price floors.

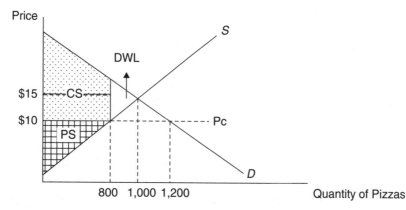

FIGURE 6-14 · The Effect of a Price Ceiling on Total Surplus

Still Struggling

What exactly does it mean to have deadweight loss, and why does it matter? Imagine that you really want to buy a T-shirt and that you are willing to pay $25 for it. You go to the store and see that the price of the shirt is only $15. If you buy the shirt, you will enjoy two things: the utility from the T-shirt and $10 of consumer surplus. You can then take the $10 you *didn't* need to spend on the T-shirt and buy something else that gives you some utility. If there were some kind of policy that prevented you from buying the shirt, you would be denied these things. At the same time, there would be a seller of T-shirts that would be denied the sale of that shirt and any producer surplus that he might have enjoyed from selling it. Deadweight loss is simply the dollar value of all the mutually beneficial transactions that are lost because of something that prevents the market equilibrium from being reached.

Excise Taxes

In addition to price controls, the government can affect the price of a product by levying a per-unit tax, or *excise tax*, on it. These taxes are often seen in the markets for goods like gasoline, tobacco, and alcohol. For each unit of a good produced, the government levies a tax, and that tax affects the price paid by consumers, the after-tax price received by producers, the equilibrium quantity, and total surplus. Unlike with price controls, an additional outcome of an excise tax is that the government collects tax revenue.

Suppose that the market for cigarettes is perfectly competitive. The market comes to equilibrium at a price of $40 per carton, and 10 million cartons are bought and sold. This market is shown in Figure 6-15. Now suppose that the government levies a $10 tax on each carton of cigarettes produced. This tax is paid by the suppliers, so in effect, the supply curve shifts vertically upward, from S_0 to S_t, by the amount of the tax.

One might initially conclude that the new price of cigarettes would be exactly $10 higher, or $50 per carton. But careful inspection of the graph shows that at a price of $50, a surplus of cigarettes exists. If the market is to clear this surplus, the price must fall to $47 and only 8 million cartons will be bought. Because the price is now $47, consumers are paying $7 more for a carton of cigarettes than they were before. This means that consumers pay $7 of the tax. Producers receive $47 at the time of purchase, but they must then send $10 to the government. Thus producers receive only $37 for each carton, or $3 less than before; sellers pay $3 of the tax. What about the government? Since 8 million cartons are sold and $10 is collected on each carton, the government collects $80 million in tax revenue.

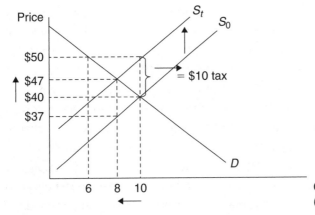

FIGURE 6-15 • Supply and Demand with an Excise Tax

In order to see what happens to total surplus, we reproduce Figure 6-15 showing the areas of consumer surplus, producer surplus, and government revenue (Figure 6-16). The impact of the tax on consumers and producers is that both consumer and producer surplus has fallen. The government revenue (G) can also be seen in the graph as the area of the rectangle ($10 × 8 million). But there is a triangle of surplus that goes to no one. This is the deadweight loss associated with the tax.

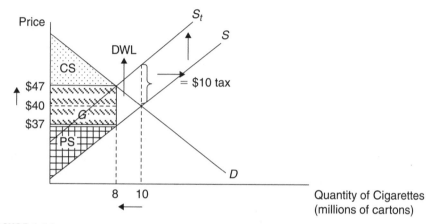

FIGURE 6-16 · Surplus and Deadweight Loss with an Excise Tax

The tax distorts the competitive market equilibrium by driving a wedge between the price that consumers pay and the price that sellers actually receive. Without the tax, if only 8 million cartons were being exchanged, an additional 2 million cartons *could be* exchanged between willing buyers and sellers. By preventing these 2 million transactions, the tax creates inefficiency.

We should point out that there may be very good social and economic reasons to tax products such as tobacco, gasoline, and alcohol, so economists do not always condemn these taxes as pure generators of inefficiency. When we discuss topics of public goods and externalities, we will address how such taxes can actually improve market efficiency, rather than diminish it.

NOTE *In the cigarette tax example, the producers were taxed, but the consumers ended up paying most of that tax. Because the price increased by $7 after a $10 tax, consumers are paying 70 percent of the tax. Producers are paying the remaining $3, or 30 percent. Interestingly, the division of the tax, or tax incidence, depends upon the relative elasticities of demand and supply.*

For example, suppose the demand for cigarettes is extremely inelastic, even perfectly inelastic. In this case, the demand curve appears as a vertical line in Figure 6-17. When the supply curve shifts upward by $10, the price increases by $10, from $40 to $50 per carton.

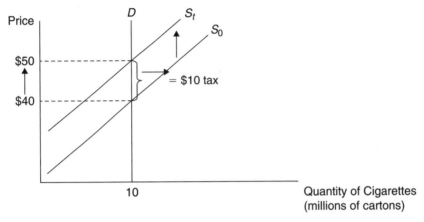

FIGURE 6-17 • Tax Incidence with Extremely Inelastic Supply

Suppose the demand for cigarettes is perfectly elastic. In this case, the demand curve is horizontal. After the supply curve is taxed and shifts upward, there is no change in the equilibrium price, but the suppliers must still pay the $10 tax to the government. In this case, consumers bear none of the burden of the tax and sellers bear 100 percent of it.

From these two extreme examples, we can conclude the following:

- *If the demand is relatively less elastic than the supply, the consumers will bear a larger share of the excise tax.*
- *If the demand is relatively more elastic than the supply, the suppliers will bear a larger share of the excise tax.*

Summary

This chapter brings both halves of the market together to show how competitive markets come to equilibrium. There is only one price at which the quantity that consumers demand is exactly the quantity that producers wish to supply.

When the demand or the supply curve shifts, the market adjusts to a new equilibrium price and quantity. So long as the competitive market remains unhindered, the outcome is efficient in maximizing the sum of the consumer and producer surplus. However, some government policies, such as quantity controls, price controls, and excise taxes, cause the market to become less efficient, and deadweight loss arises. The discussion of competitive markets continues in the next chapter by looking at the behavior of firms in the model of perfect competition.

QUIZ

Is each of the following statements *true* or *false*? Explain.

1. When the demand for candy decreases, both the equilibrium market price and the equilibrium quantity will decrease.

2. Suppose the market price of tomatoes is $1 per pound. If the government places a price ceiling at $2 per pound, we expect to see a surplus of tomatoes on the market.

3. Total surplus in the competitive market must fall if a price control is applied to that market.

For each of the following, choose the answer that best fits.

4. The market for leather basketballs is currently in equilibrium. If the cost of leather increases for basketball producers, we expect to see a _____ price and a(n) _____ quantity in the market for basketballs.
    A. higher; higher
    B. lower; higher
    C. higher; ambiguous change in the
    D. higher; lower

5. Suppose you observe that the market price of coffee has decreased and the market quantity of coffee has increased. Which of the following might have caused this?
    A. The supply curve shifted to the right and demand stayed constant.
    B. The demand curve shifted to the left and supply stayed constant.
    C. Both the supply and the demand curves shifted to the left.
    D. The supply curve shifted to the left and the demand curve shifted to the right.

Use the graph in Figure 6.18 to answer questions 6 to 8.

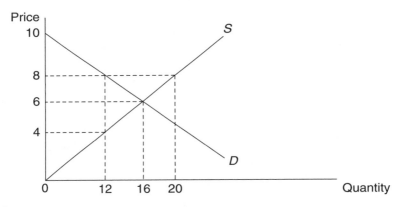

FIGURE 6-18

6. If the market in Figure 6-18 is in equilibrium, the consumer surplus is equal to:
   A. $64
   B. $32
   C. $6
   D. $8

7. Suppose a price floor of $8 is imposed in the market in Figure 6-18. This price floor will create a _____ in the market and deadweight loss equal to _____.
   A. shortage of 8 units; $16
   B. surplus of 20 units; $48
   C. surplus of 8 units; $8
   D. surplus of 8 units; $16

8. Which of the following might cause the market equilibrium in Figure 6-18 to reach a price of $4 and a quantity of 12 units?
   A. Supply falls with no change in demand.
   B. Supply rises with no change in demand.
   C. Demand rises with no change in supply.
   D. Demand falls with no change in supply.

9. Suppose the supply of tobacco is upward-sloping, but the demand for tobacco is perfectly inelastic. If the government increases the per-unit excise tax on tobacco by T, we can predict that:
   A. The price of tobacco will rise by exactly T.
   B. The price of tobacco will rise by more than T.
   C. The price of tobacco will rise by less than T.
   D. The price of tobacco will fall by exactly T.

10. Suppose the market for chocolate has reached a competitive equilibrium price and quantity. Which of the following will create deadweight loss in the chocolate market?
    A. An excise tax is imposed on the producers of chocolate.
    B. A price floor is set in the market.
    C. A price ceiling is set in the market.
    D. All of the above will create deadweight loss.

chapter 7

Perfect Competition

Markets produce goods and services, but not all markets are the same. The way in which firms within the same market interact and behave is usually a function of how many firms there are in that market, the type of products that are being produced, and how easy it is for new firms to enter the market. This chapter provides the beginnings of a framework for several theories of market structures by reintroducing the most competitive market structure, that of perfect competition.

CHAPTER OBJECTIVES

After completing this chapter, the student should be able to:

1. List and explain the key assumptions of perfect competition.

2. Understand the difference between accounting and economic profit.

3. Use the rule for profit maximization to show how much output a perfectly competitive firm will produce.

4. Draw side-by-side graphs of a competitive market and the typical perfectly competitive firm to show the price, output, and short-run economic profit (or loss) earned by the firm.

5. Describe the conditions under which a firm will choose to shut down in the short run.

6. Show how the market adjusts to long-run equilibrium and how this long-run equilibrium outcome is both allocatively and productively efficient.

Key Assumptions of Perfect Competition

Economists typically recognize several assumptions of the theory of perfect competition that together have important implications for profitability and efficiency. Although real-world markets do not often resemble perfect competition, the outcomes of this market structure provide nice benchmarks by which other markets can be measured and evaluated. The key assumptions are:

- There are many buyers and sellers.
- Firms sell a homogeneous (identical) good.
- Firms (and consumers) can easily enter and exit the market.
- Firms and consumers have perfect information.

We also assume, until later chapters, that externalities do not exist in these markets. This simply means that there is no impact on third parties when goods are exchanged in the market. Chapter 6 described a critical implication of the perfectly competitive assumptions: neither a firm nor a consumer can affect the market price through individual actions. In other words, both firms and consumers are "price takers." The market, through the forces of supply and demand, determines the price of the good, and firms and consumers take that price and make the best possible decisions given that price.

The assumptions about a perfectly competitive market give us some insight into why this is the case. Suppose a single seller of a good decides that she does not like the market price and charges a slightly higher price. Consumers who have perfect information and can buy an identical good from one of the many other sellers simply will not buy her good, and she will be forced to return to the market price. Similarly, since there are many buyers of the good, she can sell however many of the good she wants to at the market price, so if she lowers her price, all she will do is make herself worse off. (We will see in later chapters that when some of these assumptions change, firms *do* have some control over the price they charge.)

For the firms, this means that they must choose a level of output that will maximize profit at the market price. Before we go further into the theory of perfect competition, let's briefly discuss economic profit and how it is maximized.

Revenue and Costs

In Chapter 4 we discussed the costs of a firm and how they were broken down. Total costs of production are a function of output, and $TC(Q)$ can be separated into two parts:

$$TC(Q) = TFC + TVC(Q)$$

where TFC are the fixed costs that do not change as more or less is produced (and therefore TFC is not a function of Q), and $TVC(Q)$ are the variable costs, which do change as more or less is produced.

Profit is the difference between the amount of money that a firm takes in (known as total revenue) and the amount that it costs the firm to produce what it sells. *Total revenue* (TR) is equal to the product of the quantity (Q) of units sold and the price (P) at which they were sold. Mathematically,

$$TR = P \times Q$$

Mathematically speaking, then, the amount of economic profit (Π) that a firm makes from producing Q units is found in this manner:

$$\Pi(Q) = TR(Q) - TC(Q) = P \times Q - TC(Q)$$

Recall that in Chapter 4, we also found the marginal cost of production, $MC(Q)$, which was the additional amount it cost the firm to produce the Qth unit of output (for example, if we were finding MC(4), this would be the additional amount it would cost to produce the fourth unit). We are also interested in the *marginal revenue*, or $MR(Q)$, which is the additional revenue received from producing one more unit of input. $MR(Q)$ can be found using the following formula:

$$MR(Q) = \left(\frac{\Delta TR(Q)}{\Delta Q} \right)$$

Note that when we are talking about one more unit, the change in quantity is equal to 1. For instance, if a firm earns $500 from producing 10 units and $530 from producing 11 units, MR(11) = $30.

In Chapter 1, we saw that an individual's objective is to maximize utility, which she did when she found the quantity where $MB(Q) = MC(Q)$. The objective of a firm is to maximize profits. To the firm, the benefit of increasing production is to increase its revenue, but increasing production will also increase costs. A firm will increase production only as long as the additional cost incurred isn't greater than the additional revenue received. In other words, a firm will be best off if it produces the quantity where

$$MR(Q) = MC(Q)$$

Profit Maximization, Mathematically

It may be helpful to see how this works using actual numbers. Suppose that Dave operates a landscaping service. Each week he has a fixed cost of $20 for a contract he has with an advertising agency to advertise his services. He has figured out that his costs vary based on the number of lawns he mows, and this varies according to the function $TVC(Q) = \frac{1}{2}Q^2$. The going rate for having your lawn mowed in his town is $13, which he will get regardless of how many lawns he mows. He wants to figure out how many lawns to mow to make the most profit. He enters the information in a spreadsheet (see Table 7-1).

TABLE 7-1 Dave's Costs, Revenue, and Profit at $13

		Costs				Revenue		
Q	P	TFC	TVC	TC	MC	Total Revenue	MR	Profit
0	$13.00	$20.00	$ 0.00	$ 20.00	n/a	$ 0.00	n/a	−$20.00
1	$13.00	$20.00	$ 1.50	$ 21.50	$ 1.50	$ 13.00	$13.00	−$ 8.50
2	$13.00	$20.00	$ 6.00	$ 26.00	$ 4.50	$ 26.00	$13.00	$ 0.00
3	$13.00	$20.00	$ 13.50	$ 33.50	$ 7.50	$ 39.00	$13.00	$ 5.50
4	$13.00	$20.00	$ 24.00	$ 44.00	$10.50	$ 52.00	$13.00	$ 8.00
5	$13.00	$20.00	$ 37.50	$ 57.50	$13.50	$ 65.00	$13.00	$ 7.50
6	$13.00	$20.00	$ 54.00	$ 74.00	$16.50	$ 78.00	$13.00	$ 4.00
7	$13.00	$20.00	$ 73.50	$ 93.50	$19.50	$ 91.00	$13.00	−$ 2.50
8	$13.00	$20.00	$ 96.00	$116.00	$22.50	$104.00	$13.00	−$12.00
9	$13.00	$20.00	$121.50	$141.50	$25.50	$117.00	$13.00	−$24.50
10	$13.00	$20.00	$150.00	$170.00	$28.50	$130.00	$13.00	−$40.00

As we can see, when he produces 4 units, he makes a profit of $8. No other quantity will give him a higher profit.

Laying out the numbers like this allows us to make some observations.

1. When the price doesn't change, the marginal revenue doesn't change.

2. The marginal cost, however, does change. In fact, his marginal cost increases.

3. At his profit-maximizing quantity of 4, $MC(Q) = MR(Q)$ (or as close to it as you can get). This is always true mathematically, and it is sometimes called the *profit-maximizing rule*.

4. This profit-maximizing rule makes sense intuitively as well. Suppose Dave considers mowing 5 lawns instead of 4. He will get only $13 for mowing the fifth lawn, but mowing one more lawn will cost him $13.50.

Accounting Profit and Economic Profit

Computing a firm's profit is rather simple: begin with the total revenue earned from sales and subtract the total production costs. Despite this apparent simplicity of computing profit, accountants and economists have different views about what should be included in the total costs that are subtracted. Accountants, and the general public, include only the direct *explicit* costs made to employ production inputs supplied by people outside the firm. For example, most firms employ workers, and the paychecks written to those workers are an explicit cost of production. The same is true of payments made for raw materials, energy, machinery, interest on debt, rent on office space, and other such expenses. When all of the explicit (or accounting) costs are subtracted from total revenue, we have *accounting profit* as

$$\text{Accounting profit} = \text{total revenue} - \text{explicit production costs}$$

Economists agree that these payments are production costs, but they also understand that any time a decision is made, such as the decision to operate a firm, opportunity costs exist. For example, if the owner of Firm A could have earned a salary as an employee of Firm B, the owner has forgone this salary in order to operate his own firm. The forgone salary is an opportunity, or *implicit*, cost for this firm and should be included with the accounting costs in the calculation of total *economic profit*:

$$\text{Economic profit} = \text{total revenue} - (\text{explicit production costs} + \text{implicit costs})$$
$$= \text{TR} - \text{TC}$$

If economic profit is greater than zero, the owner of the firm has earned enough revenue to pay all of the explicit production costs *and* all of the things that he gave up in order to pursue this venture. The goal of the firm is to produce the level of output that maximizes economic profit.

TIP *Because economic profits include an additional cost, accounting profits will always be higher than economic profits. For this reason, we can have a situation in which an economist would say that there are zero economic profits, and an accountant would say that a firm was making a profit.*

Profit Maximization, Graphically

Since economic profit is simply the difference between total revenue and total economic cost, the firm must simply find the level of output where that difference is the greatest. Graphically, we saw the short-run total cost curve in Chapter 4, and it is reproduced in Figure 7-1. Because firms are price takers, total revenue is a straight line with a slope equal to the market-determined price. Economic profit (Π) or loss is the vertical distance between the total revenue line and the total cost curve. The graph shows two levels of output, Q_1 and Q_2, where total revenue is equal to total cost and thus economic profit is equal to zero. Below Q_1 and above Q_2, total cost exceeds total revenue, and economic losses are incurred. Between Q_1 and Q_2, economic profit is positive, and at Q^*, the economic profit is maximized.

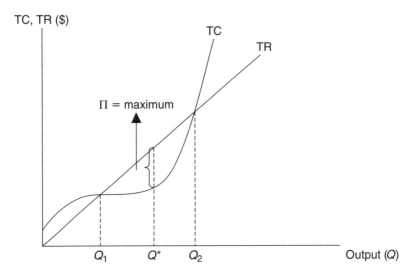

FIGURE 7-1 · Economic Profit

There's actually an equivalent way to find the profit-maximizing output that will prove to be more useful as we analyze how firms behave: compare the marginal revenue of the next unit sold to the marginal cost of producing that unit. Recall that *marginal* is synonymous with "additional," so if the additional dollars coming into the firm from the next unit are at least as great as the additional dollars leaving the firm, the firm profits from producing the next unit.

We can see the profit-maximizing output Q^* in Figure 7-2 at the intersection of the upward-sloping marginal cost (MC) curve and the horizontal marginal revenue (MR) curve. When firms are price takers, the additional revenue from selling the next unit is simply the market price (P). Because the firm cannot affect the market price by producing fewer or additional units of output, and because we assume that all units produced are sold at that price, the marginal revenue curve also serves as the demand curve (D) for this perfectly competitive firm's product. In the next section of the chapter, we discuss how we can determine how much economic profit the firm is earning and whether the firm should produce *anything* in the short run.

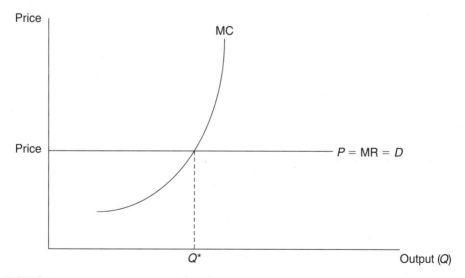

FIGURE 7-2 · Marginal Revenue and Marginal Cost

TIP *Students are sometimes confused about why the marginal revenue and demand curves are the same here. Recall that the firm can sell any quantity it chooses at the market price. So in essence, the demand curve for this firm is basically the price. We noted in Table 7-1 that the marginal revenue was the same as the price when firms don't have any control over price. Therefore, in this situation, price, MR, and demand are all the same thing.*

Economic Profit and Loss in the Short Run

A perfectly competitive firm can earn positive economic profit if the market price is high enough so that the total revenue is greater than the total economic cost. Alternatively, on a per-unit basis, profit is positive if the price per unit is greater than the total cost per unit. Recall from Chapter 4 that we had a special term for cost per unit: average total cost, or $ATC(Q) = TC(Q)/Q$. Multiplying per-unit profit by the units produced gets us back to total profit. This is seen by manipulating the earlier equation for total profit (Π):

$$\Pi(Q) = TR(Q) - TC(Q) = (Q \times P) - TC(Q)$$

Recall that $ATC(Q) = TC(Q)/Q$. If we rearrange this by bringing Q to the left side of the equation, we get $Q \times ATC(Q) = TC(Q)$, which we can then substitute into our profit function:

$$\Pi(Q) = Q \times P - Q \times ATC(Q)$$

Note that there is a common variable, Q. Let's pull the Q out to group terms:

$$\Pi(Q) = Q[P - ATC(Q)]$$

In order to show the profit or loss being earned, it is useful to draw two graphs side by side. The graph on the left, Figure 7-3, shows the market for a perfectly competitive product like wheat. The graph on the right, Figure 7-4, shows, for a typical wheat farmer, the marginal cost (MC), average variable cost (AVC), average total cost (ATC), and marginal revenue (MR) curves. To maximize profit, the firm takes the market price P_c and finds the output Q_f where $P = MR = MC$. At that output, the price is greater than average total cost, so profit per unit is positive. The area of the shaded "profit rectangle" represents the positive economic profit.

CAUTION   *It is important to remember that the "profit rectangle" is absolutely a rectangle. A common student mistake is to shade in the entire area above the average total cost curve. This creates a curvy little "bump" on the bottom of the rectangle and blows up the rectangular shape. If you find yourself drawing something that is not really a rectangle, you have not correctly identified profit in the graph. Using the formula $\Pi(Q) = Q[P - ATC(Q)]$, it is easy to see why. Recall that the formula for the area of a rectangle is length $\times$ width. In this case, the length is Q and the width is (P − ATC).*

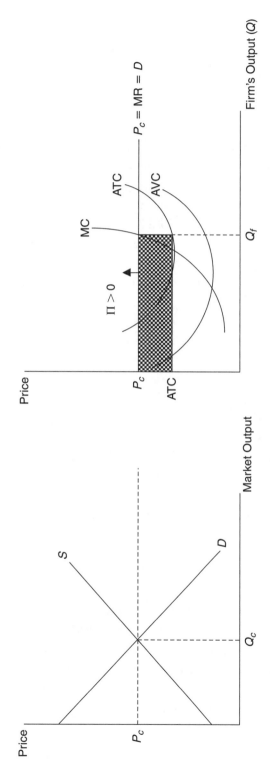

FIGURE 7-4 • Price and Quantity for a Single Firm with Economic Profits

FIGURE 7-3 • Market Price and Quantity for a Competitive Product

117

We must keep in mind that all firms in the perfectly competitive wheat industry are earning positive short-run economic profit because the market price happens to be greater than average total cost. Suppose that the market price were significantly lower. Figure 7-6 shows a wheat producer that finds the profit-maximizing output where $P = MR = MC$, but, because the market price of wheat has fallen below average total cost, economic profit is negative. The losses are again seen as the area of the shaded rectangle in the graph. The corresponding graph for the market is shown in Figure 7-5.

If all of the wheat farmers are incurring losses in the short run, why are they still in business? The reason is that the farmers are losing less money by operating at a loss than they would lose if they ceased production altogether. Recall that we are discussing the short-run production period, and in the short run, fixed costs exist. The producers must pay the fixed cost no matter what the level of output, even if that output is zero. Because fixed costs always must be paid, the relevant production decision really boils down to whether the variable costs can be paid. If the price is high enough so that total revenue exceeds total variable cost, the firm minimizes its losses by producing at the point where $P = MR = MC$. On a per-unit basis, if the price is greater than or equal to the average variable cost, the firm should continue to produce in the short run, even at a loss. This is known as the *shutdown decision: if $P < AVC$, then the firm should choose $Q = 0$.* The firm in Figure 7-6 is minimizing short-run losses by producing Q_f units of output because the market price is greater than average variable cost. If the price were to fall below the minimum of average variable cost, the firm would shut down, producing zero units in the short run, and lose only the total fixed costs that must always be paid. If the price does not soon rise, many of these firms will cease to exist in the long run.

To see why this is, consider Dave's production decision again. Suppose the market price of lawn service fell to $10. Now his spreadsheet looks like Table 7-2.

Dave has to face an unhappy fact: there is no way he will make a profit at a price of $10. Should he not mow any lawns? Well, he still has a contract with the ad agency, so he has to pay $20 to it no matter what. If he produces nothing, he is producing $Q = 0$, which would give him a profit of $-\$20$. If, on the other hand, he produces 3 units, he loses only $-\$3.50$, which isn't as bad. So in the short run, at least until the contract expires, he will continue to produce.

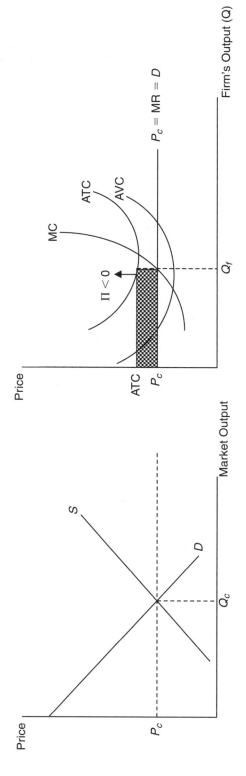

FIGURE 7-5 • Market Price and Output for a Competitive Product

FIGURE 7-6 • Price and Quantity for a Single Firm with Economic Losses

TABLE 7-2 Dave's Costs, Revenue, and Profit at $10

		Costs				Revenue		
Q	P	TFC	TVC	TC	MC	Total Revenue	MR	Profit
0	$10.00	$20.00	$ 0.00	$ 20.00	n/a	$ 0.00	n/a	−$20.00
1	$10.00	$20.00	$ 1.50	$ 21.50	$ 1.50	$ 10.00	$10.00	−$11.50
2	$10.00	$20.00	$ 6.00	$ 26.00	$ 4.50	$ 20.00	$10.00	−$ 6.00
3	$10.00	$20.00	$ 13.50	$ 33.50	$ 7.50	$ 30.00	$10.00	−$ 3.50
4	$10.00	$20.00	$ 24.00	$ 44.00	$10.50	$ 40.00	$10.00	−$ 4.00
5	$10.00	$20.00	$ 37.50	$ 57.50	$13.50	$ 50.00	$10.00	−$ 7.50
6	$10.00	$20.00	$ 54.00	$ 74.00	$16.50	$ 60.00	$10.00	−$14.00
7	$10.00	$20.00	$ 73.50	$ 93.50	$19.50	$ 70.00	$10.00	−$23.50
8	$10.00	$20.00	$ 96.00	$116.00	$22.50	$ 80.00	$10.00	−$36.00
9	$10.00	$20.00	$121.50	$141.50	$25.50	$ 90.00	$10.00	−$51.50
10	$10.00	$20.00	$150.00	$170.00	$28.50	$100.00	$10.00	−$70.00

Still Struggling

It's not always easy to understand the shutdown decision. As with most things in economics, try to think about it as another example of how we weigh the benefits and costs of any decision. The decision is whether to produce Q_f units of output in the short run. Two things happen when Q_f units are produced:

1. The firm receives total revenue (TR) from the sale of those units.
2. The firm incurs total variable cost (TVC) from the production of those units.

Now the decision is easy:

- If TR < TVC, those units should *not* be produced.

On a per-unit basis, the decision becomes:

- If P < AVC, those units should *not* be produced.

Long-Run Adjustments

We have seen that perfectly competitive firms can earn either positive or negative short-run profits, but a key assumption guarantees that these profits will not last. With free entry of new firms and easy exit of existing firms, long-run profits will be driven to zero. Let's see how this works. Again suppose that producers in the wheat market are earning short-run positive economic profits. In the long run, with enough time to mobilize the necessary land, labor, and capital, new wheat farmers will emerge and begin to produce wheat. As more producers offer wheat to the market, the market supply curve shifts to the right. And as the supply curve shifts to the right, the price begins to fall, each producer produces less, and the rectangle of profit shrinks. When will the last new firm enter the market? When the price is reduced to where it equals average total cost and economic profit is equal to zero.

Figures 7-7 and 7-8 show how the market, and the firm, will adjust from short-run economic profits to the long-run equilibrium. Through the entry of new firms, the short-run price of P_{SR} has been driven downward to the long-run price P_{LR}, which intersects the marginal cost curve at the minimum of the average total cost curve. More total output is being produced in the market, but each firm produces fewer units in the long run than it did when the short-run price was higher.

A similar adjustment takes place when short-run losses are incurred. In the long run, some firms will exit the wheat market. When there are fewer producers, the supply curve shifts to the left, and the market price begins to rise. As the price rises, each firm produces more wheat and the rectangle of losses gets smaller. The exit of firms ends when the losses are eliminated and all remaining firms are breaking even. The long-run price, whether there were short-run profits or losses, is always the same and is the price that is equal to average total cost.

TIP *How do we know when the long run has been achieved? Well, since short-run profits will spark entry and short-run losses will prompt exit, the only time when there is no incentive for firms to come or go is when there are no profits and no losses—in other words, when firms are breaking even.*

Efficiency

We discussed the efficiency of competitive markets in Chapter 6, but the long-run outcome for perfectly competitive firms allows an opportunity to provide a little more detail. Economists see two important sources of efficiency in this

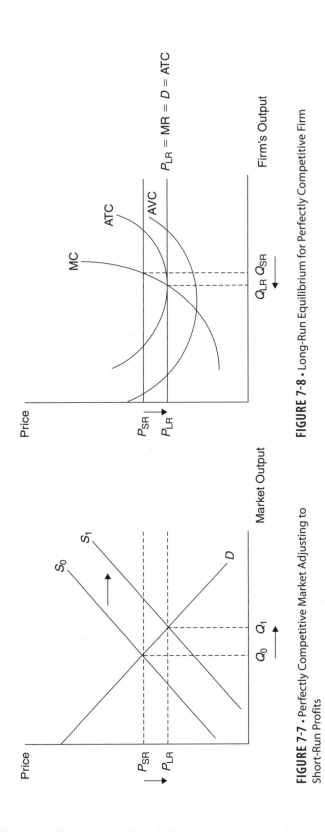

FIGURE 7-8 • Long-Run Equilibrium for Perfectly Competitive Firm

FIGURE 7-7 • Perfectly Competitive Market Adjusting to Short-Run Profits

model: allocative and productive efficiency. *Allocative efficiency* is achieved because each firm is producing the level of output at which price is equal to marginal cost. By producing this quantity, the firm is producing neither too much nor too little. Because each firm is producing the efficient output where price equals marginal cost, the market produces the "right" level of output where supply intersects demand. In other words, in perfect competition, there is no deadweight loss. Firms also achieve *productive efficiency*. The long-run equilibrium ensures that each firm produces at the level where the average total cost is minimized. If there were firms that could not produce the same product, sold at the same market price, for the minimum average total cost, they would be forced to exit the market. Thus each remaining firm must be as productively efficient as possible. We soon discover that, when the market structure turns from competitive to monopolistic, these efficiencies cease to exist.

Summary

This chapter introduced the model of perfect competition, the key assumptions of that model, and the difference between accounting and economic profit. Firms maximize profit by finding the level of output where the marginal revenue of the next unit sold (which is equal to the price in this model) is equal to the marginal cost of producing it. If the price is greater than average total cost, short-run economic profits will be made. If the price is less than average total cost, short-run economic losses will be incurred. However, the firm will shut down in the short run if the price falls below average variable cost. In the long run, entry and exit of firms will return economic profits to the breakeven level and long-run equilibrium. In this equilibrium, the market and the firm achieve both allocative and productive efficiency. We see in the next chapter that the model of monopoly has very little in common with the outcomes seen in perfect competition.

QUIZ

Is each of the following statements *true* or *false*? Explain.

1. If economic profit is equal to zero, accounting profit is positive.

2. If the price is less than the average total cost, the firm must shut down in the short run.

3. A key assumption of perfect competition is that firms can set the price.

4. In the long run, the following is true: $P = MR = MC = ATC$.

For each of the following, choose the answer that best fits.

5. Which of the following is an accurate statement about perfect competition?
   A. In the long run, the price is equal to average variable cost.
   B. There are no barriers to entry or exit.
   C. Firms can increase the price to increase profits.
   D. Price is greater than marginal revenue in the short run, but equal to marginal revenue in the long run.

6. Suppose firms in a perfectly competitive market are earning positive short-run economic profits. Which of the following statements is accurate?
   A. Long-run profits in this market will be positive.
   B. In the long run, exit of firms will increase profits to zero.
   C. In the long run, entry of firms will decrease profits to zero.
   D. Long-run profits in this market will be negative.

7. Josie is a perfectly competitive soybean farmer who is currently producing 100 bushels at the market price of $50 per bushel. Her average variable cost is $60, and her average fixed cost is $10 per bushel. If Josie wants to increase her short-run profit, she should:
   A. Shut down and produce nothing.
   B. Continue to produce 100 bushels.
   C. Increase the price to $70 per bushel.
   D. Increase her output.

Use the graph in Figure 7-9 for questions 8 to 10.

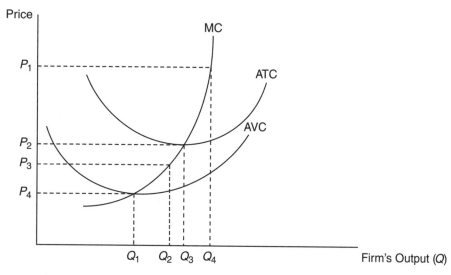

FIGURE 7-9

8. Using the labels in the graph, if the current price in the market is P_1, the firm will produce _____ units of output and short-run profits will be _____.
   A. Q_4; zero
   B. Q_1; negative
   C. Q_3; zero
   D. Q_4; positive

9. If the short-run price is P_3, the long-run price will be:
   A. P_1
   B. P_2
   C. P_3
   D. P_4

10. Which of the following prices would cause the firm to shut down in the short run?
    A. P_2
    B. P_3
    C. Any price between P_2 and P_4
    D. Any price below P_4

chapter **8**

Monopoly

Perfect competition is the most competitive of market structures, and monopoly is the least competitive. Because firms in perfect competition can only hope to break even in the long run, most of them probably would rather be monopolists, who can earn profits in the long run. As we shall see, the long-run market equilibrium for the monopolist is quite different from the outcome in the perfectly competitive market.

CHAPTER OBJECTIVES

After completing this chapter, the student should be able to:

1. List and explain the key assumptions of monopoly.

2. Understand the relationship between the price of a unit sold, the marginal revenue received from its sale, and the price elasticity of demand along the demand curve.

3. Use the rule for profit maximization to show how much output a monopoly firm will produce.

4. Use a graph to show the monopolist's output, the price it sets, and the area of profit it earns.

5. Describe how the monopoly outcome creates deadweight loss.

6. Discuss how government can regulate a natural monopolist and the pros and cons of doing so.

7. Understand price discrimination in general and one type, perfect price discrimination, in particular.

Key Assumptions

The goal of the board game Monopoly is to have only a single winner. Similarly, the assumptions of the monopoly market structure begin with the premise that there will be only one "winner." A market is deemed a monopoly if it is characterized by the following:

- Only one firm is selling a good to many consumers.
- The product has no close substitutes.
- A barrier to entry of new firms exists.

The absence of close competitors and substitute products creates a situation in which the monopolist is a "price maker" rather than a market "price taker." The ability to set the price leads to long-run economic profits and can sometimes invite regulation by the government. For now, we will also assume that the firm sets only one price to maximize profit, but there are situations in which firms with monopoly power have the ability to set different prices for different groups of consumers. We look at both regulation and price discrimination later in the chapter.

NOTE   *So how do these barriers to entry emerge? After all, they are really the crux of the monopoly power to set the price. Economists generally recognize a small list of sources of barriers to entry.*

1. ***Economies of scale.*** *As firms expand their size in the long run, average total cost can decrease. Larger firms can divide the total cost of their factories by many units, and so the per-unit costs fall. How? Larger firms can purchase raw materials at lower costs and can negotiate favorable borrowing terms and labor contracts. This implies that as a firm gets larger, per-unit costs fall. This allows large firms to sell their products at lower prices, which prevents smaller firms from entering the market and competing head to head. For example, Tonya and Mo might have a great idea for a new brand of car (Toymota), but because they are small, they can never compete with Toyota.*

2. ***Legal barriers.*** *Firms can create barriers to entry by acquiring patents and copyrights on their technological and creative inventions. If you create a new product or an original piece of intellectual property, you can apply for a patent or copyright and receive the sole right to produce, sell, and profit from it. That's a monopoly! This is why movie studios, publishers, and recording studios are so angry when their products are illegally downloaded.*

3. ***Strategic barriers.*** *Long-established firms have spent lots of money on advertising and research to create products that consumers will long remember. Because firms like Nike, Apple, and Coca-Cola have made strong strategic decisions in the past, they have created barriers to entry in the present.*

Demand, Marginal Revenue, and Elasticity

When we discussed the perfectly competitive market for wheat, we recognized that there were two demand curves: the downward-sloping market demand for wheat and the perfectly elastic (horizontal) demand curve for each farmer's wheat. The horizontal demand curve was equal to the market price because each farmer was a price-taking seller. Under the assumptions of monopoly, there is only one firm selling a product with no close substitutes. This implies that the demand for the firm's product is the same as the market demand for the product.

Suppose that on a lonely stretch of rural highway, there is only one gas station for miles in all directions. Table 8-1 provides the demand schedule for this monopoly seller of gasoline. The table also includes a column that calculates the total revenue earned by the monopolist at each price and the marginal revenue from selling each additional hundred gallons of gas. Recall that marginal revenue is the change in total revenue divided by the change in the quantity of units sold. A couple of things are clear from the table. First, total revenue rises until 300 gallons have been sold, but then falls as more gallons of gasoline are sold. Second, with the exception of the first 100 gallons sold, the marginal revenue of the last gallon sold is less than the price at which it was sold. We will show that these two results are related.

CAUTION *Students will sometimes claim that a monopolist can charge "whatever price it wants" or "the highest possible price." Table 8-1 tells us why this is not the case. If this monopolist charged any price higher than $6, it wouldn't sell any gasoline at all. Moreover, if it charged the highest price that anyone was willing to pay for gasoline, $5, it would make less money than it would by charging a slightly lower price.*

TABLE 8-1 Demand Schedule for Monopoly Seller			
Price per Gallon (P)	Quantity of Gallons Demanded (Q_d)	Total Revenue (TR = P × Q_d)	Marginal Revenue $\left(MR = \dfrac{\Delta TR}{\Delta Q_d} \right)$
$6	0	$ 0	
$5	100	$500	$5
$4	200	$800	$3
$3	300	$900	$1
$2	400	$800	−$1
$1	500	$500	−$3
$0	600	$ 0	−$5

Why does total revenue not continue to increase as more gallons of gasoline are purchased? It's because the monopolist must lower the price to sell those additional gallons of gas. Recall the simple definition of total revenue:

$$(TR = P \times Q_d)$$

In Chapter 3, when discussing the price elasticity of demand, we described how lower prices have two competing impacts upon total revenue. These are referred to as the price effect and the quantity effect:

- **Price effect.** After a price decrease, each unit sold sells at a lower price, which tends to decrease revenue.
- **Quantity effect.** After a price decrease, more units are sold, which tends to increase revenue.

Between zero and 300 gallons of gasoline, lower prices cause total revenue to rise. It must be the case that in this portion of the demand curve the quantity effect is stronger than the price effect, and this can happen only when demand is price-elastic. Beyond 300 gallons of gasoline, lower prices cause total revenue to decrease. This can happen only when demand is price-inelastic. When demand schedules are linear, like the one depicted in Table 8-1, the upper half of the demand curve is price-elastic and the lower half is price-inelastic. Total revenue along the demand curve will be maximized at the midpoint. Figure 8-1a shows the demand curve from the data in Table 8-1, and Figure 8-1b shows the total revenue curve associated with the demand. A marginal revenue curve is also added to Figure 8-1a, and we now turn to the relationship between marginal revenue and price. (You might notice that the marginal revenue curve does not *exactly* match the data from the table. For a more mathematical explanation of the relationship between marginal revenue, total revenue, and the demand curve, we invite you to peruse the appendix to this chapter.)

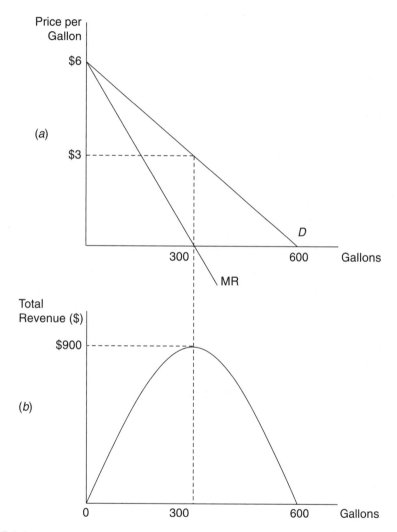

FIGURE 8-1 • Demand, Marginal Revenue, and Total Revenue for a Monopolist

TIP *Marginal revenue is the change in total revenue divided by the change in the units sold. Recall the formula:*

$$\left(MR = \frac{\Delta TR}{\Delta Q_d} \right)$$

Upon inspection of Figure 8-1b, we can see that total revenue is on the vertical axis (y) and quantity of gasoline demanded is on the horizontal axis (x), so this formula is really the change in y over the change in x. In other words, marginal revenue is the slope of total revenue. We see in Figure 8-1a that when marginal revenue is positive (below 300 units), the total revenue curve is rising. When marginal revenue is negative (more than 300 units), the total revenue curve is falling. At the peak of total revenue, its maximum point, marginal revenue is equal to zero.

But why does the marginal revenue curve lie below the demand curve? In other words, why is price always greater than marginal revenue for the next unit sold? The relationship between price and marginal revenue is caused by the pricing behavior of the monopolist. When the monopolist wants to sell additional units, he must lower the price not just for the next one unit, but for all the units sold. For instance, the monopolist cannot sell the first 100 units at $4 and the next 100 units at $3. If he wants to sell 200 units, he must charge the lower price for all of them. While revenue is gained on the additional units, some revenue from the previous units is lost because of the lower price.

Another simple graphical example can help show how this works. Figure 8-2 replicates the demand curve for gasoline but omits the marginal revenue curve. At a price of $5, 100 gallons are sold, and the area of total revenue ($500) is seen

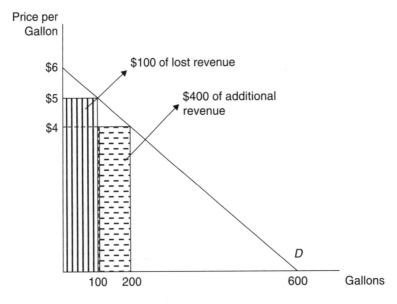

FIGURE 8-2 · Effects of Price Decreases on Revenues

as the tall shaded rectangle. Now suppose the monopolist wishes to sell 200 gallons. He must lower the price to $4 to sell this quantity. This earns the monopolist $400 of *additional* revenue, and this is shown as a slightly smaller rectangle. However, he must also lower the price by $1 for the first 100 gallons, and this costs him $100 of revenue. The net gain from lowering the price to $4 is $300 per 100 gallons, or $3 per gallon. In a similar way, the price of the next unit of a good will always exceed the marginal revenue earned from selling that unit.

Still Struggling

It's not easy to understand why marginal revenue is less than price and lies below the demand curve. Let's revise Table 8-1 by adding columns to show where the total revenue (TR) is lost and gained when the price falls along the demand curve for gasoline (see Table 8-2). When we subtract the lost revenue from the gained revenue, we can see whether total revenue will rise or fall.

Table 8-2 shows that the quantity effect that increases total revenue gets smaller and smaller as more gasoline is added, but the price effect that decreases total revenue gets larger and larger as the price falls. Once the price falls below $3, total revenue actually falls and marginal revenue becomes negative.

TABLE 8-2 Monopolist's Loss and Gain of Total Revenue				
Price per Gallon (P)	Quantity of Gallons Demanded (Q_d)	TR Gained from Sale of More Gas	TR Lost from Lowering the Price	Net Change in TR = TR Gained − TR Lost
$6	0	$ 0		
$5	100	$500	$ 0	$500 − $0 = $500 or $5 per gallon
$4	200	$400	$100	$3 per gallon
$3	300	$300	$200	$1 per gallon
$2	400	$200	$300	−$1 per gallon
$1	500	$100	$400	−$3 per gallon
$0	600	$ 0	$500	−$5 per gallon

On a more intuitive level, think about what marginal revenue actually *is*: the additional revenue that a firm gets from selling one more unit. Consider if a firm raises its price to $3. The marginal revenue is the additional amount of money that the firm will put in its cash register. When people incorrectly state that marginal revenue is greater than the price (or above the demand curve), they are basically saying that the firm charged $3, but somehow more than that amount made it into the cash register. This is clearly impossible.

Profit Maximization

Any firm, whether it is perfectly competitive or a monopolist, maximizes profit in the same way: by setting marginal revenue equal to marginal cost. For all types of firms, we expect the marginal cost to be upward-sloping. As discussed in the previous section, we expect the monopolist's marginal revenue to be downward-sloping and below the demand curve. The monopolist's profit-maximizing decision is shown in Figure 8-3, and the output that maximizes profit is Q_m. The price P_m that is necessary to sell Q_m units is found from the demand curve, and, because the average total cost curve lies below P_m, a rectangle of economic profit is shaded. These economic profits are likely to last into the long run because new entrants are faced with significant barriers to entry. The area of consumer surplus has also been shown as the area under the demand curve and above P_m.

CAUTION   *A common mistake that students make is, upon finding the intersection of marginal revenue and marginal cost, to go straight over to the y axis and label that point P_m. It is important to remember that price is always found from the demand curve, so you must go straight up from the point where MR = MC to find the demand curve and then move to the y axis of your graph. There is also an intuitive reason for this as well—the MR is lower than what consumers are willing and able to pay (i.e., that point on the demand curve). Why would a firm sell a good for less when people are more than happy to pay a higher price?*

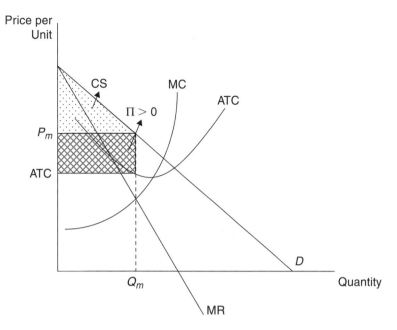

FIGURE 8-3 · Monopolist's Profit-Maximizing Decision

Deadweight Loss

The efficiency of perfect competition was discussed in Chapter 7. Perfectly competitive firms and markets are allocatively efficient because output is produced at the level where marginal cost is equal to the price. At this quantity, neither too much nor too little is being produced. In Figure 8-4, we see that at Q_m, the price P_m is greater than marginal cost.

From society's point of view, producing one more unit is beneficial so long as price exceeds marginal cost, because total surplus will rise. In fact, society would maximize total surplus under perfectly competitive conditions if output were increased to the point where the marginal cost curve intersects demand at the output of Q_e. If that efficient level of output were to be produced, the price would be much lower at P_e, and consumers would certainly be better off because there would be a larger area of consumer surplus. From the monopolist's perspective, however, producing one more unit would decrease profit, and so that unit will not be produced. Because the units between Q_m and Q_e will not be produced, deadweight loss exists as the area below demand and above marginal cost.

The monopolist is also not producing the output that provides technical efficiency, as average total cost is not minimized at Q_m. Because of these inefficiencies, and because the monopoly price exceeds the competitive price, monopolies have frequently been the target of government regulation. This is the topic of the next section.

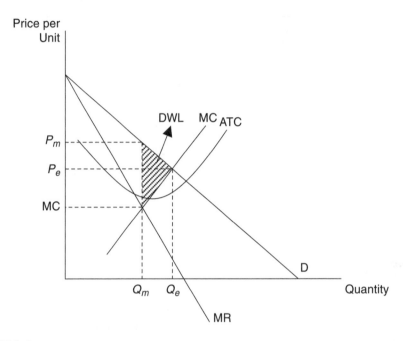

FIGURE 8-4 • Deadweight Loss from Monopoly

Government Regulation

We have seen a couple of monopoly outcomes that can be problematic. First, the absence of competition allows the monopolist to reduce output below the competitive output and increase the price above the competitive price. This outcome reduces consumer surplus and creates inefficiencies. The monopolist also earns long-run economic profit, which further reduces consumer surplus, and this could raise issues of equity. After all, some people become concerned when the consumer surplus enjoyed by many households is transferred to a single entity (the monopolist).

Regulation becomes important to government when the monopolist is producing something that is critical to society, like electricity or other public utilities.

In fact, economists refer to these firms as *natural monopolies*. A natural monopoly exists when a very large firm, such as an electric company, has such vast economies of scale that electricity can be produced at the lowest possible average total cost when there is one producer of electricity rather than several smaller producers.

We can address two broad goals for regulating a monopolist such as a public utility: regulate to the efficient level of output, or regulate so that economic profit is equal to zero. Figure 8-5 shows both regulatory options. The unregulated monopolist is still producing Q_m, where marginal revenue equals marginal cost, and setting the monopoly price of P_m. To regulate the monopolist to produce the efficient level of output, the output must be at Q_e, where marginal cost equals price. This level of output would eliminate deadweight loss, but it might also cause the firm to incur losses, as the price P_e may actually lie below average total cost. To avoid this outcome, the government may instead choose to regulate the firm in a way that causes the firm to earn zero economic profit. This occurs at the output Q_0, where the price P_0 is equal to average total cost. Some deadweight loss would exist, but not as much as would exist if the monopolist were unregulated. Neither regulatory option is perfect, but the latter has advantages in that it allows the firm to earn a fair rate of return, lessens the inefficiency, and lowers prices to the consumer.

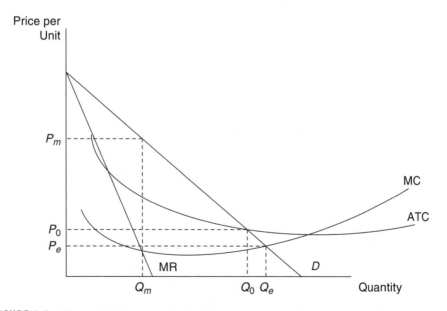

FIGURE 8-5 · Effects of Different Methods of Government Regulation of Monopolies

Price Discrimination

So far, we have assumed that the monopolist sets only one price, the one associated with selling the profit-maximizing level of output. But sometimes there are opportunities to increase profit by selling the same product to different groups of consumers and charging different prices to those different groups. This behavior is known as *price discrimination*, and we are familiar with several common examples. Suppose that Becky takes her grandfather to see the latest Harry Potter movie. When Becky's ticket costs $9 and her grandfather's costs $7, the theater is engaging in price discrimination. Suppose that Dorothy buys a plane ticket from Portland to San Francisco a month in advance of the flight, and Ray buys a ticket for the same flight two hours prior to takeoff. If Ray and Dorothy compared receipts, they would discover that Ray paid much more for the same flight. In both of these situations, the seller has charged different prices to different persons for the same product.

How is this possible? Each firm knows that it can increase its profit by doing so, and each must have three important characteristics to make it work. First, each seller must have some monopoly ability to set the price. Second, the seller must be able to differentiate the two consumers. The theater knows that Becky is not a senior citizen, and the airline knows that Ray has waited until the last minute to buy his ticket. Finally, the sellers must be able to prevent resale of the good. If Becky's grandfather could buy senior tickets and resell them in the parking lot to Becky's friends for a tidy profit, the theater's pricing strategy would fall apart.

CAUTION   *It is easy to get confused whether something that charges different prices is in fact price discrimination. For example, when Melanie takes her young child Max out to lunch at an all-you-can-eat buffet, the buffet charges Melanie a higher price. This is not price discrimination—this is charging different prices based on different costs, as Melanie is likely to eat more food than Max. On the other hand, when she takes him to the movie theater afterward, they both occupy exactly one seat each.*

The real differentiating characteristic that allows price discrimination to exist is that each group of consumers has a different price elasticity of demand for the good. Take the Dorothy and Ray example. The airline offers Ray a very high price for the last-minute ticket because it knows that Ray has a very low price elasticity of demand and that he has no choice but to pay the high price. He may be a business traveler who has suddenly discovered a very important reason to be in San Francisco, whereas Dorothy is traveling for pleasure and could afford to shop around and buy her ticket well in advance. In any price discrimination strategy, the group with the more elastic demand curve will pay a lower price than the group with the least elastic demand curve for the same good.

A special kind of price discrimination is known as *perfect price discrimination*. In this hypothetical situation, each consumer is charged the maximum price that she is willing to pay. Figure 8-6 shows this situation. The person represented at the top of the demand curve is charged the very highest price P_1 because he will pay it; the next person is charged a slightly lower price, and so on until the last person is charged the price P_e that equals the firm's marginal cost. When this happens, the demand curve is also the marginal revenue curve. Because each person is charged exactly the maximum price that she would pay, total consumer surplus is equal to zero. All the surplus goes to the monopolist. Ironically, while this sounds unfair to each individual consumer, it provides the efficient level of output to society because price is equal to marginal cost and no deadweight loss exists.

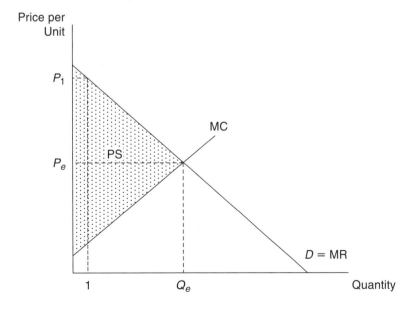

FIGURE 8-6 • Perfect Price Discrimination

Summary

This chapter introduced the model of monopoly, the key assumptions of that model, and how it greatly differs from perfect competition. A monopolist sets the price at the output where marginal revenue equals marginal cost. Unlike firms in perfect competition, marginal revenue declines as more output is sold and is always less than the price at which the output is sold. Because barriers to entry exist, monopoly profits can last in the long run, yet because monopolists reduce output below the level where price equals marginal cost, deadweight loss emerges. Because monopolies create both positive profits and deadweight loss they are often the targets of government regulation designed to lower the price and increase efficiency. Some firms with monopoly power also engage in price discrimination by charging two groups of consumers different prices for the same products. By doing this, these firms are able to increase profit, and reduce consumer surplus, even more than a single-price monopolist. In the next chapter we will discuss two market structures that fall between the two extreme cases of perfect competition and monopoly.

Appendix

When demand is linear, there is a very clear relationship between the demand curve and the marginal revenue curve. Let's use a simple example to illustrate. (Warning: a little calculus is required.)

Suppose demand is linear and is given as:

$$P = 10 - Q_d$$

This demand function is indeed a straight line with a y intercept of 10 and a slope of -1, and it is shown in Figure 8-7. The marginal revenue is also included in the graph, but to get that marginal revenue function, we must first develop the total revenue function.

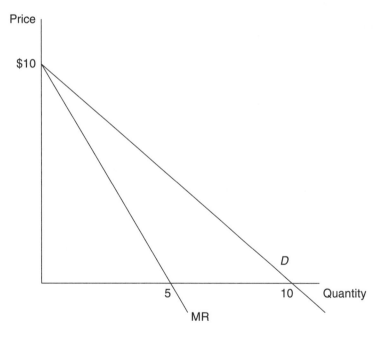

FIGURE 8-7 • Demand and Marginal Revenue Curves

Total revenue is price multiplied by quantity demanded, so with the demand function just given, we get the following total revenue function:

$$TR = P \times Q_d = (10 - Q_d) \times Q_d = 10Q_d - Q_d^2$$

Notice that this is a quadratic function; it is depicted in Figure 8-8.

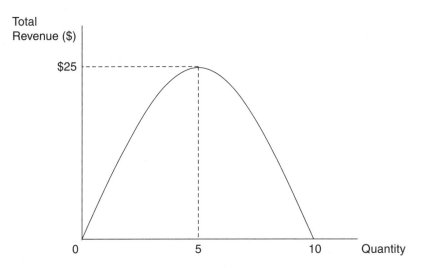

FIGURE 8-8 • The Total Revenue Curve When Demand Is Represented by $P = 10 - Q_d$

Figure 8-8 shows that total revenue is maximized at a quantity of 5 units and that total revenue is equal to $25 at that quantity. How do we know this? In order to maximize a function, we need to take the first derivative, set it equal to zero, and solve for quantity. Why do we take this approach? The first derivative gives us the slope of the function, and the slope of the total revenue function is equal to zero at the point where it is maximized. The slope of the function is also marginal revenue, so total revenue is maximized when marginal revenue is equal to zero.

$$\frac{\partial TR}{\partial Q} = MR = 10 - 2Q_d$$

If we set marginal revenue equal to zero and solve for Q_d, we can clearly see that a quantity of 5 units maximizes total revenue.

Finally, let's look at the original demand equation side by side with the marginal revenue function.

Demand:

$$P = 10 - Q_d$$

Marginal revenue:

$$MR = 10 - 2Q_d$$

Both functions are straight lines with a y intercept of 10; the only difference between these two functions is that the marginal revenue function has a slope of -2. In other words, the slope of the marginal revenue curve is twice as steep as the slope of the demand curve. And at any value of quantity demanded (except zero, of course), the marginal revenue will be less than the price. For example, at the midpoint quantity of 5 units, the price from the demand curve is $5, but the marginal revenue is zero. The results of this simple example can be generalized for any linear demand curve:

- The marginal revenue function lies below the demand function and is twice as steep.
- Total revenue is maximized at the quantity that serves as the midpoint of that demand curve.

QUIZ

Is each of the following statements *true* or *false*? Explain.

1. When compared to prices in perfectly competitive markets, monopoly prices are higher and fewer units are produced.

2. As with perfect competition, entry of new firms will cause short-run monopoly profits to fall to zero.

3. If the monopoly price is $8 at the profit-maximizing output, the marginal revenue is greater than $8.

4. If a natural monopoly is regulated in such a way that price equals average total cost, deadweight loss is eliminated.

For each of the following, choose the answer that best fits.

5. Which of the following statements is true of monopoly markets?
   A. Barriers to entry exist in the short run, but not in the long run.
   B. Price is greater than marginal revenue but less than marginal cost.
   C. Demand is more elastic than the demand for a perfectly competitive firm's output.
   D. Demand for the firm's product is also the market demand for the product.

6. Which of the following is *not* an example of price discrimination?
   A. Joe rents a two-bedroom apartment, and Susan rents a three-bedroom apartment. Susan's rent is higher than Joe's.
   B. Joe and Susan each buy a bottle of shampoo at the grocery store. Because Joe is a member of the store's "super saver" club, he receives a discount, whereas Susan does not.
   C. Joe and Susan each buy the same pancake breakfast at Denny's. Because Joe is a senior citizen, he receives a discount on his pancakes, but Susan does not.
   D. Joe and Susan are each planning a trip to Mexico. Susan buys her hotel and plane tickets together as a package and receives a discount. Joe buys the same hotel and plane tickets, but he buys them separately and pays a higher price.

7. Deadweight loss in a monopoly market is the result of:
   A. Price exceeding marginal cost at the profit-maximizing monopoly output
   B. Price equaling marginal cost at the profit-maximizing monopoly output
   C. Price equaling average total cost at the profit-maximizing monopoly output
   D. Marginal cost exceeding price at the profit-maximizing monopoly output

Give a short answer to the following questions.

8. **Draw a graph showing a profit-maximizing monopolist earning positive economic profit. In the graph, label the following:**
   - The monopoly output Q_m
   - The monopoly price P_m
   - The area of monopoly profit
   - The area of consumer surplus
   - The area of deadweight loss

9. **Referring back to the monopolist in problem 8, suppose the government taxed the monopoly profit and gave it back to the consumers as a refund. How would this affect the level of deadweight loss in the monopoly market?**

10. **Table 8-3 shows the demand schedule for a monopolist. Complete the total revenue and marginal revenue columns of the table. If the marginal cost and average cost are a constant \$5, how much output will be produced, what price will be charged, and how much profit will be earned?**

TABLE 8-3 Demand Schedule for a Monopolist			
Price	Quantity Demanded	Total Revenue	Marginal Revenue
\$8	0		
7	1		
6	2		
5	3		
4	4		
3	5		
2	6		
1	7		
0	8		

chapter 9

Imperfect Competition: Monopolistic Competition and Oligopoly

We have seen that in perfectly competitive markets, many small price-taking firms earn zero economic profit in the long run, prices to consumers are low, and output is at the socially efficient level. We have also seen that in monopoly markets, one large firm maintains positive economic profit in the long run, prices are high, and output is reduced so that deadweight loss is created. Both of these outcomes are uncommon in the real world because the basic assumptions of these two models are very strict. Markets in the real world operate somewhere in between perfect competition and monopoly, and we investigate these imperfectly competitive markets in this chapter.

CHAPTER OBJECTIVES

After completing this chapter, the student should be able to:

1. Describe the key assumptions of monopolistic competition and oligopoly.

2. Draw a graph that shows the monopolistically competitive firm maximizing short-run profit and a graph that shows the long-run outcome.

3. Describe the key assumptions of oligopoly.

4. Understand the basics of strategic games between two players, including the concepts of dominant strategies, the prisoners' dilemma, and Nash equilibria.

Key Assumptions of Monopolistic Competition

In many communities, markets such as the retail clothing market and the restaurant market can be described as good approximations of *monopolistic competition*. Let's look at the key assumptions of this model to see how this might be the case.

- Many sellers exist in the market.
- Each seller produces a good that is similar, but not identical, to the goods produced by its competitors. This is known as *product differentiation*.
- Very few barriers to entry exist.

Before we dive straight into the theory and the graphs, consider some of the restaurants in a community. The Mexican, Italian, and Chinese restaurants all produce dine-in meals for customers, but the menus are clearly distinct. In fact, the dining experience, which is an important part of the meal, is also differentiated by the décor, the music, and the members of the service staff. Because of the deliberate product differentiation each restaurant has created for its product, each has a small degree of price-setting ability. In other words, they are not price takers like firms in perfect competition, and if demand for their product is strong enough, they might earn positive economic profits.

However, as we will see, because of the low barriers to entry, those profits will exist only in the short run. In the long run, as new firms enter, each firm will find it more difficult to attract enough demand for its product to maintain the profits. In addition, we will find that the entry of new firms stops when firms are earning breakeven profits, as in the perfectly competitive model. Let's see how this works.

Short-Run Equilibrium in Monopolistic Competition

Suppose that Suzy Q's BBQ is one of many dining options in town. Because it sells a product that is differentiated from that of all the other restaurants, Suzy Q's is not a price-taking firm. The demand curve for its product is downward-sloping, and thus, like a monopoly firm, it has a marginal revenue curve that is below the demand curve and twice as steep. However, because we know that there are many close substitutes for its product, the demand for its product is probably quite elastic. Like all firms, Suzy Q's maximizes profit by finding the output level where marginal revenue equals marginal cost and then finding the corresponding price from the demand curve. Suzy's short-run situation is shown in Figure 9-1.

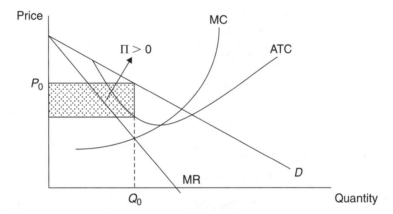

FIGURE 9-1 • Suzy Q's Short-Run Situation

At the moment, the demand for Suzy's BBQ is strong enough so that she earns positive economic profit, shown by the rectangle in Figure 9-1, and the model of monopolistic competition predicts that all the restaurants in this town will be experiencing similar profits of their own. However, what happens when entrepreneurs outside of the restaurant market notice that profits are being made? To answer that, we need to explore the long-run adjustment process.

Long-Run Equilibrium in Monopolistic Competition

Since there are minimal barriers to entry, new restaurateurs will open up to compete for customers and profits in the market. When they do, the demand for existing restaurants, like Suzy Q's, will start to decrease and probably become even more elastic. When the demand and marginal revenue curves shift to the left, the rectangle of profit from Figure 9-1 will begin to shrink. When firms like Suzy Q's are breaking even, the entry of new firms will cease. We can see the long-run outcome in Figure 9-2. The only way for firms to break even is when the output (Q_{LR}) is such that price (P_{LR}) is equal to average total cost. When the demand for Suzy's is downward-sloping, this will appear as a point of tangency between the demand curve and the average total cost curve.

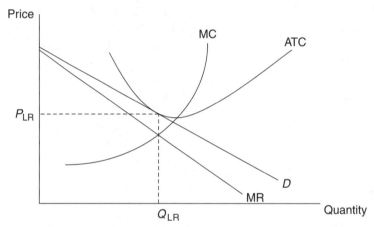

FIGURE 9-2 • Suzy Q's Long-Run Outcome

CAUTION   *When a new firm entered the market in our supply and demand model, the supply curve shifted to the right. But here, the demand curve shifts to the left when a new firm enters! The reason is that the demand we show in Figures 9-1 and 9-2 is the demand for a single good. When a competitor enters the market, the market is being divided up into ever-smaller chunks.*

So what do we make of this outcome? It tells us that monopolistically competitive markets will be extremely competitive and that firms will find it very difficult to maintain long-run profits. We also predict that there will be a lot of turnover in the market, with firms coming and going, and that firms will make vigorous attempts to continually differentiate their product from those of the other firms. These attempts can be costly (for example, advertising expense can be high), and they may not always actually provide the consumer with a better product (for example, beer cans that turn blue when they're cold).

From an efficiency standpoint, there is still deadweight loss because firms are still producing below the level where price equals marginal cost. However, because the price-setting power of these firms is not as strong as that of a monopoly firm, we can expect that the deadweight loss is not as severe. Firms in monopolistic competition are also not producing the output at which the average total cost curve is minimized. This means that prices will be higher than they would be in a perfectly competitive market. However, consumers are probably willing to pay a little bit more, despite the loss of both consumer surplus and efficiency, to have more product differentiation in their lives. After all, wouldn't it be boring if every restaurant in the market were exactly the same?

Still Struggling

Profits are zero in the long run in monopolistic competition, just as they are in perfect competition. Some students see this similarity and wonder why Figure 9-2 doesn't show output at the minimum of average total cost, just as it was in perfect competition. The explanation lies in the difference between the demand curves in the two models. In perfect competition, the demand for each firm's product is horizontal, so the only place where price is equal to average total cost is at the minimum of average total cost. In fact, this is where the horizontal demand curve is tangent to the average total cost curve. In monopolistic competition, the demand for each firm's product is downward-sloping, so that tangency with average total cost must come within the range of downward-sloping average total cost. Both types of firms earn zero long-run profit, but it happens at different points on the ATC curve.

Yet another way to look at it is mathematically. Note the profit-maximizing level of output, Q_{LR}, in Figure 9-2. The price that buyers are willing to pay for Q_{LR} is P_{LR}. Note that the average total cost of producing Q_{LR} is also P_{LR}. Whenever $P = ATC$, profit equals zero.

Oligopoly

Think about the companies that advertise during the Super Bowl or during any prime-time television show. They include companies that produce goods and services like cars, soft drinks, gasoline, beer, pizza, pharmaceuticals, financial planning, cell phones, and airlines. What do these major companies have in common? They operate in market structures known as *oligopolies*. Let's look at the key assumptions of this market structure.

Key Assumptions of Oligopoly

The small number of oligopolistic markets just listed share the following characteristics.

- There is a small number of large firms in the market (or a small number of firms make up the majority of sales in the market).
- The product may be homogeneous (for example, oil and gas) or differentiated (for example, cars and pizza).
- There are strong barriers to entry.

And there is one more important assumption about the behavior of firms in an oligopoly:

- Firms recognize their mutual interdependence and engage in strategic behavior.

So while oligopolies are markets that involve just a few large firms, this last assumption gives us a hint as to how they act. They act strategically to increase their own market share at the expense of their rivals' market share. And they know that these actions (such as advertising) will cause a response from their rivals. When my firm takes action, it affects your firm, and you will then react, which affects my firm. This is mutual interdependence. In fact, it is some of these strategic behaviors, like advertising, that create the barriers to entry. After all, could a new soft drink company enter the market and compete with Coke and Pepsi? The advertising expense required would be impossible for a new company to afford. Because of the complexity surrounding firms in an oligopoly, there really is no single model of this market, and no single graph that describes how it works. Despite this, or perhaps because of this, economists have begun using *game theory* to model the strategic interactions of these firms. We will discuss some of the simpler versions of this field of economics.

Game Theory

Though the French mathematician Antoine Augustin Cournot published work on the interaction of two firms (a duopoly) as far back as 1838, modern game theory as an academic discipline probably originated with John von Neumann and Oskar Morgenstern, who published a book in 1944 titled *Theory of Games and Economic Behavior*. The discipline has been advanced by both mathematicians and economists, and some of the work involves some seriously complicated theoretical mathematics. However, we can study some of the strategic interactions between two firms with a couple of simple games.

The Prisoners' Dilemma

Imagine two thieves, Bob and Patrick, who have robbed a jewelry store. The police have captured them in possession of the stolen property (jewelry), but, without a confession from at least one of them, cannot convict them of the more serious crime of armed robbery. Bob and Patrick are interrogated in separate rooms, and each is offered a deal: if one of you confesses to the armed robbery and the other does not, the one who confesses will go free and the other will spend 20 years in prison. If you both confess, you will each receive a lesser sentence of 5 years in prison for cooperating. If neither of you confesses, you will both spend 1 year in prison for possessing the stolen jewelry. The choices available to Bob and Patrick can be summarized in a *strategic game matrix* like Table 9-1. The outcomes, or payoffs, are found at the intersection of Bob's and Patrick's choices. For example, if both stay silent, the game ends in the top left corner of the game matrix, and both will receive 1 year in prison.

TABLE 9-1 Game Matrix for Prisoners' Dilemma

		Patrick's Choices	
		Silent	**Confess**
Bob's Choices	**Silent**	Bob: 1 year Patrick: 1 year	Bob: 20 years Patrick: go free
	Confess	Bob: go free Patrick: 20 years	Bob: 5 years Patrick: 5 years

If both Bob and Patrick make their choices at the same time, and in isolation, they must each determine the best choice (the one that assures fewer years in jail) given the choice of the other. If we were the attorney for Bob, what advice would we give him? If Patrick is going to stay silent, we would suggest that Bob confess. Confessing while Patrick stays silent allows Bob to go free, while staying silent sends Bob to jail for a year. But if Patrick were to confess in the other room, what should Bob do? Again he should confess. If Patrick is confessing, Bob can go to jail for 5 years by confessing, or he can go to jail for 20 years by remaining silent. Because the choice to confess is the best choice no matter what Patrick is doing, this is Bob's *dominant strategy*. Because Patrick is looking at the same deal, confessing is also his dominant strategy. The game ends with both players confessing.

This outcome is known as a *Nash equilibrium*, after Nobel laureate John Nash, who proposed it. A Nash equilibrium exists when both players cannot improve upon their payoff, given the choices made by the rival players. In other words, a Nash equilibrium reflects a best response to another player's best response. Given that Patrick had a dominant strategy to confess, Bob is satisfied with his decision to confess.

Obviously, as both are being "perp-walked" away to spend 5 years in prison, it appears that both of them would like to have a do-over so that they could both stay silent and receive a lesser sentence. But would this work? Not unless there was a way in which they could cooperate and figure out how to ensure that the other lives up to the agreement. After all, it's very tempting to choose the dominant strategy, thereby cheating on the agreement, and go free. In our next game, a pricing version of the prisoners' dilemma, we can see how this might happen.

Still Struggling

A helpful way to figure out what the Nash equilibrium is in a table like the one we made for Bob and Patrick is to isolate each strategy for each player and decide what the best response for that player is, and then underline the payoff to that strategy.

Step 1: Suppose we are advising Patrick. He is trying to decide what he would do if Bob picks the strategy "Silent."

Step 2: Cover up Bob's "Confess" strategy with a sheet of paper or your hand.

Step 3: Now that we have isolated Patrick's choices to only those that exist when Bob is "Silent," we can advise Patrick to find his *best response* to Bob's strategy.

Step 4: We should obviously advise Patrick to "Confess" because he prefers to go free than to spend one year in jail. We underline Patrick's payoff as shown in Table 9-2.

Step 5: Repeat this process by covering up Bob's "Silent" strategy with your hand and figure out Patrick's *best response* to Bob playing the strategy "Confess." We would again advise Patrick to "Confess" because going to jail for 5 years is a better payoff than going to jail for 20 years. We again underline Patrick's payoff.

In both cases, we advised Patrick to "Confess," and those decisions are recorded in Table 9-2 as underlined payoffs. This also reinforces that "Confess" is Patrick's dominant strategy; the strategy he chooses no matter what Bob is planning to do.

TABLE 9-2 Game Matrix for Prisoners' Dilemma—Isolating Patrick's Best Response (<u>Underlined</u>) to Bob's Choices

		Patrick's Choices	
		Silent	**Confess**
Bob's Choices	**Silent**	Bob: 1 year Patrick: 1 year	Bob: 20 years Patrick: <u>go free</u>
	Confess	Bob: go free Patrick: 20 years	Bob: 5 years Patrick: <u>5 years</u>

When you repeat this process as the advisor for Bob, you will end up underlining Bob's payoffs in the same way. You will discover that Bob always chooses to "Confess" no matter what Patrick does.

When you have underlined all best responses, the Nash equilibrium will be the outcome where the payoffs for both players are underlined in the same cell of the table. Think of this technique as "aligning" the players' strategies.

A Pricing Game

In a small town, there are two gas stations located on opposite sides of the highway. Snooki's Stop and Go and Vinny's Gas and Guzzle sell identical products, so consumers care only about who has the lowest price. Table 9-3 summarizes the daily revenue that each station would earn at each of two prices, one low (P_L) and one high (P_H). Naturally, Snooki's revenue also depends upon Vinny's pricing choice. We assume that they set the price in the morning simultaneously, and it cannot be changed.

TABLE 9-3 Game Matrix for Pricing Game			
		Vinny's Choices	
		P_H	P_L
Snooki's Choices	P_H	Snooki: $1,000 Vinny: $1,000	Snooki: $500 Vinny: $2,000
	P_L	Snooki: $2,000 Vinny: $500	Snooki: $750 Vinny: $750

Let's examine the situation. Once again we see dominant strategies in this game. No matter what price Vinny sets, Snooki's revenues are higher if she sets the low price. No matter what price Snooki sets, Vinny's revenues are higher if he also sets the low price. Setting the low price at the beginning of the day is a dominant strategy, and that is the Nash equilibrium.

Can they get out of this pricing dilemma? Not if the game is played only once. If the game is played repeatedly, like every day, Snooki and Vinny might learn to cooperate and set high prices every day. This cooperation, or *tacit collusion*, is believed to be common in oligopolies with a very small number of competing rivals. However, as in the prisoners' dilemma, the temptation to "cheat" on the unspoken agreement by setting the low price one day is quite high. In repeated games, a firm that cheats one day can be punished the next day when the other firm also sets the low price. Such behavior is sometimes seen in industries like the airline industry when one company offers a discounted fare between two cities and rival airlines quickly counter with the same low fare.

NOTE   *Why don't Snooki and Vinny just meet for pancakes every morning and discuss which price, high or low, they will set that day? Once they agree, they can go back to their gas stations and post the price. If one of them "waffles" on the agreement, the other can either revoke the agreement or punish him or her tomorrow. This sounds really straightforward, but it's quite illegal for this explicit price fixing to occur. The Sherman Antitrust Act of 1890 outlawed, in very broad language, behavior that would constitute a "restraint of trade" or is anticompetitive. Over time, the courts have had to specify what actions might, under some* *circumstances, qualify as anticompetitive, and collusive price fixing has certainly fit that definition. So while it is more difficult for these two firms to collude tacitly, it is more likely to keep them out of the slammer than the explicit collusion at the pancake house.*

A Slightly More Complicated Game

Both of the games previously discussed had two players with the same dominant strategy, and when dominant strategies converge, a Nash equilibrium outcome is clear to see. What happens if one or both firms do not have a dominant strategy? Table 9-4 shows the profits earned by two firms that can choose a high level of advertising (A_H) spending or a low level (A_L) of spending. Advertising is supposed to increase revenue, but it is also very costly and usually benefits larger firms with more customer loyalty. Firm 1 is a more established firm that will always earn more profit than Firm 2, so the payoffs are not symmetrical the way they were in the previous games.

TABLE 9-4 Game Matrix for Advertising Spending			
		Firm 2's Choices	
		A_H	A_L
Firm 1's Choices	A_H	Firm 1: $5,000 Firm 2: $1,500	Firm 1: $10,000 Firm 2: $3,000
	A_L	Firm 1: $3,000 Firm 2: $2,000	Firm 1: $4,000 Firm 2: $1,000

Firm 1 has a clear choice: choose a high level of advertising spending. No matter what Firm 2 does, Firm 1's profits are always higher when it chooses A_H rather than A_L. However, the decision isn't so clear for Firm 2. The owner might have deliberations that go something like this:

- If Firm 1 is going to choose A_L, I should choose A_H because $2,000 is better than $1,000.

- But if Firm 1 is going to choose A_H, I should choose A_L because $3,000 is better than $1,500.

While it seems as if the owner of Firm 2 might flip-flop back and forth between her choices, because she can see that Firm 1 will always choose A_H, Firm 2 will choose A_L. Again this is a Nash equilibrium because, given the rival's choice, neither firm would decide to change its choice away from the one that was made.

TIP   *Reading these game matrices is difficult at first. Here's a way to focus the decision making until you feel more comfortable with the process. Let's start with a similar advertising game as one final example (see Table 9-5).*

TABLE 9-5 Game Matrix for What If Analysis			
		Firm 2's Choices	
		A_H	A_L
Firm 1's Choices	A_H	Firm 1: $5 Firm 2: $1	Firm 1: $10 Firm 2: $3
	A_L	Firm 1: $3 Firm 2: $2	Firm 1: $4 Firm 2: $5

One way to walk through a solution to a game such as this one is to look at each potential scenario faced by both firms. You might refer to this as "what if?" analysis.

Let's assume that we are Firm 1.

- *What if Firm 2 is going to choose A_H? We can choose A_H and have profits of $5, or we can choose A_L and have profits of $3. We choose A_H.*
- *What if Firm 2 is going to choose A_L? We can choose A_H and have profits of $10, or we can choose A_L and have profits of $5. We choose A_H.*

No matter what, Firm 1 chooses A_H.
Now let's assume that we are Firm 2.

- *What if Firm 1 is going to choose A_H? We can choose A_H and have profits of $1, or we can choose A_L and have profits of $3. We choose A_L.*
- *What if Firm 1 is going to choose A_L? We can choose A_H and have profits of $2, or we can choose A_L and have profits of $5. We choose A_L.*

No matter what, Firm 2 chooses A_L.
Once you have worked through the "what if?" analysis for both firms, you can see that the outcome will be that Firm 1 chooses A_H and Firm 2 chooses A_L, and the Nash equilibrium outcome is in the upper right corner of the matrix.

Summary

This chapter presented the imperfectly competitive market structures of monopolistic competition and oligopoly. Monopolistic competition shares characteristics of both perfect competition and monopoly. Because each firm has some product differentiation, the demand for the firm's product is downward-sloping, and this gives the firm some degree of pricing power. It is possible for profits to be positive (or negative) in the short run, but in the long run, entry and exit of firms will bring profits back to zero. Oligopoly is a market structure that describes a broad group of real-world markets. The vast diversity of such markets makes it impossible to produce one general model that predicts how firms strategically behave when there is mutual interdependence. Game theory has been used to predict how a small number of rivals can either compete with each other or cooperate with each other. The simple prisoners' dilemma and a related pricing game were presented to show how two rivals can pursue dominant strategies and how the outcome produces a Nash equilibrium.

QUIZ

Is each of the following statements *true* or *false*? Explain.

1. Like those in perfect competition, firms in monopolistic competition earn zero profit in the long run and, as with monopolies, deadweight loss is created.

2. The following is true of monopolistic competition in the long run: $P = ATC = MR = MC$.

3. Because of an absence of barriers to entry, firms in an oligopoly earn zero economic profit in the long run.

4. A Nash equilibrium is an outcome of a game such that each player earns the greatest payoff possible, no matter what the other player chooses.

For each of the following, choose the answer that best fits.

5. Which of the following is true of firms in monopolistic competition?
   A. Product differentiation leads to a perfectly elastic demand curve for the firm's product.
   B. Barriers to entry ensure that long-run profits are positive.
   C. Many firms exist, each with a small degree of price-setting ability.
   D. Firms produce the allocatively and productively efficient level of output.

6. Doug's Duds is a monopolistically competitive retail clothing store in Freshville. Doug is currently maximizing his profit, but that profit is negative. Given this, firms will _____ the Freshville retail clothing market, causing the demand for Doug's Duds to _____, and causing prices to _____ until profits are _____.
   A. exit; increase; increase; zero
   B. exit; increase; decrease; zero
   C. exit; decrease; increase; zero
   D. enter; decrease; decrease; zero

7. Which of the following is true of firms in oligopoly?
   A. In the long run, an absence of barriers to entry produces breakeven profits.
   B. Firms are price takers.
   C. The goods produced can be either identical or differentiated.
   D. Firms act independently of one another.

8. Suppose Coke and Pepsi are deciding whether to charge a high price or a low price for a case of soda. The game matrix in Table 9-6 shows the choices and payoffs for this game. If the game is played only once, are there any dominant strategies?

TABLE 9-6

Coke's Choices		Pepsi's Choices	
		P_H	P_L
	P_H	Coke: $5	Coke: $10
		Pepsi: $1	Pepsi: $3
	P_L	Coke: $7	Coke: $4
		Pepsi: $2	Pepsi: $5

A. Yes. Choosing P_H is the dominant strategy for both firms.
B. Yes. Choosing P_L is the dominant strategy for Pepsi.
C. Yes. Choosing P_L is the dominant strategy for both firms.
D. No. Neither firm has a dominant strategy.

9. Suppose Coke and Pepsi are deciding whether to charge a high price or a low price for a case of soda. The game matrix in Table 9-6 shows the choices and payoffs for this game. If the game is played only once, what is the outcome?
A. Both firms choose P_H.
B. Both firms choose P_L.
C. Coke chooses P_H and Pepsi choose P_L.
D. Pepsi chooses P_H and Coke chooses P_L.

10. Nike and Reebok are rival firms in the athletic shoe industry. When we say that they are mutually interdependent, this means that:
A. Nike's actions affect Reebok, but Reebok's actions do not affect Nike.
B. Nike's actions do not affect Reebok, and Reebok's actions do not affect Nike.
C. Reebok's actions affect Nike, but Nike's actions do not affect Reebok.
D. Nike's actions affect Reebok, and Reebok's actions affect Nike.

chapter **10**

Factor Markets

We have devoted a great deal of time and space to models of product markets, but factor markets are also very important. For example, one of the most important markets you will ever encounter is the market for labor. It is in this market that you will supply your labor to firms and receive a wage for your productive efforts. While there are also markets for other factors, like capital and land, we devote most of our time investigating how labor markets in particular work.

CHAPTER OBJECTIVES

After completing this chapter, the student should be able to:

1. Discuss the decision that a worker must make between leisure and labor.

2. Understand why the supply of labor is usually upward-sloping.

3. Compute the value of the marginal product of labor and use it as the firm's demand curve for labor.

4. Show how the supply and demand for labor interact to determine the equilibrium wage and employment in a labor market.

5. Determine the combination of two inputs that produces a given amount of output at the least possible cost.

The Choice Between Labor and Leisure

Economists who study labor markets begin with the assumption that individuals can choose to divide their waking hours between two things: labor and leisure. When a person chooses to work, she earns a wage that she can use to purchase things that provide her with utility. When a person chooses to consume some leisure, she forgoes that wage, but the leisure also provides utility. What is leisure? Basically, leisure is all things that are not work. Thus, an author who spends hours writing a book is engaging in labor. When that same author reads a mystery novel before bed, he is engaging in leisure.

At first glance, it seems that reading a book before bed (consuming leisure in this framework) is "free," but we must remember one of the key lessons from Chapter 1: the cost of doing something is what you give up in order to do it. In this case, the individual reading the book is giving up a wage that he could have earned. If a person can receive a high wage in his chosen field of work, higher and higher wages will cause leisure to become more and more costly. And as leisure becomes more costly, people will choose to work more and consume less leisure.

An Individual's Labor Supply

Because there is an important relationship between the wage and the number of hours spent consuming leisure, it's reasonable to assume that there is a relationship between the wage and the number of hours spent supplying labor. For the most part, economists assume that there is a positive relationship, so that more hours of labor will be supplied as the hourly wage rises. But there are circumstances in which a person might choose to work *less* if the wage were to increase. To see how this might occur, we need to introduce something called the income and substitution effects.

When her wage rises, a person is faced with two effects that influence her labor and leisure decisions.

1. **The substitution effect.** When the wage rises, the price of another hour of leisure rises, and the person will decrease leisure and increase hours of labor supplied.

$$\uparrow \text{wage}, \uparrow \text{labor}, \downarrow \text{leisure}$$

2. **The income effect.** At all levels of work (except for zero, of course), when the wage rises, the person's income rises. Assuming that leisure is a normal good, more income increases leisure consumption and therefore must decrease the hours of labor supplied.

↑wage, ↓labor, ↑leisure

The two effects of a higher wage predict different impacts on the decision to supply hours of labor to the labor market. If the substitution effect is stronger than the income effect, the labor supply curve is upward-sloping; higher wages increase the hours of labor supplied. But at very high wages, the income effect might be stronger than the substitution effect, so that the supply of labor may be downward-sloping; higher wages decrease the hours of labor supplied. Figure 10-1 shows a labor supply (S_L) curve that is "backward-bending" (downward-sloping) at high wages. Although this may indeed exist for some individuals, for most of us the labor supply curve is upward-sloping, and we will draw it as such throughout this chapter.

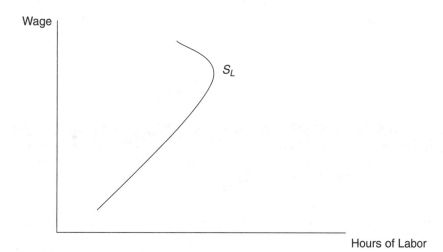

FIGURE 10.1 • Backward-Bending Labor Supply Curve

TIP *Another way to remember why people may begin to substitute away from labor (and the utility that people get from the fruits of that labor) and toward unpaid leisure is to recall that we get diminishing marginal utility from consumption. As each additional unit of labor yields less and less utility, we may switch to consuming a good that we aren't consuming much of (leisure) because the marginal utility we get from one more unit of that is higher.*

Labor Demand

The other side of the labor market is, of course, labor demand. When deciding whether the next unit of labor should be hired, employers weigh the marginal benefits of hiring against the marginal costs of hiring. By now this decision-making process should sound familiar, but in this context we have slightly different names for the marginal benefits and costs. On the benefit side of the decision, employers are interested in two key variables: how much additional output the next unit of labor brings to the firm (the *marginal product of labor*, or MP_L), and the market value of that output. For now, we assume that the firm sells its output in a perfectly competitive product market, so the market value of the output is simply the price (P). When we combine these two variables, we get the *value of the marginal product of labor* (VMP_L):

$$VMP_L = P \times MP_L$$

Let's use a quick example to show how this is computed. Suppose that Dora sells maps of historic sites to tourists that visit her city. The market for the maps is competitive, and the market price of a map is $5. Dora can employ workers, and the marginal productivity of each worker is shown in Table 10-1.

TABLE 10-1 Marginal Productivity of Labor

Workers	Total Product of Labor (TP_L)	Marginal Product of Labor (MP_L)	Price of Maps	Value of Marginal Product (VMP_L)
0	0			
1	16	16	$5	$80
2	30	14	$5	$70
3	42	12	$5	$60
4	52	10	$5	$50
5	60	8	$5	$40
6	66	6	$5	$30
7	70	4	$5	$20
8	72	2	$5	$10

Like any profit-maximizing employer, Dora will not employ a worker if the marginal cost of employing that worker exceeds the value of the marginal product. Suppose the market wage is $40. At this wage, Dora will employ 5 workers to maximize her profit. Figure 10-2 shows this hiring decision as the intersection of the downward-sloping VMP_L curve and the constant market wage. If the market wage rises to $50, Dora will reduce her hiring from 5 workers to 4. This inverse relationship between the wage and hiring is another example of the law of demand, and the VMP_L curve serves as Dora's demand for labor (D_L) curve.

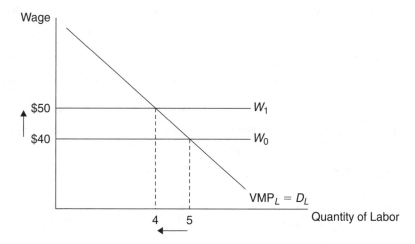

FIGURE 10-2 · Demand for Labor Curve

Still Struggling?

How do we know that Dora's employment of five workers at the wage of $40 is the profit-maximizing employment decision? Think of it marginally. If the marginal dollars of revenue earned from a hire at least exceed the marginal dollars of cost incurred from that hire, she should hire that worker because marginal profit is greater than or equal to zero. Table 10-2 shows this hiring decision again.

TABLE 10-2 Marginal Productivity of Labor and Profit

Workers	Total Product of Labor (TP$_L$)	Value of Marginal Product (VMP$_L$)	Wage (MC)	Marginal Profit = VMP$_L$ − W	Total Profit
0	0				
1	16	$80	$40	$80 − $40 = $40	$ 40
2	30	$70	$40	$30	$ 70
3	42	$60	$40	$20	$ 90
4	52	$50	$40	$10	$100
5	60	$40	$40	0	$100
6	66	$30	$40	− $10	$ 90
7	70	$20	$40	− $20	$ 70
8	72	$10	$40	− $30	$ 40

If we sum up all of the marginal profit gained from the first five workers, we get a total profit of $100. We can see from the table that employment of the sixth worker will actually cause profit to fall by $10.

In addition to wage-related movements along the labor demand curve, the labor demand curve can shift if one of several determinants of labor demand changes. We typically recognize four demand determinants in factor markets such as the market for labor.

1. **The price of the output.** If the price of the output increases, the VMP$_L$ will increase at all levels of employment, shifting the demand for labor to the right. The demand for a factor is described as a *derived demand* because it is derived from the demand for the goods that are being produced by the factor. For example, if the demand for steel increases, the price of steel increases, thus increasing the demand for steelworkers.

2. **The price of substitute factors.** All else equal, if the price of a substitute factor (like some forms of capital) increases, the firm's demand for labor increases. This also works in reverse. If the price of industrial sewing machines decreases, the demand for textile workers decreases.

3. **The price of complementary factors.** All else equal, if the price of a complementary factor increases, the demand for labor decreases. If the price of diesel fuel increases, the demand for truck drivers decreases.

4. **Productivity.** If the marginal productivity of labor increases, the VMP_L increases, and the demand for labor shifts to the right.

NOTE *We have assumed that the firm sells its output in a perfectly competitive product market, but what if it operates as a monopoly or in monopolistic competition or oligopoly? In that case, we know that the firm receives the marginal revenue for each unit sold, and that marginal revenue is less than the price. This marginal revenue product of labor (MRP_L) is therefore smaller than the value of the marginal product of labor and is equal to:*

$$MRP_L = MR \times MP_L$$

The hiring decision is to hire to the point where $MRP_L = W$, and Figure 10-3 shows that this firm is going to hire fewer units of labor (Q_m) than would be hired if the firm produced in a perfectly competitive market (Q_c). This should make sense. Firms with price-setting ability reduce output below the level of a perfectly competitive market, so they employ fewer units of labor.

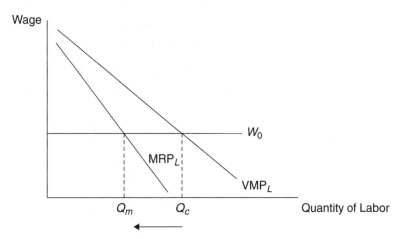

FIGURE 10-3 · Quantity of Labor Demanded in Competitive and Monopoly Markets

How Wages Are Determined

When factor markets are assumed to be competitive, wages are determined by the forces of supply and demand for that factor. In the example of Dora's map-selling business, the market wage was $40, and Dora employed five workers. Suppose that there are 100 firms selling the maps in this competitive environment and that each firm is making the same hiring decision as Dora. We can then deduce that there are 500 workers employed in this labor market at the market wage of $40. Figure 10-4 shows equilibrium in the labor market.

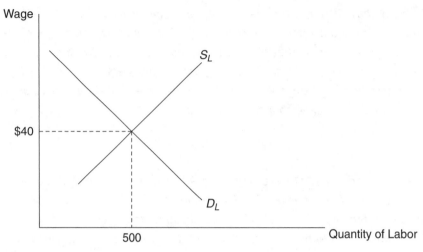

FIGURE 10-4 • Labor Market Equilibrium

Equilibrium wages in factor markets are determined in the same way as equilibrium prices in output markets. If the demand for labor rises or the supply of labor falls, the wage rises. If the demand for labor falls or the supply of labor rises, the wage falls. For example, suppose that the population of the city declines, thus reducing the size of the labor force. As the supply of labor shifts to the left in Figure 10-5, employers like Dora find it more difficult to find people who are

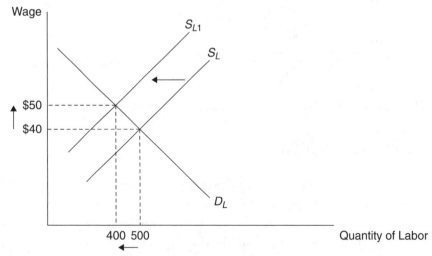

FIGURE 10-5 • A Shift to the Left of the Labor Supply Curve

willing to work at the wage of $40. Because there is a shortage of workers at this wage, there is upward pressure on the wage. If the wage rises to $50, Dora will employ 4 workers and 400 will be employed in the entire market.

TIP *In Chapter 6, we had a table showing a quick way to determine the impact of market shifts on equilibrium price and quantity. We modify that table here for labor markets.*

TABLE 10-3 Shorthand for Effect of Supply and Demand Changes on Wage and Employment		
Change	**Effect on W^***	**Effect on L^***
$D_L \uparrow$	$W^* \uparrow$	$L^* \uparrow$
$D_L \downarrow$	$W^* \downarrow$	$L^* \downarrow$
$S_L \downarrow$	$W^* \uparrow$	$L^* \downarrow$
$S_L \uparrow$	$W^* \downarrow$	$L^* \uparrow$

Again, we show only one curve changing at a time in this table. If you see arrows going in the same direction, you know for sure what is happening to the wage and employment. If the arrows are going in opposite directions, then the effect is ambiguous. For instance, if demand for labor and supply of labor are both decreasing at the same time, the employment arrows are both pointing down, so we know for sure that employment will decrease. However, the arrows on wage go in opposite directions.

NOTE *If the labor market isn't competitive, wages are not going to be determined at the intersection of market supply and demand. For example, suppose that Dora is the only employer in this labor market. As the only demander of labor, she is a monopsonist. The supply of labor is still upward-sloping, but the additional cost of employing the next unit of labor is no longer the wage because the wage must be increased to all units of labor, not just the next unit of labor. This* marginal factor cost *exceeds the wage and is equal to:*

$$MFC_L = \frac{\Delta(\text{total labor cost})}{\Delta \text{hiring}}$$

Suppose that the labor supply curve is described by Table 10-4. The total labor cost is equal to the wage (W) multiplied by the quantity of labor supplied (Q_s). The MFC_L is simply the change in TLC when the next unit of labor is hired.

TABLE 10-4	Labor Demand Curve for a Monopsonist			
Quantity of Labor Supplied	Wage	Total Labor Cost	MFC_L	Value of Marginal Product (VMP_L)
0	$10			
1	$20	$ 20	$ 20	$80
2	$30	$ 60	$ 40	$70
3	$40	$120	$ 60	$60
4	$50	$200	$ 80	$50
5	$60	$300	$100	$40
6	$70	$420	$120	$30
7	$80	$560	$140	$20
8	$90	$720	$160	$10

Dora now hires up to the point where $MFC_L = VMP_L$, and this occurs at three workers and a wage of $40 in Figure 10-6. The graph of a monopsonist's hiring decision shows that the MFC_L curve lies above the supply of labor. We can see that the monopsonist reduces employment below the level where the supply curve intersects the demand curve and the firm actually pays a wage ($40) that is lower than the third worker's VMP_L ($60). Monopsony, like its output market parallel, monopoly, generates deadweight loss because of this reduction away from the competitive quantity. This deadweight loss is seen as the shaded triangle in Figure 10-6.

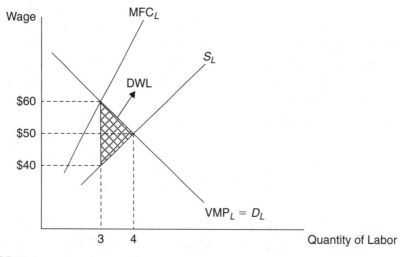

FIGURE 10-6 • Deadweight Loss from Monopsony

Least-Cost Hiring of Two Inputs

In the long run, employers can adjust the hiring of all inputs. Suppose a firm can hire labor (L) at the market wage (w) and capital (K) at the market rate (r). For any level of output, the firm wishes to hire labor and capital to produce that output at the lowest possible cost. After all, if you could produce 100 maps at a cost of $500 or 100 maps at a cost of $1,000, you would be wise to avoid the second of these two situations. We have actually seen a similar problem in Chapter 2 when we studied how a consumer could choose quantities of two goods to produce as much utility as possible while being constrained by his budget line.

Suppose Dora can employ labor at the market wage of $40 and capital at the market rate of $10. If Dora needs to produce 100 maps each day, she has several different combinations of labor and capital from which to choose. Table 10-5 shows a few combinations and the total cost of employing each combination.

TABLE 10-5 Possible Combinations of Labor and Capital

Labor (*L*)	Cost of *L*	Capital (*K*)	Cost of *K*	Total Cost
1	1 × $40 = $40	100	100 × $10 = $1,000	$1,040
2	$ 80	50	$500	$ 580
4	$ 160	25	$250	$ 410
5	$ 200	20	$200	$ 400
10	$ 400	10	$100	$ 500
20	$ 800	5	$ 50	$ 850
25	$1,000	4	$ 40	$1,040
50	$2,000	2	$ 20	$2,020
100	$4,000	1	$ 10	$4,010

If she is limited to the choices in this table, clearly Dora should choose to employ 5 units of labor and 20 units of capital because the total cost of that combination is $400, the lowest in the table.

Let's take a look at the hiring decision in a slightly different way and simplify the mathematics quite a bit. Suppose that both labor and capital can be hired at $1 per unit. In the current combination of labor and capital, Dora realizes that the marginal product of labor (MP_L) is 50 units and the marginal product of capital (MP_K) is 10 units. Should Dora maintain this hiring combination? No. If Dora hires one more unit of labor, output will rise by 50 units. To keep total costs the same, she must hire one less unit of capital, with the result that output will decline by 10 units. So this small adjustment increases output by 40 units and doesn't increase total cost. What is happening here? The additional dollar spent on the next unit of labor was more productive than it would have been if she had spent it on capital, so it was best spent on labor.

Let's compare the marginal product per dollar:

$$\frac{MP_L}{w} > \frac{MP_K}{r}$$

In Dora's situation, she wisely increased labor and decreased capital, thus readjusting her hiring decision. When would Dora find that such a readjustment would not pay dividends? To answer this, we need to introduce something known as the least-cost hiring rule. To produce a given level of output at the lowest possible cost, inputs should be hired to the point where:

$$\frac{MP_L}{w} = \frac{MP_K}{r}$$

By rearranging the equation, we see an alternative way to think about the rule.

$$\frac{MP_L}{MP_K} = \frac{w}{r}$$

This looks very similar to the rule for maximizing utility in Chapter 2. In that situation, the consumer used his budget to buy goods X and Y to the point where the marginal utility per dollar was equal. The same logic is true here. When the additional output per dollar (the "bang for the buck") is the same for both factors, there is no way to readjust the hiring to increase output at the same cost.

Still Struggling?

Let's use an alternative example to see if we can find the least-cost combination of labor and capital. Suppose that your hiring budget cannot exceed $80, and so your goal is to produce as many units of output as possible for that budget. The price of labor is $20, and the price of capital is $10. The marginal products of labor and capital are given in Table 10-6.

TABLE 10-6 Marginal Products of Labor and Capital			
Quantity of Labor Employed	**MP$_L$**	**Quantity of Capital Employed**	**MP$_K$**
1	40	1	16
2	35	2	15
3	30	3	14
4	25	4	13
5	20	5	12
6	15	6	11
7	10	7	10
8	5	8	9

Let's begin with the least-cost hiring rule:

$$\frac{MP_L}{\$20} = \frac{MP_K}{\$10}$$

This tells us that we need to find combinations of labor and capital such that the marginal product of labor is twice the marginal product of capital. There are two possibilities in Table 10-6.

Combination A: 3 units of L (MP$_L$ = 30) and 2 units of K (MP$_K$ = 15). The total cost of this hiring combination is indeed $80 (3 labor at $20 each and 2 capital at $10 each = $80), and the output is 136 units (Total output = ΣMP$_L$ + ΣMP$_K$ = 40 + 35 + 30 + 16 + 15 = 136).

Combination B: 5 units of L (MP$_L$ = 20) and 7 units of K (MP$_K$ = 10). The total cost of this hiring combination is $170, which is beyond our hiring budget.

There are other combinations of labor and capital that would spend exactly $80. For example, let's consider one final combination.

Combination C: 2 units of labor (MP$_L$ = 35) and 4 units of capital (MP$_K$ = 13). While it's true that this spends the $80 hiring budget, it's also true that

$$\frac{35}{\$20} > \frac{13}{\$10}$$

If we left this hiring decision unchanged, total output would be only 133 units. But if we spent just a little more on labor and a little less on capital (Combination A) we could get 3 additional units of output and keep hiring costs the same.

Summary

When the wage rises, most people find that leisure becomes too costly, and they increase the hours of labor supplied to the labor market, thus giving us an upward-sloping labor supply curve. The downward-sloping labor demand curve comes from combining a downward-sloping marginal product of labor with the market price to compute the value of the marginal product. Because the profit-maximizing firm hires labor to the point where the market wage is equal to VMP_L, this serves as the firm's demand for labor. The competitive labor market determines the equilibrium wage and employment at the intersection of the demand and supply curves. Wages in this market rise and fall with the typical patterns of any competitive market. In the long run, when the firm can adjust both labor and capital, the firm seeks to find the least-cost combination of labor and capital to produce a given level of output. This occurs when the marginal product per dollar is equal for both factors.

This chapter concludes our coverage of what is typically seen as microeconomics. The next several chapters introduce and develop macroeconomics and show how all of the micro decisions affect the broader macro economy.

QUIZ

Is each of the following statements *true* or *false*? Explain.

1. There is no theoretical justification for a downward-sloping labor supply curve.

2. When markets are perfectly competitive, the VMP$_L$ curve is downward-sloping because of diminishing marginal returns to production.

3. If the VMP$_L$ curve shifts to the right, the firm will increase hiring to increase profits.

4. If the demand for labor increases and the supply of labor decreases, the wage will certainly rise.

5. The least-cost combination of labor and capital occurs when the marginal product of labor is equal to the marginal product of capital.

For each of the following, choose the answer that best fits.

6. When Eric's wage falls, we predict that he will:
   A. Decrease his hours of labor supplied because the substitution effect is greater than the income effect
   B. Increase his hours of labor supplied because the substitution effect is greater than the income effect
   C. Decrease his hours of labor supplied because the income effect is greater than the substitution effect
   D. Increase his hours of labor supplied because there is no substitution effect when wages fall, there is only income effect

Use Table 10-7 to respond to questions 7 and 8.

TABLE 10-7	
Number of Employees	**Marginal Product of Labor**
1	14
2	12
3	10
4	8
5	6
6	4
7	2

7. This firm sells each unit of output in a perfectly competitive product market at a price of $10. The value of the marginal product of labor for the sixth worker is equal to:
   A. $10
   B. $14
   C. $40
   D. $16

8. If the competitive market wage is equal to $30 and the competitive price of the output is $3, how many workers will be employed to maximize profit?
   A. 1
   B. 2
   C. 3
   D. 4

9. The labor market for fast food workers is perfectly competitive and is currently in equilibrium. Suppose the cost of restaurant equipment (such as stoves, ovens, and dishwashers) falls. In the market for fast food workers, we predict that:
   A. Wage rises and employment falls if the workers are substitutes.
   B. Wage and employment both fall if the workers and equipment are substitutes.
   C. Wage and employment both fall if the workers and equipment are complementary.
   D. Wage falls and employment rises if the workers and equipment are complementary.

10. Stanley is currently employing labor at a wage of $5 per unit, and capital at a rate of $25 per unit. The marginal product of labor is currently equal to 20 units, and the marginal product of capital is equal to 100 units. Stanley should:
    A. Increase hiring of both labor and capital.
    B. Increase hiring of labor and decrease hiring of capital.
    C. Decrease hiring of labor and increase hiring of capital.
    D. Do nothing; he has already hired the least-cost combination of labor and capital.

chapter 11

Introduction to Macroeconomics

The first 10 chapters of this book dealt with *microeconomic* issues, that is, issues involving the performance of individual markets. Microeconomics seeks to answer questions like, "How much is produced and sold?," "Is that amount efficient?," and "Will intervention improve this outcome?" The second half of this book deals with *macroeconomic* issues. Macroeconomics, from the Greek root *macro* meaning "large," deals with the performance of entire economies and studies issues such as economic growth, the total amount of production within an economy (usually called *aggregate output*), inflation, unemployment, trade, and the monetary system. The goal of a macroeconomist is to understand the mechanisms that drive the trends in these measures.

CHAPTER OBJECTIVES

After completing this chapter, the student should be able to:

1. Describe the difference between microeconomics and macroeconomics.
2. Understand what the study of macroeconomics attempts to accomplish, and what it does not try to do.

3. Discuss the circular flow diagram.

4. Describe GDP, including the components of GDP and how much of U.S. GDP each component makes up.

5. Explain the two methods of calculating GDP.

6. Discuss the difference between GDP and GNP.

History tells us that crises can lead to major developments and advances in thinking as people try to understand what led to a particular crisis and how to prevent another similar event from happening. Economics is no exception, and modern macroeconomics has its roots in the Great Depression of the 1930s.

Expansions and contractions of business activity were not new at that time, and economists had long studied business cycles, inflation, and growth. However, the scope and scale of the events of the early 1930s were unprecedented. The failure of the "invisible hand" to correct the economic Armageddon of the Great Depression led to a fundamental shift within economics and a schism that divided economics into two distinct fields. Other major events over the past century have further pushed the development of macroeconomics, but we will address those in later chapters.

Before we move on to what macroeconomists do, we need to make the following points about macroeconomics:

- **Macroeconomics uses models.** Like microeconomics, macroeconomics uses graphs and equations to create a stylized (or simplified) idea of how something is supposed to work.

- *Ceteris paribus* **still holds.** There are countless moving parts within an economy. When we are studying the impact of a specific phenomenon on an economy, we still assume that only *that* phenomenon is changing so that we can focus on what the effect of *that* thing changing will be.

- **The goal of macroeconomics is not to fine-tune the economy.** Macroeconomics does not set out to keep business cycles from occurring. To do so would be not only impossible, but perhaps even detrimental to an economy (remember that major advances can come from turning points). The study of macroeconomics is more concerned with understanding how the economy as a whole works, so that policy makers can try to keep major swings in business activity and economic catastrophes, such as the Great Depression, from occurring again.

A Model of the Economy as a Whole: The Circular Flow Diagram

Imagine that you just got your paycheck. You take that money and use it to pay rent, buy food, and maybe buy a few books at a store. To your landlord, the grocer, and the bookstore owner, the money you have just spent is money that they receive as income. They use that income to pay for the loan to build your apartment, the frozen food manufacturer who supplied the grocer with chicken nuggets, and the clerk to work at the bookstore. In turn, each of those people uses that money to pay some other entity, which then uses that money to pay yet another entity.

This is the basis of our first model of the macroeconomy: the *circular flow diagram*. This model breaks up the macroeconomy into two main entities, households and firms. Households are buyers of goods, but sellers of the factors of production. Firms are sellers of goods, but buyers of the factors of production. Households take money in exchange for providing labor services, savings, and other resources. They then spend that money for the purchase of goods and services from firms.

Figure 11-1 illustrates this idea. The goods and services being exchanged move clockwise. The payments for the goods and services move counterclockwise. In the figure, the clockwise arrows signify households that sell labor in the factor market; the labor is then used by firms to make goods, which are then sold to the households. In the figure, the counterclockwise arrows show that households receive money for their labor, and they use that money for consumer spending, which becomes revenue for firms.

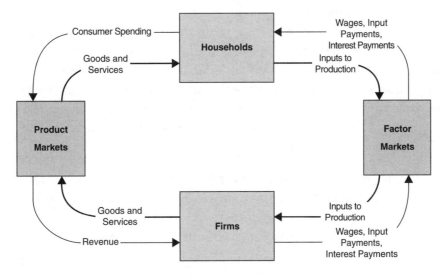

FIGURE 11-1 • The Circular Flow Diagram

The circular flow diagram illustrates several key concepts:

- This is a snapshot of production within an economy. When macroeconomists are talking about the goods and services produced by the economy, this is the picture they have in mind.

- One entity's income is another entity's spending. Economists would say that income equals expenditures. Basically, income and expenditures are two sides of the same coin.

TIP   *This second point brings up an important fact: if we are interested in counting production, we can count either all the income that is received by the entities in an economy, or all the expenditures that entities in the economy make. Either way, we will get the same result.*

Measuring the State of the Economy

When you go to the doctor for an annual exam, the doctor generally does more than take a glance at you to determine whether you are "healthy" or "sick." The doctor will take various measurements to attempt to quantify your health. She might take your temperature, your pulse, your blood pressure, and your weight. Each of these measurements individually provides the doctor with useful information, but taken collectively, they give a more complete idea of your health status. Similarly, we take measures of the macroeconomy to determine how well an economy is doing.

The most important of these measures is the *gross domestic product (GDP)*. This is a measure of the market value of the final goods and services produced within an economy. It gives information on how much economic activity is occurring within the economy. It is also reflects the standard of living within the economy, as our collective income depends on how many goods and services are being produced in the economy. Before we continue to how it is measured, let's take the definition apart. Gross domestic product is:

- **The market value.** Gross domestic product is measured in terms of money, the market prices at which goods are sold. This is a necessity because we need some sort of common denominator to add up all of the chicken nuggets, cars, and window-washing services that an economy might produce.

- **Of final goods and services.** We want our measure of the production within an economy to be as accurate as possible. In particular, we want to avoid overcounting or undercounting. Take, for example, the cars produced in an economy. If we counted the car at its market price, this includes the value of the parts of the car, such as the tires. If we *also* counted the tires that Ford used when it made the car, we would be claiming that the economy had produced eight tires, when in fact it had produced only four. By counting only final goods, we avoid double-counting.

- **Produced within an economy**. GDP measures the production of goods within the geographic borders of an economy, regardless of the nationality of the person who owns the factors of production used to make those goods. For instance, if Ford Motor Company operates a plant within Canada, that production is counted as part of Canadian GDP, not U.S. GDP. Similarly, if Volkswagen, a German carmaker, operates a plant in Tennessee, that production is counted in U.S. GDP.

Counting GDP: The Expenditures Approach

There are two ways to calculate GDP. The simpler way is the expenditures approach. As the name suggests, it involves simply adding up all of the expenditures on final goods and services in an economy. Using this approach, GDP has five components:

$$GDP = C + I + G + (X - M)$$

- **Consumption (C).** This is the amount of money that individuals and households spend on final goods and services. In other words, this is the amount of money spent on things like food, rent, jewelry, toys, and pretty much anything else that individuals and households buy. This category is sometimes further broken down into durable goods (goods that are expected to last longer than three years), nondurable goods (goods that are expected to last for less than three years), and services. There is, however, one notable exception in which household purchases, rather than being counted as consumption, are instead counted as investment spending.

- **Investment (I).** This is the amount of money that is spent on things such as new business equipment, factories, software, and other productive assets. It also includes new houses purchased by households. It can be broken down into residential investment (houses, apartments, and so on), nonresidential investment (office buildings, machinery, and so on), and changes in inventories.

- **Government (G).** This is the amount of money that is spent by local, state, and federal governments on the purchase of goods and services, such as paying government employees or purchasing missiles. It does not include government spending that merely involves transfers of money, such as social security checks.

- **Exports (X).** This is the value of goods and services produced in the United States for sale outside the United States. Recall that the purpose of GDP is to capture all production, not just what we consume. Thus, we want to count the goods that we produce and send elsewhere.

- **Imports (M).** Similarly, we want to take out the goods and services that are produced elsewhere but consumed here. Therefore, we subtract the value of the goods that are produced outside the United States and consumed within the United States. When imports are subtracted from exports, we get the nation's *net exports*.

Still Struggling

You might be confused about why a few things you think you know about the economy aren't found in that list. Let's go through some common misperceptions.

- **Investment.** Why aren't stocks included in investment? When people use the term *investment* colloquially, they are usually talking about stocks, bonds, and other financial instruments. That is not what economists mean when they talk about investment. In economics, investment refers generally to the ability to create production or business activity. For instance, when Margaret "invests" in $100 of Google stock, she is purchasing a financial instrument; basically, she is letting Google use that $100 to purchase equipment, inventory, or the like. If we counted that $100 purchase of equipment *and* the $100 stock purchase, we would be double-counting that $100 and overstating the true production of the economy.

- **It's the change in inventories that matter.** You might wonder why purchases of inventory aren't double-counting. For instance, doesn't a store with inventory eventually sell that inventory, and wouldn't that sale be counted in consumption? Well, the answer is, yes, it would, if what we counted wasn't the *change* in inventory. For instance, suppose a store purchases $100 worth of T-shirts to put in its stockroom in 2009. That would be counted in the investment category in 2009 because the purchase added $100 of production. If the store sold half of those T-shirts in 2010 for $80, −$50 would be counted in investment in 2010, and $80 would be counted in consumption in 2010 (the net change of +$30 to GDP reflects the value added of the store selling the T-shirts, such as the services of the worker who helps you pick out a shirt).

- **Government.** Government's contribution to GDP includes government purchases, but not necessarily all government spending. The category *G* does not include every time the government spends money; it includes only actual productive activity. For instance, suppose the government spends $1,000 on your grandmother: a $900 social security payment and a $100 payment to her doctor through Medicare spending. The Medicare spending is a purchase of a service—there was actual productive activity involved (a doctor visit). However, the $900 social security payment is what is called a *transfer payment*—the government is sending your grandmother a check simply because she is retired, not because she is providing the government with a good or service. Moreover, if your grandmother then took that $900 and spent it on food, that would be double-counting.

Table 11-1 gives the breakdown of U.S. GDP and its components from 2008 to 2011. From this, we can take away some key points:

- Consumption is the largest component of GDP, and most of that consumption is in the form of services.

- The United States is a net importer, meaning that we typically import more goods and services than we export.

- The greatest variation from year to year is in investment. This is key: the investment category is spending by businesses to produce in the future. If this is going up or down, it reflects how much business activity firms expect to do in the future. It is particularly noteworthy to see the drop in investment in 2009 following the start of the recession in 2008. Even though consumption dropped, it dropped by only about 1.7 percent. Investment fell by 25.9 percent. This is particularly apparent in the change in inventories—it appears that businesses were more interested in getting rid of inventory than in adding to it.

TABLE 11-1 U.S. GDP, 2008–2010 (in Billions of Dollars)

	2008	2009	2010	Percent of Total (2010)
Gross domestic product	14,291.5	13,939.0	14,526.5	100%
Consumption (C)	10,035.5	9,866.1	10,245.5	70.53%
Goods	3,381.7	3,197.5	3,387.0	
Durable goods	1,108.9	1,029.6	1,085.5	
Nondurable goods	2,272.8	2,167.8	2,301.5	
Services	6,653.8	6,668.7	6,858.5	
Private domestic investment (I)	2,087.6	1,546.8	1,795.1	12.36%
Nonresidential	1,656.3	1,353.0	1,390.1	
Residential	472.4	354.7	338.1	
Change in private inventories	−41.1	−160.8	66.9	
Net exports of goods and services (X − M)	−709.7	−391.5	−516.9	−3.56%
Exports	1,846.8	1,583.0	1,839.8	
Imports	2,556.5	1,974.6	2,356.7	
Government consumption expenditures and gross investment (G)	2,878.1	2,917.5	3,002.8	20.67%
Federal..................	1,080.1	1,142.7	1,222.8	
State and local.......	1,798.0	1,774.8	1,780.0	

Source: Bureau of Economic Analysis

TIP *What isn't counted in GDP?*

Recall that GDP is the sale of all final goods and services within the geographic borders of a country. However, there are some notable exceptions that need to be remembered. Only final goods are counted, and they are counted in the year in which they were produced. Resold goods such as used homes, used cars, and used clothing are not counted this year, as they were already counted in the year in which they were produced. Also, goods that are bought, sold, or produced illegally or informally are not counted. For instance, during the Prohibition era, the sale of alcohol was prohibited. It was still produced and bought and sold on the black market, but it was not included in official GDP calculations. Informal production includes the unpaid work that is done around the house. For example, if a working parent washes his own laundry at home, this activity is not counted in GDP. However, if the person pays to send the dirty clothes out to a laundry service, this would be counted.

Counting GDP: The Income Approach

A somewhat less intuitive, but nonetheless important, approach to measuring GDP is the income approach. As its name suggests, this is computed by adding up the various components of national income, called *factor incomes*. This reflects the fact that these are the incomes that accrue to the various factors of production in the economy. Using this approach, GDP is referred to as *national income*.

$$NI = Wages + Rents + Interest + Profits$$

- **Wages.** This refers to wages, salaries, and benefits earned by labor. It also includes income that comes from social security and unemployment benefits.

- **Rents.** This includes rental income that households receive from property and capital. It includes rental properties, such as a house that a household may own and rent to someone else, but it also includes royalties from patents and copyrights.

- **Interest.** This includes interest income that households receive from providing money to corporations, such as returns on stock or bond investments. Interest paid by governments or by households to businesses (such as for mortgages or car loans) is not included in this category.

- **Profits.** This is the amount of money that firms have left over after paying wages, rent, interest, and other expenses.

Either way you calculate GDP, you should end up with roughly the same number. There is sometimes a slight difference because of the way things are measured and calculated, and slight variation as a result of rounding error, but in practice the differences are negligible. This should not be at all surprising—recall from the circular flow diagram that expenditures simply go in one direction, and income flows in the opposite direction.

GNP Versus GDP—What's the Difference?

Occasionally you may see a different, but similar-looking, measure called gross national product (GNP) reported. GNP is the measure of all final goods and services that are produced by the productive assets of a country, whereas GDP is the measure of all final goods and services that are produced within the geographic borders of a country, regardless of who owns the resources. For example, consider Toyota Motor Manufacturing, Kentucky (TMMK), an automotive factory in Georgetown, Kentucky. The firm TMMK is located within the geographic borders of the United States, and so its production would be counted in various parts of U.S. GDP. However, TMMK is wholly owned by the Toyota Motor Company, which is headquartered in Japan. Therefore TMMK's production would be counted not in U.S. GNP, but in Japan's GNP.

The intuition behind GDP and GNP is similar, but the uses and interpretations differ slightly. Gross domestic product is a good measure of how the local economy of a country is doing, whereas GNP gives a better picture of how well off the nationals of a country are economically. For instance, if a very large share of a country's resources is foreign-owned, the proceeds from that production are likely to go elsewhere. Certain subfields of economics, such as development economics, use this measure because they are ultimately more concerned with the well-being of the individuals within a country.

Summary

This chapter described the difference between microeconomics and macroeconomics, and why we distinguish between the two. It introduced one of the key measures of the health of a macroeconomy, GDP, and how it is calculated. Gross domestic product was broken down into its five components, and we explained some common misconceptions concerning what production is and is not included in the nation's official GDP calculations. Finally, we introduced the concept of GNP, and why this slightly different measure is sometimes used. The key idea in this chapter is that a country's well-being depends on its ability to produce goods and services. Of course, in order to produce those goods and services, you need to hire workers. In the next chapter, we extend our discussion of trying to measure the health of an economy by looking at the employment picture, specifically, how and why we measure employment and unemployment.

QUIZ

Is each of the following statements *true* or *false*? Explain.

1. **Microeconomics and macroeconomics are different names for the same study of economies.**

2. **In the United States, government spending makes up the greatest percentage of GDP.**

3. **Investment spending is the most volatile portion of GDP.**

4. **Gross national product is an indication of what is produced within a country's borders.**

5. **Gross domestic product counts all goods and services that are produced within a country.**

Give a short answer to the following questions.

6. **A store purchases grogs to put in its storeroom in 2009 for a total of $200. In 2010, the store sells those same grogs for a total of $300. Explain how each of these appears in the calculation of GDP.**

Use the following information to answer questions 7 through 10.

Within the nation of Maxistan in 2010, all of the sales of goods and services can be described as follows: durable goods of $500, new homes of $1,000, used homes of $200, inventories of $300, nondurable goods of $900, and government purchases of $400. In addition, Maxistan imported $150 worth of goods and exported $280 worth of goods.

7. **Describe which category of GDP each item sold in Maxistan would fall into, using the expenditures approach to calculating GDP.**

8. **Calculate the GDP of Maxistan.**

9. **Which items sold in Maxistan aren't counted in GDP? Why aren't they counted?**

10. **Is Maxistan a net exporter or a net importer? Explain.**

chapter 12

Unemployment

Unemployment, like GDP, is an important indicator of the health of the macroeconomy. In order to make the goods and services that a country produces, firms need workers. All else equal, then, we expect more people to be working when an economy is making more goods and services and fewer people to be working when an economy is making fewer goods and services. Thus, it's intuitive that the number of people working, or rather *not* working, can be a good indicator of how close an economy is to producing its full potential. While everybody is familiar with the idea of the unemployment rate, many people lack a real understanding of what unemployment is, how it is measured, how to interpret it, and the caveats we need to consider in drawing conclusions about it.

CHAPTER OBJECTIVES

After completing this chapter, the student should be able to:

1. Understand what the labor force is and calculate the labor force participation rate.

2. Describe the term *unemployment* and how to calculate the unemployment rate.

3. Describe the differences between structural, frictional, seasonal, and cyclical unemployment.

4. Describe three theories on why labor markets fail.

5. Describe what is meant by full employment and the natural rate of unemployment.

6. Understand what is meant by underemployment and discouraged workers.

What Is Unemployment?

When reporters, politicians, and pundits talk about the state of the economy, one of the numbers that they are likely to hold up as a sign of its success or failure is the degree of *unemployment* that exists in an economy. Unemployment refers to a situation in which people are not working, even though they are *willing* and *able* to work.

These two italicized words are an important clue to understanding what we mean by unemployment. It is not merely everyone who is not working. For instance, if a family decides that one parent will stay home and take care of the kids while the other parent works, and both parents are happy with this situation, we would hardly think of the nonworking parent as being a reflection of a bad state of the economy. When we talk about unemployment, we are really talking about a person who wants to work but for some reason is unable to find work.

Despite the ubiquity of unemployment reports, it is easy to argue that most people still do not understand unemployment very well. We tend to think of unemployment as "bad." Unemployment can be a difficult, painful time for those who are experiencing it, and the existence of unemployment may even represent a market failure. However, a certain amount of unemployment not only is good for an economy, but may be necessary if that economy is to grow at a healthy pace without large increases in the prices of goods and services.

The Labor Force

Before we start to calculate who should (and should not) be counted as unemployed, we need to limit ourselves to people who might possibly be employed. This might seem silly—shouldn't everyone be counted? Of course not. Remember, ultimately we want to capture the extent to which the market for labor is failing. We don't want to include people in our count who wouldn't be participating in this market even if it operated perfectly. If we counted three-year-old children, stay-at-home parents, or people in prison as potential workers, this could seriously distort a measure of who is willing and able to work.

Before we continue on to our measures of work, we need to identify the agency that is responsible for producing these measures. In the United States, the Bureau of Labor Statistics (BLS) has collected and analyzed employment data since 1940. Each month, the BLS conducts the Current Population Survey (CPS) in order to track trends in employment and the labor force. All of the statistics included in this chapter are from annual CPS reports.

Those who are considered potential workers are called the *labor force*. The definition of those included in the labor force varies by country, but in the United States, to be counted as being in the labor force, you must:

- Be of working age (over 16 years)
- Not be part of the "institutionalized population" (that is, not be in prison, jail, a mental institution, or the military)

And have either:

- Worked at least one hour in the previous week *or*
- Not worked at all in the previous week and been actively looking for work

As of July 2011, there were 153.2 million people in the U.S. labor force. According to the U.S. Census Bureau, the U.S. population in July 2011 was approximately 307 million people. Thus, roughly half of the U.S. population isn't counted as potential workers.

This leads us to our first measure of the health of a nation's labor market, the *labor force participation rate* (LFPR). The LFPR tells us the percentage of the population that is participating in the labor market, either by working or by trying to get a job. To find the LFPR, we simply divide the labor force by the civilian, noninstitutionalized, working-age population:

$$\text{LFPR} = \frac{\text{labor force}}{\text{civilian, noninstitutionalized, working-age population}}$$

The LFPR can tell us much more than a simple percentage. First, it can tell us how the full employment rate of an economy is changing over time—the more people who are participating in the labor force, the more potential for jobs there is over time (we will discuss this more in Chapter 14). Second, it can also indicate changes in the composition of the labor force over time. If people tend to stay in school for longer periods of time, or if large numbers of the population are incarcerated or in the military, this will lower the LFPR. On the other hand, if more people are drawn into the workforce because there are better opportunities available to them or because incomes are increasing, the LFPR will increase.

As of July 2011, the U.S. LFPR was 63.9 percent. For the past 30 years or so, the labor force participation rate in the United States has hovered around 64 to 67 percent. However, in the 1940s, the LFPR was only around 48 percent. The majority of this dramatic increase is due to the increased labor force participation by women as single-earner; two-adult households have become the exception rather than the norm.

Measuring Unemployment

Every month, on the first Friday of the month, the BLS releases the monthly *unemployment rate*, the percentage of people that were unemployed during the previous month. Ultimately, the purpose of the unemployment rate is to capture the *true* employment situation. An important question for a nation is this: are the people who are willing and able to work able to find jobs? The higher the unemployment rate is, the more likely it is that the answer to that question is no.

Our measure of unemployment should therefore focus on those who are willing and able to work. Just as the labor force doesn't include people who have no interest in working or no ability to work, we don't want to count people who don't have a job, but aren't really trying to get one, as unemployed. Therefore, we define *employed* and *unemployed* as follows:

Employed. A person is counted as being employed if he worked a single hour during the previous week

Unemployed. A person is counted as being unemployed if he did not work a single hour during the previous week *and* had actively looked for work during the last four weeks.

Taken together, the employed and the unemployed make up the entire labor force. To calculate the unemployment rate (UR), we simply divide the number of people who are unemployed by the total number of people in the labor force:

$$UR = \frac{\text{Number of unemployed}}{\text{Number of employed} + \text{Number of unemployed}}$$

For example, in July 2011, there were 139.3 million people employed in the United States and 13.9 million people unemployed. This gives us a labor force of 153.2 million and an unemployment rate of 9.1 percent.

There is a third category used by the BLS to describe people above the age of 16 who are neither employed nor unemployed. These folks are classified as "not in the labor force" and include retirees, stay-at-home parents, and other adults who have simply chosen not to seek work or who physically cannot work. The extent of a special subset of this last group of people, the so-called discouraged workers, is something that warrants additional discussion a bit later in the chapter.

The unemployment rate tells us the percentage of people who are actively looking for work out of all of the people in the labor force. But without some additional information, we can't really interpret this number. If some unemployment is good and too much unemployment is bad, what is the "right amount" of unemployment? To better understand that, we need to discuss the different types of unemployment.

Still Struggling

Consider the fictional economy described in Table 12-1, in which it is illegal for those under the age of 16 to work and the mandatory retirement age is 65.

TABLE 12-1 Maxistan Annual Census		
Category	**Number**	***Key***
Total population	100,000	
Population by age		
0–15	20,000	*Not working age—not in the labor force*
16–45	40,000	*Working age—potentially labor force*
46–64	30,000	*Working age—potentially labor force*
65+	10,000	*Retirement age—not in the labor force*
Number of workers	35,000	*Number employed—in the labor force*
Number of unemployed and looking for work	4,000	*Number unemployed—in the labor force*
Number in military	6,000	*Not in the labor force*
Number institutionalized	2,000	*Not in the labor force*

There are a total of 100,000 people in Maxistan, and 70,000 of them are between the ages of 16 and 65. However, we need to remove those who are institutionalized (2,000) and those who are in the military (6,000). That leaves us with 62,000 who are in the civilian noninstitutionalized working-age population (CNIWAP).

The labor force consists of those who are employed (35,000) and those who are unemployed and looking for work (4,000). Therefore, the labor force (LF) = 39,000.

The labor force participation rate = LF/CNIWAP = 39,000/62,000 = 63.9 percent.

There are 4,000 people who are not currently working but are looking for work. The unemployment rate = unemployed/LF = 4,000/39,000 = 10.26 percent.

Two Types of Unemployment

The reason we tend to think of unemployment as being undesirable is that we tend to think of it in terms of losing a job or having trouble finding one; in other words, it is the involuntary nature of unemployment that we dislike. This is a valid point: an economy that cannot provide jobs for everyone who desires one has problems. However, not all unemployment is involuntary. We can divide unemployment between these two concepts. Economists generally categorize unemployment as being either *frictional unemployment* or *structural unemployment*.

Frictional unemployment, just as it sounds like, occurs when the labor market doesn't work perfectly. Basically, frictional unemployment is unemployment that results from the fact that people aren't perfectly matched with jobs. This can happen when someone quits a job that she doesn't like in order to find another one, someone is holding out for a job offer with a higher wage, or someone is fired for cause (that is, he wasn't good enough at his job). Generally, frictional unemployment exists because of the costs involved in matching workers with jobs, rather than because of some fundamental problem with the economy. In this sense, a certain amount of frictional unemployment is actually healthy for an economy—it takes time for people to find appropriate jobs for their skills. If they just took whatever job first became available, they might be poorly matched to that job and thus be less productive than they should be.

Structural unemployment is unemployment that is caused by an inherent mismatch between the skills that employers are demanding and the skills that workers can provide. This is generally involuntary unemployment (whereas frictional employment can really be either). For instance, when demand for a particular skill permanently declines (like blacksmithing, for example), workers with that skill will not be able to find employers that are willing to hire them. The mismatch may also be due to the seasonal nature of the work. Some types of work, such as agricultural work or construction, occur only at certain times of the year, and when the season is over, those workers become unemployed (this is known as *seasonal unemployment*). As we discussed in Chapter 10, the demand for labor is based on firms' expected demand for their goods. If firms expect that future sales will be bad, they may not hire workers or they may even eliminate jobs. If we extend this to the economy as a whole, whenever an economy contracts as part of the business cycle, workers tend to lose their jobs and have trouble finding new ones, a problem known as *cyclical unemployment*.

The Idea of Full Employment

The unemployment rate is a good approximation of the labor situation in a country, and it is an indicator that a country is either underproducing or overproducing goods and services. Suppose a country has a potential working population of 5,000, with 1,000 of those people not being in the labor force and 250 being unemployed. This means that the labor force is 4,000, there are 3,750 people employed, and the unemployment rate is 6.25 percent.

Suppose we knew that this economy was capable of producing $200 billion worth of goods and services, and that it takes exactly 3,750 workers to produce that amount of goods and services. In this case, this economy has just the "right" amount of unemployment. The term *full employment* refers to the situation in which an economy is fully utilizing its labor force to the extent that is supported by the other factors of production that it employs. There is therefore a *natural rate of unemployment*, that is, a level of unemployment that we would expect to see even when the economy is operating at its full potential. For the fictional nation just described, the natural rate of unemployment is 6.25 percent. If the unemployment rate were to rise above 6.25 percent, we might conclude that the state of the economy is weakening, total production is falling, and the economy may be slipping into a recessionary period. If the unemployment rate were to fall below 6.25 percent, we might conclude that the economy is actually producing more than its capacity, which could lead to a spike in prices and an inflationary period. We will discuss the causes and ramifications of recessionary and inflationary periods in Chapter 14.

Underemployment and Discouraged Workers

While the unemployment rate is a good approximation of the state of the labor situation in a country, it is not a perfect measure. In fact, in certain situations, it can even be somewhat misleading. For that reason, we sometimes need to get a bigger picture of the employment situation than merely the unemployment rate in order to draw conclusions about the labor market.

One example of this is the idea of *underemployment*. This term applies to the situation in which people take jobs for which they are overqualified and/or jobs with reduced hours when they cannot find appropriate jobs. Consider a person who has been looking for a job for a long time in the field she has trained in, such as a kindergarten teacher. However, she may find that a job in the field she trained in is not available, and she may need to take a lesser job, like one in a coffee shop, or one with fewer hours, like one as a teacher's aide, to get by until she finds the right job. In this case, even though this person is still looking for a better job and would be more productive as a kindergarten teacher, she would still be counted as employed. This means that the unemployment rate would understate the true employment situation.

Another concern is the *discouraged worker effect*. Consider an economy that is experiencing a severe recession; it currently has a labor force of 200, and 50 of those people are unemployed (yielding an unemployment rate of 25 percent). If these unemployed people have searched for at least a year and still cannot find jobs, they may give up looking for a job and exit the labor force. Suppose half of the unemployed people leave the labor force. Now, there are only 25 people who are unemployed, and there are 175 people in the labor force, yielding an unemployment rate of 14.9 percent. Note that the unemployment situation did not improve, but the unemployment rate did!

NOTE   *The BLS sometimes refers to workers who are "marginally attached to the workforce." These are workers who have technically left the workforce, but who would still like to work and have demonstrated some degree of attachment to the labor force. That means that they might not have looked for work during the previous week (the reference period for the BLS survey), but tend to* *go into and out of the labor force. Discouraged workers are part of this subset, but people who haven't looked for work because of family constraints, transportation problems, school commitments, ill health, or other reasons are also included in this category.*

For this reason, the BLS issues reports on not just the unemployment rate, but broader measures of unemployment that reflect discouraged workers and underemployment. In fact, there are six different measures of unemployment, U–1 to U–6, that the BLS reports (the official rate of unemployment that we calculated before is U–3). During recessions and other economic downturns, the difference between the reported unemployment rate and the true unemployment rate can be substantial. In July 2011, the broadest measure of unemployment (U–6), which includes the underemployed and discouraged workers, was 16.1 percent.

Theories of Unemployment

According to our analysis of markets in Chapter 6, unemployment really shouldn't happen. Recall that if markets operate effectively, the market will adjust until the quantity supplied equals the quantity demanded and markets clear at the equilibrium price. However, persistent unemployment means that the quantity of labor supplied exceeds the quantity demanded at the current market wage. That leads us to the unhappy conclusion that the labor market does not operate effectively.

As in other markets, we can usually trace this market failure to some problem in price adjustment, meaning that the wage rate does not adjust appropriately. There are many reasons that this may occur, but the following three are pretty easily recognizable and are generally accepted by economists as some of the reasons that wages don't adjust. First, the existence of minimum wage laws keeps wages from adjusting downward if they are binding (see Chapter 6). Second, when labor unions, or any group of employees, are able to negotiate wages above the equilibrium wage, this can generate unemployment.

A third and more interesting example is something known as *efficiency wage theory*. According to this theory, wages are higher than the market-clearing wage not because some outside force makes this happen, but because firms *voluntarily* pay higher than equilibrium wages. This seems strange—why would a firm pay more for a worker than it has to? Consider this: if there is no unemployment, then finding a job if you get fired is pretty easy. After all, if there is no surplus of workers, a person should have an easy time finding a new employer to give him a job. Given this, employees may have little incentive to work to full capacity, as the fear of unemployment is gone. However, if firms pay higher wages, this decreases the quantity of workers they are willing to hire and increases the quantity of workers who are willing to supply their labor at the higher wage, creating a pool of unemployed people. Now, if workers lose their jobs, they are losing a higher-paying job *and* get thrown into a pool of the unemployed.

Summary

Measures of the state of a nation's macroeconomic labor market are important indicators of the strength of the economy. Adults are classified as either employed, unemployed, or not in the labor force. The sum of the employed and the unemployed is known as the labor force. An important distinction between a person who is unemployed and a person who is out of the labor force is that a person must have actively sought a job to be counted as unemployed. The unemployment rate is simply the number of unemployed persons as a percentage of the entire labor force. If the economy is producing at its potential level of output, the labor markets are said to be at their natural rate of unemployment. Economists see unemployment as a situation in which labor markets are not clearing because the wage cannot adjust downward to the point where the supply of labor intersects the demand for labor. This may be due to minimum wage laws, workers who are under contract for a fixed wage, or the theory of efficiency wages.

Recall that one of the concerns we have is that unemployment might actually be too low. One of the reasons we are concerned about very low levels of unemployment is that in a tight job market, firms may raise wages in order to attract workers. This sounds great from a worker's point of view, but if firms have to pay more for workers, they will pass this along to the purchasers of goods and services, and prices will start to rise. This is one of the ways in which a general rise in the price level, a phenomenon known as *inflation*, might occur; we talk about this in the next chapter.

QUIZ

For each of the following, choose the answer that best fits.

1. **As a percentage of the total labor force, the unemployment rate measures:**
   A. The number of people in an economy who do not have jobs.
   B. The number of people in an economy who have jobs.
   C. The number of people who are out of work and actively looking for work.
   D. The number of people who are looking for work.

2. **According to the efficiency wage theory, which of the following leads to unemployment?**
   A. Firms are paying a wage that is higher than the market would otherwise generate.
   B. Firms are paying wages below the market equilibrium wage to cut costs and earn monopoly profits.
   C. Workers are willing to work for less than the minimum wage.
   D. All of the above.

3. **Which one of the following types of people is *not* counted as part of the labor force?**
   A. People who are too young to work.
   B. People who are in the military.
   C. People who are institutionalized.
   D. None of the above are counted as part of the labor force.

4. **Suppose there is a severe recession and unemployed people stop looking for work. All else equal, which of the following would occur?**
   I. **The labor force participation rate would decrease.**
   II. **The unemployment rate would decrease.**
   III. **The unemployment rate would increase.**
   A. I only
   B. II only
   C. III only
   D. I and II

5. **Which of the following types of unemployment may actually be both unavoidable and desirable?**
   A. Structural unemployment
   B. Frictional unemployment
   C. Seasonal unemployment
   D. Cyclical unemployment

Use the following scenario to answer questions 6 through 10.

The BLS conducted a survey of all the residents of Smallville. Of the 21 residents, 9 were age 15 and under. The following describes the rest of the residents:

Maggie, age 17, full-time student, not working, not looking for work.

Grace, age 35, works 10 hours per week but is looking for another part-time job.

Owen, age 40, works 45 hours per week.

Erin, age 29, works 40 hours per week.

Bridgette, age 25, works 35 hours per week.

Luke, age 65, works 20 hours per week.

Andrew, age 50, works 30 hours per week.

Jude, age 21, does not work but is looking for a job.

Alex, age 30, does not work but is looking for a job.

Max, age 16, full-time student, not working, not looking for a job.

Ella, age 26, works 40 hours per week as an officer in the U.S. Marine Corps office in Smallville.

Jack, age 52, does not work and gave up looking for work last month.

6. Complete Table 12-2.

Name of Person	Category (in the labor force and employed, in the labor force and unemployed, not in the labor force)	Explanation as to Why Each Is Counted This Way

TABLE 12-2 Residents of Smallville

7. What is the civilian, noninstitutionalized population? What is the labor force?

8. What is the labor force participation rate?

9. What is the unemployment rate?

10. How might this unemployment rate distort the true employment situation? (Hint: Use Jack in your explanation.)

chapter **13**

Inflation

When the price of one or two things goes up, we notice. Whether we are paying more for gasoline or for a pizza, when the price of something we want to buy goes up, it makes us feel poorer. But what happens when the price of *everything* goes up? Are we even worse off? The answer to this might be surprising.

CHAPTER OBJECTIVES

After completing this chapter, the student should be able to:

1. Explain the Consumer Price Index.
2. Define and calculate inflation.
3. Explain some of the problems that inflation may cause.
4. Explain the difference between deflation and disinflation.
5. Describe a theorized relationship between inflation and unemployment.

Introduction to Inflation

In Chapter 6, we talked about the equilibrium price of a single good or service in a single market. In macroeconomics, however, we are talking about all the goods and services that an economy produces. The corollary in macroeconomics is the *price level*, the average of all the prices of goods and services in an economy. *Inflation* is an increase in that price level, meaning that when inflation occurs, prices in general are going up.

Another way to think about inflation is not just that prices are going up, but that the value of money is going down. Consider an economy that has only one good—oranges. If the price of an orange is 20 cents, then the value of a dollar is 5 oranges (because that is what you can actually buy with a dollar). However, if the price of oranges goes up to 25 cents, the value of a dollar falls to 4 oranges.

We respond when the price of a single thing increases. Would it make sense that we would *really* respond if the prices of all things were increasing? Interestingly, the answer is, not necessarily. Recall from Chapter 11 that one of the prices that firms must pay is wages. If *all* prices are going up, firms are paying higher wages, which means that households are receiving higher incomes. In other words, if prices double, but so do incomes, nobody is any poorer or any wealthier in terms of his buying power.

NOTE *A good example of how little the price level matters is the conversion of the złoty, the official currency of Poland, in 1995. In the early 1990s, virtually every Polish citizen was a millionaire—average monthly salaries were in the millions of złoty per month. However, if you wanted to buy a soft drink at a local street vendor, it would cost you about 10,000 złoty. Why? Hyperinflation had steadily raised both the price level and wages over the previous decade.*

To combat the practical problems (such as fitting enough zeroes on a piece of paper money) that a high-denominated currency can cause, the government of Poland introduced a new złoty on January 1, 1995. The new currency could be exchanged at a rate of 10,000 old złoty for 1 new złoty. Note that suddenly being paid "only" 5,000 złoty per month instead of 50,000,000 złoty didn't impoverish you because the price level had been slashed by the same proportion.

What is important, however, is the rate at which the price level is changing. The rate of inflation is the percentage increase in prices from one period to another. To find the rate of inflation between two periods, we calculate:

$$\text{Rate of inflation} = \frac{\text{price level in new period} - \text{price level in old period}}{\text{price level in old period}}$$

The Consumer Price Index

So what exactly do we mean by a price level? A *price level* is some sort of measure that is meant to capture the overall prices in an economy at some point in time. There are actually several different measurements that are calculated that fit that description, but the one that most people are most familiar with and that is most widely used in the United States is the *Consumer Price Index (CPI)*. To understand the CPI, let's break down what the term means:

Consumer. The CPI is designed to include the goods and services that a typical consumer purchases.

Price. The CPI uses the prices that consumers actually pay for those goods and services.

Index. The prices paid for the goods and services are converted into a tool that simplifies them by showing them as movements of a numerical series. In other words, the CPI takes the prices and compares them to prices during some base period to make them easier to understand and compare.

In the United States, the Bureau of Labor Statistics (BLS) calculates the CPI. In order to calculate a CPI, you must complete five steps:

1. **Fix a basket of goods.** In order to see how prices are changing over time, we need to limit our focus to changes in the prices, not in the goods being purchased. For this reason, we need to figure out what should go into our basket of goods and always look at the prices that are paid to purchase exactly the same goods. The BLS creates a basket of goods based on surveys of thousands of households to determine what people actually buy and the quantities that they buy.

2. **Find the prices.** The next step is to determine the retail price of each of these goods and services. Each month, BLS employees call stores and firms to determine these prices. In some cases, BLS employees will walk through supermarkets and scan product bar codes to get the pricing information directly into the BLS database.

3. **Compute the cost of the basket in each period.** Once the prices of all those goods are determined, they are added together to determine the amount of money it would take to purchase the basket of goods.

4. **Choose a base year.** It doesn't matter which year you choose, but keep in mind that you are comparing all years' prices to this year. In fact, the CPI occasionally changes the base year it uses and then recalculates the CPI for all years based on a new base year.

5. **Compute the CPI.** To calculate the CPI for a particular year, say year X, the following formula is used:

$$CPI_x = \frac{\text{cost of the basket of goods in year X}}{\text{cost of the basket of goods in base year}} \times 100$$

The cost of purchasing the market basket in any given year is then compared to what it cost to purchase that basket in the base year. Currently, the BLS actually uses the average price over a three-year period, 1982–1984, to compute the cost of the basket in the base year.

Let's use an example to show how this is done. Suppose the nation of Cire conducted a survey and concluded that each month the typical household purchased 1 bar of soap, 4 loaves of bread, 2 gallons of milk, 2 dozen bagels, and a haircut. A survey of sellers found out that each of these goods sold for the prices in Table 13-1 during a four-year period.

We can then use this information to calculate the price of a basket in each year (see Table 13-2).

The next steps are to choose a base year and then calculate the CPI for each year. Let's use 2001 as our base year (see Table 13-3).

Finally, we can use the CPI to calculate the rate of inflation (see Table 13-4).

TABLE 13-1 Prices in Cire, 2000–2003

Year	Price of Soap (per bar)	Price of Bread (per loaf)	Price of Milk (per gallon)	Price of Bagels (per dozen)	Price of Haircut
2000	$1.00	$2.00	$3.00	$5.00	$20.00
2001	$1.00	$2.50	$4.00	$5.50	$21.00
2002	$1.25	$2.50	$4.25	$5.50	$22.00
2003	$1.50	$2.75	$4.50	$6.00	$23.00

TABLE 13-2 Cost of Basket of Goods in Cire

Year	Price of Soap (per bar)	Price of Bread (per loaf)	Price of Milk (per gallon)	Price of Bagels (per dozen)	Price of Haircut	Cost of the Basket
2000	$1.00 × 1	$2.00 × 4	$3.00 × 2	$5.00 × 2	$20.00 × 1	= $45.00
2001	$1.00 × 1	$2.50 × 4	$4.00 × 2	$5.50 × 2	$21.00 × 1	= $51.00
2002	$1.25 × 1	$2.50 × 4	$4.25 × 2	$5.50 × 2	$22.00 × 1	= $52.75
2003	$1.50 × 1	$2.50 × 4	$4.50 × 2	$6.00 × 2	$23.00 × 1	= $55.50

There are a couple of things that you should note immediately from these calculations. First, the CPI in the base year is always 100. Second, whenever you are comparing the CPI for future years (that is, when the CPI is over 100) to the base year, the rate of inflation since that base year is easy to calculate. For instance, the rate of inflation between 2001 and 2003 was 8.82 percent.

TABLE 13-3 CPI for Each Year in Cire, Using 2001 as Base Year

Year	Price of Soap (per bar)	Price of Bread (per loaf)	Price of Milk (per gallon)	Price of Bagels (per dozen)	Price of Haircut	Cost of the Basket	CPI
2000	$1.00 × 1	$2.00 × 4	$3.00 × 2	$5.00 × 2	$20.00 × 1	$45.00	$=\dfrac{\$45.00}{\$51.00}\times100 = 88.24$
2001	$1.00 × 1	$2.50 × 4	$4.00 × 2	$5.50 × 2	$21.00 × 1	$51.00	$=\dfrac{\$51.00}{\$51.00}\times100 = 100$
2002	$1.25 × 1	$2.50 × 4	$4.25 × 2	$5.50 × 2	$22.00 × 1	$52.75	$=\dfrac{\$52.75}{\$51.00}\times100 = 103.43$
2003	$1.50 × 1	$2.50 × 4	$4.50 × 2	$6.00 × 2	$23.00 × 1	$55.50	$=\dfrac{\$55.50}{\$51.00}\times100 = 108.82$

TABLE 13-4 Rate of Inflation in Cire

Year	Price of Soap (bar)	Price of Bread (loaf)	Price of Milk (gallon)	Price of Bagels (dozen)	Price of Haircut	Cost of the Basket	CPI	Rate of Inflation
2000	$1.00 × 1	$2.00 × 4	$3.00 × 2	$5.00 × 2	$20.00 × 1	$45.00	88.24	—
2001	$1.00 × 1	$2.50 × 4	$4.00 × 2	$5.50 × 2	$21.00 × 1	$51.00	100	$=\dfrac{100 - 88.24}{88.24} = 13.3\%$
2002	$1.25 × 1	$2.50 × 4	$4.25 × 2	$5.50 × 2	$22.00 × 1	$52.75	103.43	$=\dfrac{103.43 - 100}{100} = 3.4\%$
2003	$1.50 × 1	$2.50 × 4	$4.50 × 2	$6.00 × 2	$23.00 × 1	$55.50	108.82	$=\dfrac{108.82 - 103.43}{88.24} = 5.2\%$

Still Struggling

Let's look at what happens if we choose a different base year, such as 2000. If we recalculate Table 13-4, we get Table 13-5.

Note that the CPI for each year has changed, but the rate of inflation for each year is roughly the same.

TABLE 13-5 Rate of Inflation for Cire with a Different Base Year

Year	Price of Soap (bar)	Price of Bread (loaf)	Price of Milk (gallon)	Price of Bagels (dozen)	Price of Haircut	Cost of the Basket	CPI	Rate of Inflation
2000	$1.00 × 1	$2.00 × 4	$3.00 × 2	$5.00 × 2	$20.00 × 1	$45.00	100	—
2001	$1.00 × 1	$2.50 × 4	$4.00 × 2	$5.50 × 2	$21.00 × 1	$51.00	$= \dfrac{51}{45} \times 100 = 113.3$	$= \dfrac{113.3 - 100}{100} = 13.3\%$
2002	$1.25 × 1	$2.50 × 4	$4.25 × 2	$5.50 × 2	$22.00 × 1	$52.75	$= \dfrac{52.75}{117.2} \times 100 = 45$	$= \dfrac{117.2 - 113.3}{113.3} = 3.4\%$
2003	$1.50 × 1	$2.50 × 4	$4.50 × 2	$6.00 × 2	$23.00 × 1	$55.50	$= \dfrac{55.50}{123.3} \times 100 = 45$	$= \dfrac{123.3 - 117.2}{88.24} = 5.2\%$

CAUTION *We should point out that Tables 13-1 to 13-5 assume that the typical household continues to purchase the same quantity of each item even though the prices are rising. This, of course, may not be an accurate assumption in the real world. For example, if the typical household sees no increase in its wages, it may reduce its consumption of some or all of these items. When that happens, the composition of the market basket fundamentally changes. To account for changes in purchasing patterns, the BLS periodically updates the market basket itself so that estimates of the CPI are reasonably accurate.*

Real and Nominal Dollars

In Chapter 11, we discussed how GDP is really the product of prices and output. You take the quantity of output in a given year (Q) and multiply it by the price of the output (P) in that year. Suppose that next year prices rise, but Q stays the same. Clearly GDP will increase, but this is misleading because the true size of the economy hasn't increased; it has simply experienced inflation. The value of the output this year, using this year's prices, is called *nominal GDP*.

To adjust for changing prices (inflation) from year to year, we adjust nominal GDP by calculating the value of current production, but using prices from a fixed point in time—the base year. Once this adjustment is made, we have *real GDP*. For example, if we value 2010 production at 2009 prices, we have computed real GDP in 2010, and now we can compare it to production in 2009 (the base year) because we have held the prices constant. This is also known as "constant-dollar GDP." If real GDP is higher in 2010 than it was in 2009, then we can say that, even after adjusting for inflation, the value of the nation's output has risen.

Suppose an economy produces only three goods. Table 13-6 shows hypothetical prices and output levels for three recent years.

If we focus only on the nominal GDP column of the table, we can see that there was a large jump from 2009 to 2010 and a decrease from 2010 to 2011. But we can't determine whether these changes were due to changes in production or changes in price. In reality, both factors are changing. We eliminate the price differences by using the prices from 2009 as our base year prices and computing the column of real GDP. Table 13-7 converts these dollar figures into percentage changes.

The large jump in nominal GDP from 2009 to 2010 doesn't look so impressive when we adjust for the inflation that occurred. Likewise, the large decrease in nominal GDP from 2010 to 2011 isn't as large when we account for the fall in prices that occurred in 2011.

TABLE 13-6 Real GDP for an Economy

Year	Tons of Wheat	Price per Ton	Cars	Price per Car	Books	Price per Book	Nominal GDP	Real GDP Base Year = 2009
2009	100	$100	100	$200	50	$10	(100 × $100) + (100 × $200) + (50 × $10) = $30,500	= $30,500
2010	105	$110	125	$220	60	$12	(105 × $110) + (125 × $220) + (60 × $12) = $39,770	(105 × $100) + (125 × $200) + (60 × $10) = $36,100
2011	95	$115	120	$205	40	$ 9	(95 × $115) + (120 × $205) + (40 × $9) = $35,885	(95 × $100) + (120 × $200) + (40 × $10) = $33,900

TABLE 13-7 Percentage Changes for Table 13-6

Year	Nominal	% Change Nominal	Real	% Change Real
2009	$30,500		$30,500	
2010	$39,770	30%	$36,100	18%
2011	$35,885	−10%	$33,900	−6%

This is just one example of how to deflate nominal results to get the real values of GDP. There is also a tool called the *GDP deflator*, which is a number that modifies nominal GDP to get real GDP. The GDP deflator is sometimes used rather than the CPI to get real GDP in a given year because the CPI does not capture changes in the prices of all goods, only consumer goods. The technique, however, is the same.

TIP   *A price index can also be used to adjust nominal GDP (or any other dollar value) in some year to real GDP by using the following formula:*

$$\text{Real value} = \frac{\text{nominal value}}{\text{price index}} \times (100)$$

For example, suppose your salary was $40,000 in 2009, and it rose to $44,000 in 2010. This is a 10 percent increase in your nominal salary, and you were probably very pleased. To adjust for inflation, we need to know the Consumer Price Index in each of those years. After a little research, we find that the CPI was 214.54 in 2009 and 218.06 in 2010, and we can compute real salaries in both *years. The base year is the three-year period of 1982–1984, but this is irrelevant in comparing these two real salaries.*

$$\text{Real salary in } 2009 = \$18,644.54 = \frac{\$40,000}{214.54} \times (100)$$

$$\text{Real salary in } 2010 = \$20,177.93 = \frac{\$44,000}{218.06} \times (100)$$

After adjusting for inflation, your salary still increased, but by only 8.2 percent.

The Consequences of Inflation

In our example, we haven't really said anything normative about the prices going up from year to year. If the households of Cire are seeing similar increases in income from year to year, they aren't really any worse off. There are, however, some costs associated with inflation, which is why rapid inflation is generally viewed as being undesirable.

First, inflation is associated with *shoe-leather costs*. This funny-sounding term actually refers to the transaction costs of inflation. When prices go up, the value of the dollar goes down. Because of this, people will go out of their way to avoid holding money in their wallets, and will go out of their way to store value either in goods or in a bank account that is earning enough interest so that money keeps its real value. For example, during the hyperinflation that Germany experienced in the early 1920s, people would get paid daily and would immediately rush out to spend their money on goods before the money became worthless. The term *shoe-leather costs* is a reference to the wear and tear that people would put on their shoes in carrying out these transactions, when the running around that they were doing to avoid the loss of value of their money could have been put to productive use.

Second, inflation imposes *menu costs*. In a modern economy, there are many goods and services, each with a different price. When prices are changing, each of these prices has to be changed. Consider a restaurant menu—if prices are changing every day, someone must go and change the prices in the menu every single day, and the time spent doing that is not going toward a productive use.

Interestingly, there are winners and losers from inflation. When people borrow money, the borrower and the lender enter into a contract that specifies the amount borrowed, the time period in which it must be repaid, and the *interest rate* that will be charged to the borrower. The interest rate that is actually charged, called the *nominal interest rate*, is set so that it takes into account the expected rate of inflation over the time period of the loan and the lender also gets some sort of real payment for agreeing to lend the money (the *real interest rate*). For instance, if the expected rate of inflation is 5 percent and the nominal interest rate is 8 percent, the amount that the lender actually gets is 8 percent − 5 percent = 3 percent.

What happens if the rate of inflation turns out to be 6 percent? In this case, the lender loses out—it expected to make a 3 percent return, but it made only 2 percent in real terms. On the other hand, if the inflation rate turns out to be only 4 percent, then the borrower is worse off. If there is any uncertainty regarding inflation, people might be reluctant to enter such contracts. When there is a great deal of price volatility, or when inflation is very high (which leads to unpredictability), this can discourage investment or borrowing.

Deflation Versus Disinflation

If inflation is undesirable, then would *deflation* (a decrease in the price level or a negative inflation rate) be a good thing? The consensus is a resounding no, for several reasons. First of all, if people expect prices to fall, they may put off spending. For instance, if you know that you will have to pay only half as much for a car in six months, it makes sense to put off that purchase. However, as we will see in the next chapter, this reduction in spending puts a halt on the circular flow of goods and services.

Second, if prices are going down, the value of a dollar in the future is increasing. While that sounds good, it also means that the value of debts that are owed increases. Lenders gain from deflation because, when they are repaid by the borrowers, those dollars are worth more, not less. Of course, this means that the borrowers are hurt by this transfer of purchasing power and rising debt burden. If there is a widespread increase in the amount of debt that is owed, this may lead to increases in bankruptcies and to bank failures. (This is precisely what happened during the deflation that the United States experienced during the Great Depression.)

Finally, if prices are going down, wages will go down as well. Unfortunately, wages do not go down very easily, as people are usually reluctant to agree to work for less money. This means that sometimes the only way to lower wages is through mass unemployment. For these reasons, deflation is usually associated with severe recessions and depressions.

Disinflation, on the other hand, is something that might be desirable during periods of rapid inflation. Disinflation is a slowing of the rate of inflation—for instance, if the inflation rate had been 15 percent per year and it is brought down to 5 percent. In other words, disinflation is a lower rate of inflation. Disinflation can be a long and costly process, in terms of employment and output. This is especially true if expectations of high inflation have become ingrained in an economy.

Employment and Inflation

In 1958, an economist named William Phillips published a paper in the journal *Economica* that noted that when the unemployment rate in Great Britain was high, the inflation rate was low, and when the inflation rate was high, the unemployment rate was low. This inverse relationship between the inflation rate and the unemployment rate came to be known as the *Phillips curve*. The implication of this in terms of disinflation is clear: one of the costs of disinflation may be increasing the unemployment rate.

This trade-off between unemployment and inflation has an intuitive explanation. If the unemployment rate is very low, this will cause upward pressure on wages, leading to the cycle we described at the beginning of this chapter. Indeed, during the 1960s, economists came to believe that this was a real trade-off that policy makers had to consider. However, in the 1970s, this relationship appeared to fall apart as economies experienced *both* high inflation and high unemployment. What happened?

The culprit turns out to be expectations. Up until the 1960s, people had come to expect low inflation. By the late 1960s, inflation had begun to increase, and persistent inflation became the norm. Once employees and firms begin to expect inflation, they will incorporate these expectations into employment contracts. For instance, if firms and employees expect that there will be 3 percent inflation, they will agree to wages that are 3 percent higher. This means that the actual rate of inflation that is experienced at any given unemployment rate will be 3 percent higher.

This is illustrated in Figure 13-1. The *short-run Phillips curve* (SRPC) shows the relationship between unemployment and inflation for a particular country. When this country experiences 7 percent unemployment, it experiences 0 percent inflation. Suppose the government of this economy decides that it wants to lower the unemployment rate to 4 percent, which it achieves through a variety of policies. This will drive up the inflation rate to 3 percent.

Over time, employees and firms will come to expect this amount of inflation and begin incorporating this into their wages. By doing this, they will make the actual rate of inflation 3 percent higher, even at the same rate of unemployment. This effect is illustrated by the shift from the initial $SRPC_0$ to $SRPC_1$. Note that now people will come to expect 6 percent inflation, and will build these expectations into their wage negotiations. As a result of attempting to trade off lower unemployment for higher inflation, there will be continuously accelerating rates of inflation. If this economy wanted to create disinflation, it would have to simultaneously increase unemployment and lower expectations of inflation, which could be a difficult and painful process.

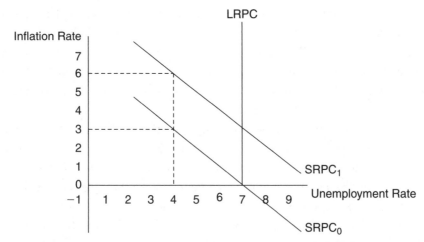

FIGURE 13-1 · Effects of Attempting to Lower Unemployment, as Shown by the Short-Run and Long-Run Phillips Curves

On the other hand, if no attempt had been made to lower the unemployment rate below 7 percent, there would be no expectation of inflation. In the long run, after expectations have time to adjust to the inflation that an economy actually experiences, we end up with a single rate of unemployment that would not be associated with ever-accelerating inflation. The *long-run Phillips curve* (LRPC) reflects the relationship between inflation and unemployment once expectations have adjusted. It is vertical at the *nonaccelerating inflation rate of unemployment* (NAIRU).

The implication of this is clear: if an attempt is made to maintain a level of unemployment below the NAIRU, the result will be ever-escalating levels of inflation. Recall from Chapter 12 the concept of the *natural rate of unemployment*. The NAIRU and the natural rate of unemployment are one and the same.

Summary

Inflation is an increase in the general level of prices in an economy. This chapter discussed the final statistical measure of the economy that we will consider, the Consumer Price Index, which captures the rate of inflation in an economy. The CPI is a measure that tracks the cost of purchasing a basket of goods that a typical urban household purchases. Unexpectedly high rates of inflation impose costs upon society and create winners and losers. There has been an observed inverse relationship between the level of inflation and the level of unemployment, and attempts to maintain a level of unemployment that is "too low" can result in ever-increasing amounts of inflation. That leads us to the question, what is the "right" amount of unemployment? Recall that unemployment and production are tied to each other. If more goods and services are produced, more workers are employed to produce those goods and services, and there is less unemployment. This implies that there may be some equilibrium level of output. We return to this idea of production in the next chapter, when we explore not the supply and demand for a single good, but the supply and demand for all goods and services in an economy. This model of aggregate supply and aggregate demand allows us to predict how the price level and unemployment can change in the macroeconomy.

QUIZ

Is each of the following statements *true* or *false*? Explain.

1. Deflation is a desirable alternative to inflation.

2. The Consumer Price Index measures the increases in prices of all goods and services produced in an economy.

3. To calculate the rate of inflation between any two years, you subtract the CPI in one year from the CPI in the previous year.

4. The rate of inflation from year to year will not change significantly if you change the base year, but the values of the CPI in each year will change.

5. When the rate of inflation is higher than expected, borrowers are better off and lenders are worse off.

Give a short answer for each of the following questions.

For questions 6 through 8, consider the following facts about the Nation of Maxistan. The typical consumer in Maxistan consumes a basket of goods consisting of 2 pounds of sliced ham, 1 case of bottled water, 6 magazines, and 4 hours of babysitting. A survey of prices for a four-year period is given in Table 13-8.

TABLE 13-8				
Year	Price of Ham (per pound)	Price of Bottled Water	Price of Magazines	Hourly Wage of Babysitters
1990	$2.00	$10.00	$1.00	$6.00
1991	$2.00	$11.00	$1.50	$6.00
1992	$2.50	$12.00	$1.75	$7.00
1993	$2.75	$13.00	$2.50	$8.00

6. Calculate the cost of the basket of goods for each year.

7. Using 1990 as the base year, calculate the CPI for each year.

8. Calculate the rate of inflation for each year.

For questions 9 and 10, consider the graph in Figure 13-2.

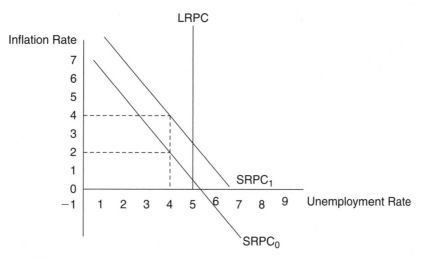

FIGURE 13-2

9. What level of unemployment is associated with the natural rate of unemployment for this economy?

10. The nation is currently experiencing 4 percent unemployment and expects 2 percent inflation. Given this expectation and the shift in the SRPC shown in Figure 13-2, what was the actual rate of unemployment and inflation that this economy experienced in the short run?

chapter 14

The Model of Aggregate Demand and Aggregate Supply

In Chapters 11, 12, and 13, we discussed the three most widely used measures of macroeconomic performance: GDP, unemployment, and the price level. However, these are just measures of the macroeconomy, the outcomes of how an economy works, rather than a model to tell us *how* it works. In this chapter, we turn our attention to the model of aggregate supply and aggregate demand, which helps us understand how the price level is determined and the fluctuations that we tend to see in unemployment and GDP.

CHAPTER OBJECTIVES

After completing this chapter, the student should be able to:

1. Describe the business cycle.

2. Describe aggregate demand and aggregate supply.

3. Use the aggregate demand and aggregate supply model to show how economic fluctuations occur.

4. Relate full-employment production to the natural rate of unemployment.

5. Describe and graph what is meant by economic growth.

Macroeconomic policy has three major goals: price stability, an appropriate amount of unemployment, and *economic growth*, which is the ability of an economy to produce more goods and services. As we have discussed in the previous three chapters, however, there is fluctuation in prices and employment as GDP fluctuates. In fact, even though output has increased over time, this increase doesn't happen consistently or continuously. There are periods of time when output is expanding and periods of time when output is falling, but the amount of output in an economy tends to increase gradually over time. We can visualize these fluctuations in Figure 14-1.

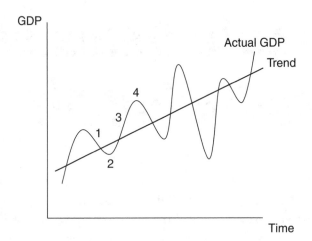

FIGURE 14-1 • The Business Cycle

Figure 14-1 illustrates *the business cycle*, which is the alternation between expansions (when GDP and employment are rising) and contractions (when GDP and employment are falling). The four stages of the business cycle are (1) contraction, (2) trough (or bottom), (3) expansion or recovery, and (4) peak. There is no strict rule, but for the most part, when output and employment have fallen for six months or more, this is called a *recession*. If a recession is severe and prolonged, it is called a *depression*. According to the National Bureau of Economic Research, which is the group that officially declares a recession, there have been 11 recessions in the United States since World War II, and the average length of the business cycle (from one peak to the next) is about five years and seven months. Despite these recessions, however, the economy is growing on average. The trend line in Figure 14-1 shows the average rate of growth over the same time period. In the United States, the economy has grown, on average, about 2.8 percent every year. This means that over the long run, the economy is able to produce 2.8 percent more goods and services every year, even if the growth is more than 2.8 percent in some years and less than 2.8 percent (or even negative) in other years.

Economic growth accumulates, so if GDP is $100 in year 1 and the growth rate is 5 percent, GDP is $105 in year 2 and will be 5 percent higher than $105 in year 3. This is a mathematical chain called an *exponential expansion*. Whenever you have an exponential expansion, there is a handy rule, called the *rule of 70,* that gives you the amount of time it takes for a number in that series to double:

$$\text{Doubling time} = \frac{70}{\text{rate of growth}}$$

So if the growth rate of GDP is 5 percent, 70/5 = 14 years. Given that the United States grows at an average rate of 2.8 percent, the U.S. economy can expect to double in about 25 years.

Real GDP and Nominal GDP

In Chapter 11, we calculated GDP using the expenditures approach, where

$$GDP = C + I + G + (X - M)$$

To do this, we added up the dollar value of all of the goods and services for each category. However, we noted in Chapter 13 that dollar values and prices change frequently. This means that if we fail to account for changes in prices, we may believe that we are producing more goods and services than we are, since prices going up would make our value of GDP go up as well.

We need to make an important distinction between *nominal GDP* and *real GDP*. Nominal GDP is the calculation of GDP using *current prices*. For example, if you are calculating GDP in 2010, you would use the prices that goods sold for in 2010. Real GDP, on the other hand, adjusts nominal GDP to account for price changes. This can be done in a few different ways. One common way is to calculate GDP using the same prices every year. Using this method, you would use the prices that exist in 2010 to calculate GDP in 2009, 2008, and any other year. If you would like to review this technique of deflating nominal values to real values, there are a few examples given in Chapter 13.

We might also make a final adjustment to GDP by finding *real GDP per capita*. According to the World Bank, the GDP of India in 2010 was about $1.7 trillion and the GDP of Canada was about $1.5 trillion. It would be incorrect to conclude based on this that India had a higher standard of living than Canada. India, with a population of more than 1.2 billion people, has to spread that output out over a lot more people than Canada, with a population of 34 million. To compute GDP per capita, we divide GDP by the population (*capita* means "head" in Latin). In fact, the GDP per capita in Canada in 2010 was $46,060, while Indian GDP per capita was only $1,477.

Understanding the Model of Aggregate Demand and Aggregate Supply

If our goal is to achieve economic growth while maintaining a healthy level of unemployment and price stability, it would be useful to have a model to help us understand how output and price level change. After all, we used the model of supply and demand in microeconomics to help us understand how a single market achieved an equilibrium price and quantity. The model that macroeconomists use to explain the short run fluctuations in output around the long-run trend is the *model of aggregate supply and demand (AD-AS model)*, and it is shown in Figure 14-2.

The AD-AS model should look familiar, as it closely resembles the supply and demand model. In the AD-AS model, however, we use *aggregate demand* (AD), *short-run aggregate supply* (SRAS), and an additional curve, *long-run aggregate supply* (LRAS). There are some other important distinctions to make as well:

1. A price level, rather than a single price, is on the vertical axis. In this model, we are talking about the price of all goods and services, so we need some measure that represents the price level (such as the CPI) to capture what the overall level of prices is.

2. The dollar value of output is on the horizontal axis. Recall that we cannot simply add together all of the output in an economy; we need to denominate

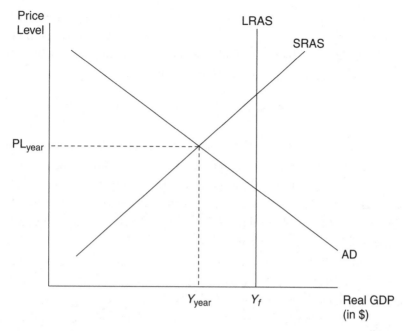

FIGURE 14-2 • The AD-AS Model

it using dollars. However, we want to capture the real value of the goods and services being produced, so we use real GDP to capture this.

3. The equilibrium in this economy is the price level (PL_{year}) that a country experiences in a given year and the actual level of output that a country produces each year (Y_{year}). For instance, if we were to use the CPI as our measure of the price level, for the United States in 2010, $PL_{2010} = 216.87$ and $Y_{2010} = \$13.2$ trillion.

4. Notice that the equilibrium in this economy is less than Y_f, which is the *full-employment level of output*. You can think of Y_f as an ideal amount of production of goods and services.

Another key difference between the AD-AS model and the supply and demand model is the curves used. As you can see, there are three curves in this model rather than two. We will discuss each of them more in depth.

Aggregate Demand (AD)

Our AD-AS model is an aggregation of all of the markets in an economy. This means that aggregate demand is the curve that represents all spending on goods and services and the relationship of that spending to the aggregate price level. Aggregate demand is thus the quantity of output that would be demanded at any possible price level by households, businesses, the government, and the rest of the world. The equation representing AD is

$$AD = C + I + G + (X - M)$$

An astute observer will note that this is the same as the equation we gave for GDP using the expenditures method. This is not surprising, as they both represent spending on all goods and services in an economy. The difference is that GDP represents a particular point on the AD curve (a particular level of GDP given the price level), and the AD curve itself represents the hypothetical GDP that would be purchased at varying price levels.

Like demand in microeconomics, AD is downward-sloping, as illustrated in Figure 14-3. However, demand in microeconomics is downward-sloping because of the law of demand. Recall that a movement along a demand curve is a change in the quantity demanded for a good *holding all other determinants of demand constant*; in the AD-AS model, we are instead considering an aggregate change in the prices of all goods and services. Our AD curve states that people will consume different amounts at different price levels. Why is this the case?

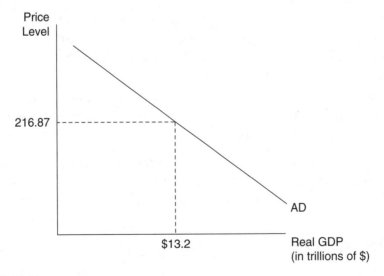

FIGURE 14-3 · The AD Curve

The AD curve is downward-sloping for three reasons:

- **The wealth effect** (aka the *Pigou wealth effect*). When there is an increase in the price level, the purchasing power of money goes down. For instance, if you had $1,000 in a non-interest-bearing account, your effective wealth would decrease when there was an increase in the price level. People are less able to purchase goods and services when the price level increases, and more able to purchase goods and services when the price level decreases, because their wealth changes.

- **The interest-rate effect.** When the price level goes up, people need to hold on to more money, as opposed to keeping it in the form of assets like a bank account, in order to purchase goods and services. Suppose you normally buy $100 in goods and services in a week, but the price level goes up 20 percent. You now need to keep 20 extra dollars on hand to purchase the same goods. However, when you keep that in your wallet instead of in the bank, the bank can no longer lend that money out; this reduces the funds available to borrowers and drives up the interest rate. When the interest rate increases, this lowers the amount of investment, the *I* part of AD. Therefore, as the price level increases, the amount of AD decreases.

- **Exchange-rate effect.** When the price level in one country increases, people naturally look to other countries to purchase goods and services elsewhere. This increases imports, which lowers aggregate demand. Remember that goods imported from other nations are subtracted from the home nation's GDP.

These three effects explain why the AD curve is downward-sloping, or what causes movements *along* the AD curve. What if more aggregate output is demanded when the price level hasn't increased? This implies that the AD curve must have shifted. When AD increases, the AD curve shifts outward (or to the right). When AD decreases, the AD curve shifts inward (or to the left). Shifts in aggregate demand are shown in Figure 14-4.

Several factors can cause a shift in AD, but the following are the most common:

- **Changes in expectations.** When firms decide to invest, either by expanding their inventory or increasing their productive capacity, they do so because they expect to sell more goods and services in the future. Likewise, consumers plan purchases based on their expectations of income,

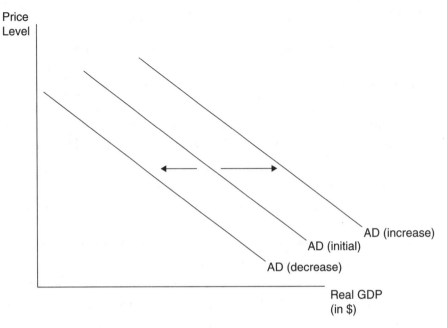

FIGURE 14-4 · Shifts in the AD Curve

expectations about needing to save, and a variety of other considerations. If consumers and firms are more optimistic, AD will increase. If consumers and firms are more pessimistic, AD will decrease.

- **Changes in wealth.** In 2008, a housing "bubble" burst. That is, the prices and values of houses suddenly and dramatically decreased. For many families, their homes are their largest asset, so a dramatic decrease in the value of a family home is a decrease in that family's wealth. Moreover, a fall in the value of a home curtails the ability to borrow against that asset for consumer spending, such as through a home equity loan. This collapse in housing prices was partly responsible for the decrease in consumer spending in 2008, and thus decreased AD.

- **Government policies.** The government can influence AD through two types of policy: *fiscal policy* and *monetary policy*. Fiscal policy is the use of government spending, which directly changes the G component of AD, or the use of taxes to influence the C or I component. If the government increases spending or reduces taxes, then AD increases. Monetary policy is the use of the money supply to influence interest rates, which in turn influences the C and I components of AD. When the government, through its central bank, increases the money supply, interest rates fall, and this increases aggregate demand. (We discuss these in more depth in Chapter 16.)

TIP *The key to remembering what shifts AD is to remember that the components of AD are same as the components of GDP. If something affects C, I, G, X, or M through something besides the price level, it will change AD.*

Aggregate Supply (SRAS and LRAS)

The counterpart to AD in the AD-AS model is aggregate supply (AS). This is a little misleading, however. We actually distinguish between two different AS curves, short-run aggregate supply (SRAS) and long-run aggregate supply (LRAS). In this model, the short run applies to the period of time in which production costs can be taken as fixed. The SRAS curve is therefore a graphical representation of the relationship between the aggregate amount of output that is supplied and the price level. The LRAS curve has a different intuition entirely from a microeconomic supply curve—it represents the potential output of an economy if all prices have adjusted. It is vertical because along the LRAS, all prices have adjusted, and therefore there is no longer a relationship between the price level and output. Moreover, it is vertical at a specific level of output—the output at which all inputs to production are used the most effectively and appropriately.

The SRAS curve is upward-sloping, which means that higher levels of GDP supplied are associated with higher price levels, at least in the short run. It isn't necessarily true, and doesn't necessarily make sense intuitively, that firms would produce more in response to higher price levels, but we do see more production at higher price levels. There are three main theories that may explain why this occurs:

- **Misperceptions theory.** According to misperceptions theory, price changes temporarily confuse or mislead firms about relative prices. For instance, a firm might mistakenly believe that the demand for its good has increased when it can sell the same quantity of goods at higher prices.
- **Sticky price theory.** The prices of some goods do not respond very quickly. Thus, if the price level decreases, firms may not adjust their prices and end up selling more goods.
- **Sticky wage theory.** Labor contracts tend to be fixed for periods of time (for instance, annual salary revisions). If there is inflation, labor is relatively cheaper in real terms and firms can produce more at lower real cost.

In the short run, output may be different at different price levels. In the long run, on the other hand, prices have had a chance to fully adjust and the level of production is independent of the price level. It will depend instead on what the economy actually uses to produce goods and services (that is, a country's stock of the inputs of production) and the technology that an economy uses to combine these inputs to create goods and services. The LRAS curve is a straight line that is vertical at the full-employment level of output. Recall that the full-employment level of output is an ideal level of output—the level of output that is produced when employment is at the natural rate of unemployment (the NAIRU).

Like AD, our SRAS and LRAS curves may shift when conditions change. LRAS depends on the stock of the inputs to production (land, labor, capital, and technology), and when the stock of one or more of these inputs increases, LRAS increases (or shifts to the right). For instance, if a country finds a new source of energy (counted in "land"), the LRAS curve would shift to the right, as shown in Figure 14-5. LRAS can also decrease if the stock of one of the factors of production goes down. This is particularly relevant to capital. Capital depreciates, which means that an economy must engage in at least some investment in order to maintain its stock of capital. If investment falls too low, the stock of capital decreases, and the economy's potential for production also decreases.

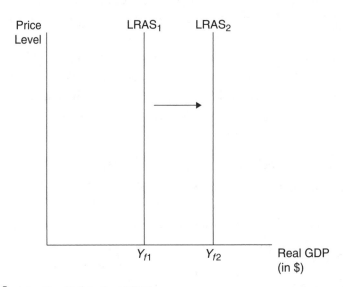

FIGURE 14-5 • A Positive Shift in the LRAS Curve

On the other hand, shifts in SRAS occur when the *prices* of one or more of these inputs to production change. For instance, Figure 14-6 shows the effect on SRAS if the price of labor increases. Here, the cost of production will increase for the entire economy, and the SRAS supply curve decreases (shifts to the left). Since the amount or stock of labor that exists in the economy hasn't changed, the LRAS remains unchanged.

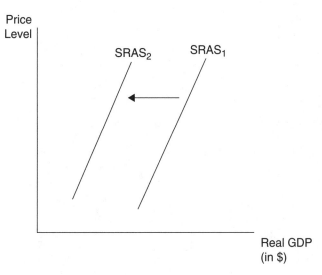

FIGURE 14-6 • A Negative Shift in the SRAS Curve

Equilibrium in the Macroeconomy

The AD-AS model uses aggregate supply and aggregate demand to analyze economic fluctuations. As in the supply and demand model we have seen, equilibrium in the macroeconomy occurs when the quantity of aggregate output supplied is equal to the quantity of aggregate output demanded. However, in the macroeconomy, we have two outcomes that we are concerned about: *short-run macroeconomic equilibrium* and *long-run macroeconomic equilibrium*.

In the short run, there is a short-run aggregate price level and a short-run aggregate output associated with the short-run macroeconomic equilibrium. As shown in Figure 14-2, this occurs at the intersection of AD and SRAS. The intuition here is similar to the supply and demand model in that if the amount of aggregate output demanded differs from the amount of aggregate output supplied, the price level will adjust to restore macroeconomic equilibrium.

If there is a shock to the macroeconomy, the short-run equilibrium will change, leading to fluctuations in the price level and output. Consider a negative aggregate demand shock that occurs because consumers become pessimistic about the future. Such a shock would shift the AD curve to the left, as shown in Figure 14-7. As a result, aggregate output in the economy would decline as well as the price level. Note that this also has implications for employment: if there is less GDP being produced, there is less need for workers, and the unemployment rate will increase.

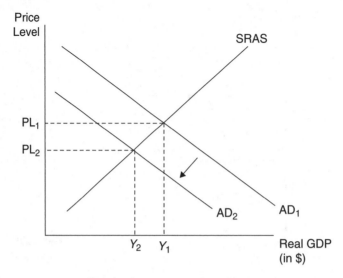

FIGURE 14-7 • A Negative Demand Shock

Similarly, there can be positive economic shocks. For instance, if people become relatively wealthier, aggregate demand will increase, as shown in Figure 14-8. As a result, output and price levels increase. This also has an effect on unemployment, as more production requires more workers. This is an important fact about our measures of macroeconomic performance: output and employment tend to move in the same direction (conversely, output and unemployment move in opposite directions).

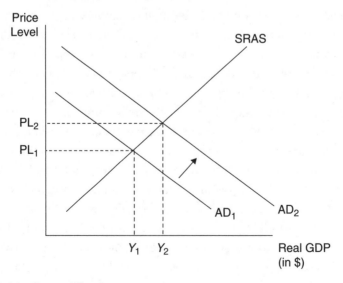

FIGURE 14-8 • A Positive Demand Shock

Macroeconomic fluctuations can also be the result of fluctuations in SRAS. Consider what happens to our model if the price of energy increases—SRAS decreases (shifts to the left), which results in a higher price level and a lower output, as shown in Figure 14-9. This combination of stagnation of output and inflation even has a special term, *stagflation*. This is a particularly bad situation—falling output means rising unemployment and falling incomes even while people have to pay higher prices (we will see in Chapter 16 that this is particularly problematic for policy makers who are attempting to solve these dual problems).

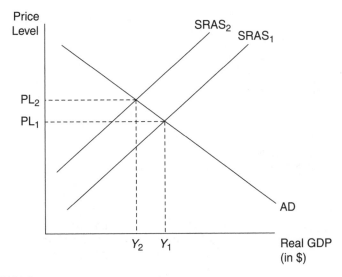

FIGURE 14-9 • A Negative Supply Shock

Long-run macroeconomic equilibrium is shown in Figure 14-10. This occurs when the actual amount of production is at the ideal level. Here, prices have fully adjusted, the economy is operating at its full potential, and unemployment is at the natural rate.

To understand why events like recessions or expansions occur, let's consider what happens when an economy that is in long-run equilibrium experiences a shock, as in Figure 14-11. The economy is initially in long-run equilibrium with a price level of PL_1 and an output of Y_1. Suppose consumer confidence in the economy falls, as in our previous example. As a result, AD shifts to the left, and the economy is now in short-run equilibrium at Y_2 and PL_2. Output has decreased, which leads to higher unemployment. The difference between the current output (Y_2) and the full-employment output

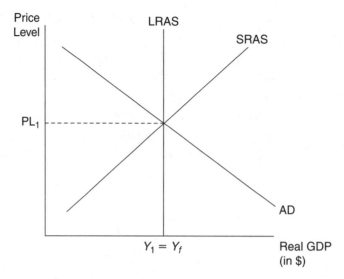

FIGURE 14-10 · Long-Run Macroeconomic Equilibrium

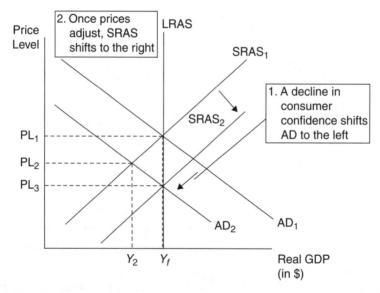

FIGURE 14-11 · Effects of a Negative Demand Shock

(Y_f) is called a *recessionary gap*; it can be caused by either a negative supply shock or a negative demand shock.

Over time, one of two things will happen. One possibility is that something restores AD to its initial position, either a change in consumer confidence or some sort of policy (as we will discuss in Chapter 16). Another possibility is that, since the unemployment rate has increased, people become willing to work for lower wages in order to get jobs. This would shift the SRAS curve to the right, returning output to the full-employment level, but at a lower price level. It should be noted that this self-correction back to full employment might take quite some time. Because lengthy recessions are quite painful for households and businesses, the government will rarely sit idly by and wait for the SRAS curve to return the economy to full employment.

Conversely, an *inflationary gap* occurs when the current output exceeds the full-employment output. An inflationary gap is caused by either a positive supply shock or a positive demand shock. Consider an economy that is currently in long-run macroeconomic equilibrium, but an increase in consumer confidence increases AD. This would cause a rightward shift in the AD curve, as shown in Figure 14-12. As a result, unemployment drops below the NAIRU, placing upward pressure on wages, which increases production costs and shifts SRAS to the left, returning the economy to long-run equilibrium.

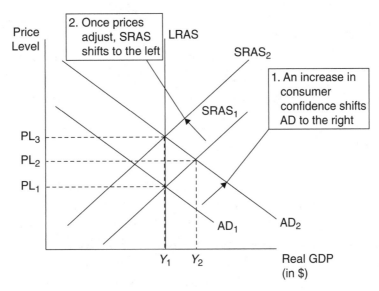

FIGURE 14-12 • Effects of a Positive Demand Shock at Long-Run Equilibrium

Still Struggling

Table 14-1 will help you keep track of how changes in the factors affecting SRAS and AD will lead to macroeconomic fluctuations. Note that all of these are short-run changes—in the long run, output will return to the full-employment level of output and the natural rate of unemployment, although there may be a different price level.

TABLE 14-1 Effects of Changes in Factors Affecting SRAS and AD				
Change	Effect	Resulting Change to Price Level	Resulting Change to Output	Resulting Change to Unemployment
Prices of inputs fall	SRAS shifts right	Price level decreases	Output increases	Unemployment decreases
Prices of inputs rise	SRAS shifts left	Price level increases	Output decreases	Unemployment increases
Expectations are optimistic	AD shifts right	Price level increases	Output increases	Unemployment decreases
Expectations are pessimistic	AD shifts left	Price level decreases	Output decreases	Unemployment increases
Wealth increases	AD shifts right	Price level increases	Output increases	Unemployment decreases
Wealth decreases	AD shifts left	Price level decreases	Output decreases	Unemployment increases

Economic Growth

The fluctuations that cause recessions and expansions are explained by shifts in AD and/or SRAS. But in Figure 14-1 we show that even with fluctuations, there is an increase in GDP over time. This *economic growth* reflects an increase in the ability of an economy to produce goods and services, not merely a temporary spike in production. The only way an economy can grow, therefore, is to increase its capacity. This is reflected in our AD-AS model as a shift to the right of the LRAS curve as a result of an increase in the stock of inputs or an improvement in technology. This can occur in the following ways:

- **An increase in labor.** An increase in either the quantity of labor or the quality of labor (sometimes called *human capital*) expands the potential labor force of an economy.

- **An increase in natural resources.** This would result from things such as the discovery of new energy sources or more efficiency in using energy resources.

- **An increase in the capital stock.** This occurs through investment.
- **An improvement in technology.** This occurs if better ways of combining resources are developed to produce more goods and services using the same technology.

One special branch of macroeconomics called growth theory is interested in determining which of these changes have led to economic growth and how to create more economic growth. Recall that real GDP per capita is a better indicator of the well-being of a country than merely real GDP. This means that if a population is growing, an economy must continue to expand if it is to maintain or improve its well-being. The relative importance of each of these factors in economic growth has changed over time. During the Industrial Revolution, much of the economic growth that occurred was due to increases in the stock of capital. More recently, improvements in human capital and technology seem to be better explanations for economic growth.

Summary

In this chapter, we introduced the AD-AS model to explain the fact that economies experience contractions and expansions of output. Shifts in SRAS and AD explain the temporary fluctuations around a long-run trend of economic growth, which is explained by shifts in LRAS. One of the factors that shift aggregate demand is government policies in the form of monetary policy and fiscal policy. In order to understand monetary policy, however, we need to explore money in a little more depth. This is the focus of the next chapter.

QUIZ

Is each of the following statements *true* or *false*? Explain.

1. **A decrease in LRAS is not possible.**

2. **All else equal, if consumer confidence increases, inflation will occur.**

3. **Long-run equilibrium is associated with an unemployment rate of zero.**

4. **It is not possible to produce beyond the full potential employment.**

5. **A recession is any decrease in a nation's output.**

For each of the following, choose the answer that best fits.

6. **The point in the business cycle when an economy is at "rock bottom" is called the:**
    A. Peak
    B. Expansion
    C. Contraction
    D. Trough

7. **Which of the following leads to an initial increase in the aggregate demand of an economy?**
    A. An increase in the price of energy
    B. A decrease in consumer wealth
    C. An increase in investment
    D. An increase in the wage rate

8. **Which of the following is a possible explanation for why SRAS is upward-sloping?**
    A. Sticky wages
    B. The wealth effect
    C. The exchange-rate effect
    D. The interest-rate effect

9. **Which of the following would lead to economic growth?**
    A. A decrease in the wage rate
    B. An improvement in education
    C. An increase in consumer confidence
    D. An decrease in investment

10. **An inflationary gap would be caused by which of the following changes?**
    A. An increase in the price of energy
    B. An increase in the wage rate
    C. An increase in the price of capital
    D. An increase in consumer wealth

chapter 15

Money and the Money Market

Money surrounds us, we use it daily, and it affects our lives in both seen and unseen ways. However, it is certainly the least understood aspect of the economy. In this chapter, we discuss money—what it is, why we want it, and how it influences the macroeconomy. We introduce the money market, which affects the interest rate and in turn the investment that we discussed in previous chapters. We conclude by talking about the role of a central bank in an economy.

CHAPTER OBJECTIVES

After completing this chapter, the student should be able to:

1. Describe the functions and types of money.

2. Calculate the money multiplier and describe how banks create money.

3. Describe and model the money market, including how interest rates are determined and how the money supply is increased and decreased.

4. Relate the money supply to inflation.

5. Describe the role of the central bank and the structure of the central bank in the United States.

The Functions and Types of Money

When most people refer to money, such as how much money they have in their wallet or their bank account, they are really talking about *wealth*, the ability to convert some store of value into consumption. To an economist, however, *money* is defined by what it does. Money is any kind of asset that fulfills the *functions of money*. The three functions of money are:

- **A unit of account.** To be considered money, an asset must be able to serve as a standard unit of measurement of the value or prices of goods. That is, we must be able to say that a television is worth a certain amount of dollars, or a certain amount of pieces of metal.

- **A store of value.** To be considered money, an asset must be able to reasonably maintain that unit of value. Ice, for example, would do very poorly at this function, as it would be extremely difficult for it to remain ice. Metal or paper or even salt, however, could easily maintain its value.

- **A unit of exchange.** To be considered money, an asset must be accepted in exchange for goods or services. Note that this is the basis of why we want it to store value.

Anything that can perform all three of these functions can serve as money, and many different things have served as money since humans began using money several thousand years ago. In fact, everything from giant rocks, to seashells, to salt has been used as money (in fact, the word *salary* is derived from the Latin word for salt, which was used to pay Roman soldiers).

The items that are used for money fall into two categories, *commodity money* and *fiat money*. Commodity money, such as gold or salt, is something used as a medium of exchange that has use value of its own. Fiat money, on the other hand, is money with no intrinsic or commodity value (or whose intrinsic value is minuscule compared to its face value). The paper and coin money that are in circulation today are fiat money.

A great example of what money is and how it works is illustrated in a 1945 article by R. A. Radford in the journal *Economica*. Radford was an economist who was captured during World War II and spent time in a German prisoner-of-war camp. There was an official currency circulating in the camp, the Reichsmark, but it was not used for trade between prisoners; it could be used only to purchase items from the canteen (which frequently meant that it had no exchange value at all, as relatively little was available at the canteen).

However, each of the prisoners in this camp had a regular allotment of goods in the form of his rations and Red Cross packets that contained items like milk, chocolate, and cigarettes, and occasionally some prisoners received private packages of things like clothing and toiletries. At first, trade was carried out through barter, but this was very inefficient (if you wanted to trade chocolate for bread, you had to find someone who was willing to trade bread for chocolate). Nonsmokers would trade their cigarettes for something that was of value to them. Soon, however, the cigarettes arose as a single unit of account. Someone might walk through the camp offering to sell "cheese for seven [cigarettes]." People were willing to accept cigarettes in trade because they knew that they could, in turn, use cigarettes to acquire goods that they wanted.

An interesting aspect of this cigarette money system is that it soon experienced a problem that all commodity money faces: *Gresham's law.* The gist of Gresham's law is that bad money will chase out good. The cigarettes worked well as money because they were an easily recognizable unit of exchange, not because they had intrinsic value. In fact, people would frequently pinch tobacco out of the cigarettes and hand-roll cigarettes to smoke. This took the part of the money with commodity value (the tobacco) out of the money and left the shells of cigarettes (the bad money) to be traded.

NOTE *The earliest money was commodity money, but virtually all money today is fiat money. You might wonder how something like fiat money ever came into existence. Consider the situation several hundred (or even several thousand) years ago, when banks were nonexistent and law enforcement was unreliable. If you had wealth, such as gold, that you wanted to keep, you needed to find a place to put it. Goldsmiths and blacksmiths were among the few places where you could store gold, as they had safes. The smith would give you a receipt for your gold that would enable you to retrieve it. If you wanted to make a purchase of something like a horse, you would go to the smith, give him your receipt, and take your gold to the person selling the horse; he, in turn, would deposit the same gold and get a receipt. Eventually it was realized that if you just exchanged the receipt, the entire process was less cumbersome because there were fewer transaction costs.*

The Money Supply

Many things can be money, but above all else, what makes something money is the belief that it can serve the functions of money. If we suddenly were in doubt that the paycheck we received from an employer could be converted into goods and services, we would be unwilling to exchange our labor for it. In a sense, money is money only as long as we believe it is money.

This raises a question: where does money come from? Before we describe how money is created, let's be specific about what we count as money in the United States. In the United States, the stock of money on hand, or the *money supply*, is tracked by the Federal Reserve, the central bank of the United States. The Federal Reserve breaks the money supply into two categories according to its *liquidity*, meaning the relative ease with which an asset can be converted into cash. The second category is less liquid than the first:

- M1 = cash (currency) outside of banks + coins + checking deposits + traveler's checks.

  M1 is the most liquid category. Cash can easily be converted into itself; checking accounts have relatively few restrictions on taking money out; traveler's checks are widely accepted, and when you make a purchase with a traveler's check, you receive change in cash.

- M2 = M1 + savings accounts + small time deposits (that is, certificates of deposit that are under $100,000) + money market deposits + money market mutual funds.

The instruments in the category M2 are slightly less liquid than those in M1. Many of these types of accounts have more restrictions on them, such as savings accounts that have a 10-day hold before you can withdraw money deposited. M2 is sometimes referred to as *near money*, because although it is not directly convertible as a medium of exchange, it can be converted into money fairly easily. According to the Federal Reserve Economic Data (FRED), in mid-August 2011, M1 was $2,085.8 billion (or about $2.085 trillion) and M2 was $9,521.8 billion.

Fractional Reserves

If you were under the impression that the institution that creates money in the United States is the Treasury Department, the agency that prints currency, then you would be wrong. Only about half of the money supply is made up of currency. Banks create money when they issue loans. The basis of how banks create money is a banking practice known as *fractional reserves*. A bank does not keep all of the money that is deposited on hand; instead, it keeps a fraction of what is deposited. This fraction of reserves, called a *reserve ratio*, is used to meet the day-to-day cash needs of depositors. The remainder is used to make loans.

To understand how fractional reserve banking works, and how it leads to the creation of money, let's walk through an example using a *T account*. A T account is a way of keeping track of a bank's *liabilities*, that is, its obligations to pay out money, and its *assets*, that is, the things it holds that are of value. For a bank, any deposit that an individual makes is a liability, because that person may withdraw it at any time. On the other hand, a loan is something that has value, as it is income that the bank will be taking in (in fact, loans are sometimes even sold to another financial institution). A T account has two sides, with assets on one side and liabilities on the other side (it is called a T account because that is what it looks like).

Let's start with an economy with $1,000 in currency and no banks. Then City National Bank opens. Suppose that an initial deposit of $1,000 is made, and the bank is required to keep at least 20 percent of deposits on hand (known as a *reserve requirement*). We note how this affects the bank's T account, and the money supply, in Table 15-1. The $1,000 deposit is a liability for the bank, but the $1,000 that the bank now has in its vault is an asset.

TABLE 15-1			
	Assets	**Liabilities**	**Money Supply = M1**
Initial deposit	$1,000 (currency)	$1,000 (deposit 1)	(currency held outside of banks + checking deposits)
			$ 0 currency not in bank
			+$1,000 deposits
			$1,000 = M1

The bank is required to keep only 20 percent of that deposit on hand, so it really needs to have only $200 in its vault. In essence, it has an extra $800 on hand that it can lend and earn interest on. When the bank lends money, it appears in the T-account as shown in Table 15-2.

TABLE 15-2			
	Assets	**Liabilities**	**Money Supply = M1**
Initial deposit	$ 200 (currency)	$1,000 (deposit 1)	(currency held outside of banks + checking deposits)
	$ 800 (loan 1)		$ 800 currency not in bank
			+$1,000 deposits
			$1,800 = M1

There are two things to note about this action. First, it is important that the bank remain *solvent*, that is, its liabilities must not exceed its assets. Second, the action of making the loan increased the money supply. When we say that banks create money, this is exactly what we are talking about. Interestingly, this process doesn't end here. Suppose the borrower uses that $800 loan to purchase equipment from Bob's Tractor Supply. Bob then deposits that money in the only bank in town, as shown in Table 15-3.

TABLE 15-3		
Assets	**Liabilities**	**Money Supply = M1**
$ 200 (currency)	$1,000 (deposit 1)	(currency held outside of banks + checking deposits)
$ 800 (loan 1)		$ 0 currency not in bank
$ 800 (currency)	$800 Bob's account (deposit 2)	+$1,800 deposits $1,800 = M1

Once again, the bank is holding more cash than it is required to. It must keep 20 percent of the initial deposit and 20 percent of Bob's deposit (or $160), so it needs only $360 in its vault. This means that it has an extra $640 that it can lend. If it does this, its T-account changes, as shown in Table 15-4.

TABLE 15-4		
Assets	**Liabilities**	**Money Supply = M1**
$ 200 (currency)	$1,000 (deposit 1)	(currency held outside of banks + checking deposits)
$ 800 (loan 1)		$ 640 currency not in bank
$ 160 (currency)	$800 Bob's account (deposit 2)	+$1,800 deposits
$ 640 (loan 2)		$2,440 = M1

Again, note that this loan expanded the money supply. This process can be repeated over and over again, leading to multiple expansions of deposits. We could continue forward, redepositing $640 and keeping $128 on hand, then lending $512, and so on to figure out what the money supply will be. However, it turns out that there is a mathematical shortcut. We can find the *money multiplier* to figure out what the amount of the money supply will be if we assume that banks keep only the required reserves on hand (that is, they do not keep excess reserves), and that all loans are redeposited (that is, someone doesn't take out a loan and do something like stick the money under her mattress). The money multiplier (MM) is:

$$MM = \frac{1}{\text{reserve requirment}}$$

In our case, the base money is the initial amount of currency in the economy, $1,000. With a reserve requirement of 20 percent, this becomes

$$MM = \frac{1}{0.2} = 5$$

To find out what the final impact of the multiple expansion of deposits will be, we multiply the money multiplier by our initial stock of money. In this case, $5 \times \$1,000 = \$5,000$, so we will end up with a money supply of $5,000.

Still Struggling

Whenever you are dealing with a mathematical calculation, it's useful to work through more than one example. In the case of the multiple expansion of the money supply, this is even more critical to help you "wrap your head around" something that seems pretty far-fetched. To help you convince yourself that this is actually how the money supply is determined, do the following as you are walking through the steps: (1) keep track of what the money supply is at each step, and (2) remind yourself that money in the vault (reserves) doesn't count as part of the money supply because it can't be used to purchase goods and services. Money in circulation does count, as does what is in a bank account, because those monies *can* be used to buy goods and services.

Take another example of an economy that starts with an injection of $5,000 into its economy, has a reserve requirement of 10 percent, and requires that banks fully lend (that is, they do not keep excess reserves) and that all loans are redeposited. The first five iterations of the multiple expansion are in Table 15-5. Try doing them on your own to test yourself.

TABLE 15-5

	Assets	Liabilities	Money Supply = M1
Acct. 1 reserve	$500	$5,000 (account 1)	(currency held outside of banks + checking deposits)
	$4,500 (loan 1)		M1 (after first loan) = $9,500
Acct. 2 reserve	$450	$4,500 (account 2)	
	$4,050 (loan 2)		
Acct. 3 reserve	$405	$4,050 (account 3)	
	$3,195 (loan 3)		
Acct. 4 reserve	$319.50	$3,195 (account 4)	
	$2,875.50 (loan 4)		
Acct. 5 reserve	$287.55	$2,875.50 (account 5)	
	$2,587.95 (loan 5)		M1 (after fifth loan) = $19,620.50
	(which would become acct. 6)		

The Role of a Central Bank

So how is the money supply in an economy actually determined? This process indicates that there are two pieces of the economy that determine what the money supply will be. The first and most important piece is the Federal Reserve System, which determines the amount of base money in the economy and sets reserve requirements for banks. The second piece is the banks themselves, which decide whether or not to keep reserves above the required amount and whether or not to make loans. The *Federal Reserve System* is the *central bank* in the United States. A central bank is an institution that oversees and regulates the banking system in an economy and controls the *monetary base*.

The Federal Reserve (or the Fed for short) was created by an act of Congress in 1913, largely in response to many banking panics that had occurred in the late 1800s and early 1900s. It consists of two parts, the Board of Governors and

12 regional Federal Reserve Banks. The Board of Governors oversees the entire system from its location in Washington, DC, and has seven members, including a chair. The governors are appointed by the president with the approval of the Senate for 14-year terms, except for the chair, who is appointed for a four-year term. The 12 Federal Reserve Banks each serve a region of the country called a Federal Reserve District. For instance, the Federal Reserve Bank of Dallas serves all of Texas, southern New Mexico, and northern Louisiana. Each of the 12 banks is operated by a board of directors that is made up of local banking and business leaders. The president of each bank is appointed by its board and approved by the Board of Governors.

The Fed has an unusual place in the economy, as it is neither a government agency nor a truly private institution. The Fed is independent of the government in the sense that its decisions do not have to be approved by any of the three branches of government (judicial, legislative, or executive). Another interesting aspect of the Fed is that its operations expenses are paid for out of the fees charged for the services that the Fed performs, and any profits are turned over to the Treasury.

The Federal Reserve System has two main objectives. First of all, it is charged with maintaining the operation of a healthy banking system. It does this by serving as a clearinghouse for checks, auditing banks within each district, setting the reserve requirement for banks, and serving as a lender of last resort for banks. For instance, if a bank finds itself short of funds to meet its reserve requirements, it can borrow from other banks to cover this shortfall or, if no other banks are willing to lend to it, from the Fed. The second objective is to maintain the money supply and carry out *monetary policy*, which is the attempt to manage macroeconomic performance through the control of the money supply.

The Money Market

At least eight times a year, the Federal Reserve announces what the federal funds rate will be. The federal funds rate is the rate that banks charge each other for short-term, even overnight, loans. This is usually announced in news outlets with headlines such as "the Federal Reserve moved today to lower interest rates to…" or "the Federal Reserve raised interest rates." The truth is that the Fed doesn't, as some people mistakenly believe, set interest rates. Rather, a committee within the Fed called the Federal Open Market Committee (FOMC) uses the *money market* to achieve a target rate of interest. The committee's name implies that it does this on a market, much like the ones we have seen in our chapters on microeconomics. This is, in fact, exactly what it does.

The supply side of the money market is the money supply we have developed in this chapter. Recall that the Federal Reserve decides on what the amount of money in the economy should be. At any point in time, the amount of money in the money supply is a fixed amount. Therefore, the money supply curve is vertical at a single point, as shown in Figure 15-1. The process by which the money supply changes is somewhat complicated, and we address this in the next chapter.

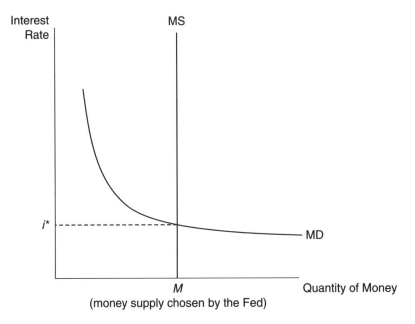

FIGURE 15-1 • The Money Market

The other side of the money market is the *money demand curve*. The money demand curve illustrates how much money people are willing to hold at various interest rates. At first it might not be intuitive that people would decide on how much money to have based on the interest rate. The key to this is to remember that there is an opportunity cost of holding money—the interest rate. Consider the decision on whether to take money out of savings and have it on hand to spend, either in your pocket or in a non-interest-bearing checking account. The higher the interest rate on your savings account, the more interest income you lose by keeping that money in your pocket.

The demand for money will depend on a number of factors, and changes in these can shift the demand curve for money in (decrease the demand for money) or out (increase the demand for money). First of all, changes in the aggregate price level will increase the demand for money. If everything you purchase costs more, you need to keep more money on hand to maintain the same amount of consumption, regardless of the interest rate you might otherwise be earning. Second, if GDP changes, so does the demand for money. Intuitively, if people are purchasing more goods and services, they will need more dollars with which to do that, and the demand for money will increase. Finally, technology and habits play a role in the demand for money. For instance, the demand for money usually increases during the winter months, as people tend to buy more for holiday celebrations. Also, technological changes such as the introduction of ATM machines have made it easier to get money as needed and made it less necessary for people to keep larger amounts of money on hand.

According to *liquidity preference theory*, the interest rate is determined by the interaction of the supply and demand for money, as illustrated in Figure 15-1. In other words, the interest rate will adjust to bring the amount of money that people want in line with the amount of money that actually exists. Consider what would happen if the current interest rate was higher than the equilibrium interest rate. In this case, people would not be as willing to hold money because they would be able to earn a higher interest rate by placing that money into something like a CD (remember that a CD is a near-money asset). Banks that were selling such assets would find that they could sell them at a lower price and still find willing buyers. This would place downward pressure on the interest rate until it reaches equilibrium. Conversely, if the going interest rate were lower than the equilibrium rate, people would be willing to hold more money than actually exists and would be less willing to hold on to near-money assets. Gradually banks would have to offer higher and higher interest rates on the near-money assets in order to get people willing to hold on to less wealth in the form of cash.

Summary

In this chapter, we discussed the purpose of money in the economy. We began with a discussion of the fact that an asset is considered money because of the functions that it performs, rather than by being a particular kind of paper or coin. We continued by introducing the concept of a money supply, how the practice of fractional reserve banking creates money, and what role a central bank such as the Federal Reserve System plays in the creation of the money supply. Finally, the role of money in determining interest rates through the money market was introduced. The fact that a central bank can manipulate the money supply, thus shifting the money supply curve and changing the interest rate, has an important implication. The interest rate influences household spending decisions and business investment decisions. Changes in the interest rate, then, can be used to change our macroeconomic variables such as GDP. We turn our attention to how and why this might be done in the next chapter.

QUIZ

Is each of the following statements *true* or *false*? Explain.

1. Anything that cannot perform all three functions of money will not be able to be used as money.

2. Something must have intrinsic value in order to be used as money.

3. Something is money because we believe it to be money.

4. M2 is sometimes called "near money."

5. If the reserve requirement is 5 percent, then an injection of $1,000 will definitely result in an increase of $20,000 in the money supply.

6. The Federal Reserve sets interest rates.

7. The Federal Reserve was created in response to the Great Depression.

8. According to the theory of liquidity preference, the Federal Reserve should set an interest rate that clears the money market.

9. If all of a sudden debit cards were made illegal, the demand for money would probably decrease.

10. If the Federal Reserve increased the money supply, the interest rate would increase.

chapter 16

Fiscal Policy and Monetary Policy

Fluctuations in the macroeconomy are common, but large or prolonged swings in unemployment, output, and inflation can have serious effects on an economy. Traditionally, economic theory held that the best course of action when these things happened was to take no action at all. The Great Depression was a dramatic illustration of why this is not always the best idea. The alternative, to "do something," generally takes the form of using either fiscal policy or monetary policy (or a combination of the two) to affect macroeconomic variables. In this chapter, we examine the classical approach, the methodology involved in using fiscal and monetary policy, and some criticisms that remain of using either to affect the macroeconomy.

CHAPTER OBJECTIVES

After completing this chapter, the student should be able to:

1. Describe the role of the interest rate and investment in the business cycle.

2. Describe and contrast the classical and Keynesian approaches to macroeconomic intervention.

3. Describe and graph the loanable funds market, and describe what effect government spending may have on the interest rate in this market.

4. Understand how fiscal policy is carried out and how this is reflected in the AD-AS model.

5. Define the terms *crowding-out effect* and *multiplier effect*, show how they affect aggregate demand in the AD-AS model, and be able to calculate the multiplier effect.

6. Understand how central banks undertake monetary policy and how this is reflected in the AD-AS model.

7. Describe and graph how monetary and fiscal policies affect macroeconomic variables such as GDP, unemployment, and inflation.

8. Describe the neoclassical synthesis and continuing debates in macroeconomics.

The Interest Rate

Before we move on to the different things that might be done to manage macroeconomic fluctuations, we need to revisit the role of the interest rate and investment. Investment is a critical part of GDP. Even though consumption typically makes up the largest share of GDP, investment plays a greater role in macroeconomic stability, and investment is much more volatile than consumption. Table 16-1 compares the average quarterly changes in the consumption and investment components of GDP during each of the previous six recessions. As you can see, not only did investment decline by significantly more than consumption, but consumption even *increased* during a few recessions!

TABLE 16-1 Changes in Consumption and Investment During Recessions

Recession	1973– 1975	1980	1981– 1982	1990– 1991	2001	2007– 2009
% change in consumption	−0.65%	−4.75%	2.2%	−0.9%	2.825%	−1.74%
% change in investment	−13.27%	−17.2%	−9.85%	−15.8%	−12.55%	−21.06%

The amount of investment in the economy will depend on a number of factors, but foremost among them is the interest rate. There are two models of how the interest rate is determined in the short run. One of them, liquidity preference, we introduced in Chapter 15. There is another model for how interest rates are determined that is slightly different from the liquidity preference theory, the *market for loanable funds model.*

As the name *market* suggests, this model is based on the supply and demand structure that we are by now very familiar with. The supply of loanable funds is upward-sloping, and it originates from the savings that exist in an economy. Individual households and businesses supply their savings through financial intermediaries. The price that savers receive for their savings is the interest rate, and as the interest rate increases, the amount of savings that households are willing to supply increases (as the opportunity cost of consuming increases, households will decrease their consumption and save more). Demand is downward-sloping because loanable funds are used for investment, and the interest rate is the price of investing. The more expensive it is to borrow money, the lower the rate of return on an investment is going to be, and therefore the less investment you will do. For instance, suppose you have four projects with rates of return of 4 percent, 3 percent, 2 percent, and 1 percent. If the interest rate is 2.5 percent, you will invest in only two of those projects, but if the interest rate is 1.5 percent, you will invest in three of them.

Shifts in the supply curve for loanable funds occur when there are changes in savings behavior or changes in savings from other countries (we abstract from this in this chapter and revisit it in Chapter 17). Demand for loanable funds is basically a derived demand. Firms demand funds to invest, but they do so because they believe that the investment will be productive in the future. In addition, if a government runs a budget deficit, it must borrow money in order to pay for the amount of government spending above the amount of tax revenues that it collects. Therefore, changes in the demand for loanable funds occur when there are changes in the investment climate or changes in the government's budget balance.

Let's examine what the effect on the interest rate would be if there were an increase in the savings rate, using both the loanable funds model and the liquidity preference model from Chapter 15. Savings is an important aspect of investment. In fact, unless we have an influx of savings from another country, any investment that is done has to come from savings. This is reflected in the *savings-investment identity, S = I.* What would be the effect of an increase in savings on the interest rate in the short run, then? According to the liquidity preference model, an increase in savings would decrease the demand for money; since people would need less money on hand to carry out transactions (they are consuming less and saving more). As shown in panel a of Figure 16-1, this would lead to a decrease in the interest rate. Since we know that a lower interest rate will spur investment, this would lead to an increase in investment in the short run. On the other hand, in the market for loanable funds model, an increase in the savings rate would lead to an increase in the supply of loanable funds, as shown in panel b of Figure 16-1. Here, we see that an increase in the savings rate will lower the interest rate and increase the quantity of funds borrowed in the economy.

You might notice that in both panels of Figure 16-1 the interest rate on the vertical axis is simply labeled as i, which would imply that the same equilibrium interest rate is observed in both markets. However, economists believe that the most appropriate interest rate to use in the money market model is the nominal interest rate, and the best interest rate to use in the loanable funds market is the real rate (which is frequently abbreviated as r). The nominal rate is equal to the real rate of interest plus expected inflation (or, $i = r +$ inflation). In Chapter 13 we discussed how nominal and real values differ. Real values, whether they are interest rates or dollars, are adjusted for the effects of inflation. In a short-term period of time, we assume that there is no inflation; thus there is no difference between the real and the nominal interest rates, so in all of our graphs we use i to denote interest.

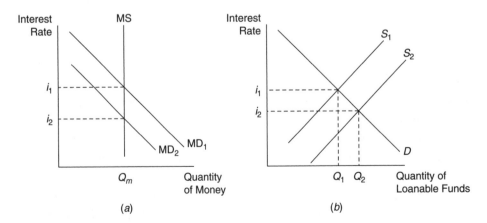

FIGURE 16-1 • (a) Liquidity Preference Model of the Interest Rate; (b) Loanable Funds Model of the Interest Rate

NOTE   *To understand how we get something like the savings-investment identity, let's return to our model of GDP. Recall that GDP = C + I + G + (X − M). For simplicity, we will assume that the economy is closed, meaning that there is no trade (so X = 0 and M = 0, and don't worry, we drop this unlikely assumption in the next chapter). In this case, GDP becomes GDP = C + I + G.*

Recall that the income approach is an equivalent way of calculating GDP, so let's use income (Y) in the previous equation:

$$Y = C + I + G$$

Since we are currently interested in investment, let's isolate investment on one side:

$$Y - C - G = I$$

We know, of course, that in such a closed economy, any government spending (G) will have to be paid for somehow. Usually, taxes are collected from households and firms and used for G. In order to change this equation to reflect taxes, without fundamentally altering it, we need to both add and subtract taxes (T) from the equation (which is the same as adding 0):

$$Y - C - G + T - T = I$$

Why would we do such a thing? Well, if we now rearrange this a little bit, we get something that actually makes sense intuitively:

$$(Y - C - T) + (T - G) = I$$

The term (Y − C − T) is the income (Y) that households and firms earn, less what they pay in taxes and less what they consume. In other words, if you have income left over after you pay your taxes and spend, the only thing left to do with it is to save it. Therefore, Y − C − T represents private savings. *The other term is what the government has left over from the tax revenue it collects after subtracting government spending. In recent U.S. history, this number has been negative because the government has spent more than the tax revenue it has taken in. This is known as a* budget deficit. *On the other hand, if the government spends less than the tax revenue it collects, this term is positive and there is a* budget surplus. *Therefore, T − G represents* public savings. *Taken together, the entire left side of the equation is all of the savings in an economy, leading us to the savings-investment identity S = I.*

The Classical Theory of Economics

Up until the 1930s, there was relatively little dissent among economists about models of the macroeconomy. The *classical theory of economics* referred to an understanding that the following were eternal truths:

- Prices fully adjust.
- Production will generate enough income to support the same level of demand.
- Savings and investment will equal each other.

In other words, short-run aggregate supply was almost an afterthought. Since prices always fully adjust, any change that affected short-run aggregate supply or aggregate demand would ultimately be neutral, and the macroeconomy would return to the full-employment level of output on its own. Additionally, the theory asserts that the full-employment level of output would always produce enough income for that output to be purchased, an idea known as *Say's law*. In fact, this price adjustment is exactly what we showed in Chapter 14 as the short-run aggregate supply curve and the aggregate demand curve adjusted in response to changes in factors affecting the macroeconomy.

The implication of this is clear: any attempt to affect macroeconomic variables is at best unnecessary and at worst damaging. For instance, any attempt to change aggregate demand by using the money supply to lower the interest rate would not actually result in more output. This idea is embodied in another model used by classical economists, the *quantity theory of money*. According to the quantity theory of money, the amount of money that is used to purchase goods and services in an economy, which you can find by multiplying the price level, P, by the real GDP, Y, is equal to the dollar amount of the money supply multiplied by its *velocity*. The velocity of money is how often a unit of the money supply changes hands. Mathematically, the quantity theory of money is simply:

$$MV = PY$$

The classical theory of money states that prices fully adjust, so P is able to change, but Y is fixed in the short term. It also assumes that the velocity of money is relatively stable and reflects the spending habits and existing technology in the money supply. The implication here is also clear: if the money supply is changed, the only effect will be an increase in the price level (that is, inflation) with no effect on the variable we really care about, Y. In other words, according to the classical theory, money is neutral and has no effect on real variables (real GDP or unemployment). We could further argue that according to classical economics, there really is no such thing as a SRAS curve; the only supply curve in the macroeconomy is the LRAS.

Still Struggling

The velocity of money is a tricky concept. Let's explain this using a simple economy. Suppose an economy has only two goods, jelly and toast. There are four units of jelly and five units of toast in the economy.

First, suppose that the price of jelly is $1 and the price of toast is $2. In this case, total spending in the economy $PY = 14. If the money supply in the economy is only $7, each of those dollar bills will have to change hands twice in order for $14 worth of goods to be sold. Thus we say that the velocity of money (V) is equal to 2.

If a dollar bill always changes hands twice in our economy, and the amount of jelly and toast are fixed (that is, V and Y are known), what happens if the money supply doubles to $14? We can use the quantity theory of money equation to predict that if the left side doubles, the right side must also double. And since it is assumed that output Y is constant, prices must also double. Thus classical economists believe that when more money is in circulation and chasing after the same goods, prices will be bid up.

Keynesian Theory

As we alluded to in the first chapter, history proved that the classical theory had some problems. According to the classical theory, the Great Depression should never have been possible. The individual actions of private producers did not aggregate into an efficient macroeconomic outcome. Say's law had fallen apart: supply did not create its own demand. Instead, allowing the macroeconomy time to self-adjust had led to a downward spiral. Such a spiral starts with something spooking aggregate demand and output going down, but since wages and other prices are not flexible downward, SRAS doesn't adjust. In fact, the AS curve is completely horizontal up to the full-employment output.

The implication of this is also clear: any decrease in aggregate demand can potentially lead to a permanent reduction in output. Once an economy has started on a downward spiral, it cannot correct itself, and some sort of intervention is not just desirable, but necessary. Equally important is the implication about the impact of any action to correct aggregate demand—it will have no effect on the price level unless aggregate demand expands beyond full employment. In other words, according to Keynesian theory, any shift in aggregate demand will not cause inflation as long as output is below the full-employment level.

Figure 16-2 illustrates how the different assumptions of the classical and Keynesian models translate into an AD-AS model, and the consequences in terms of the price level of a shift in aggregate demand. In the classical model, there is only one aggregate supply curve, since prices always fully adjust. Any shift in aggregate demand will not actually increase output; it will only cause an increase in price level. On the other hand, aggregate supply in the Keynesian model has "sticky" prices that do not adjust. In this case, when aggregate demand increases, output will increase and the price level will not.

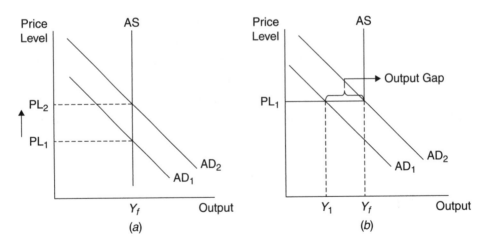

FIGURE 16-2 · (a) Classical Theory; (b) Keynesian Theory

Consider, then, an output gap as shown in panel b of Figure 16-2. The aggregate demand curve AD_1 is currently below full-employment output. According to classical theory, if we left this economy to adjust on its own, it would return to full output. Keynesian theory, however, says that some sort of intervention is necessary. Efforts to return output to the full-employment level are known as *stabilization policy*. There are two types of macroeconomic intervention: *fiscal policy*, which is the use of government spending and/or taxes to change output, and *monetary policy*, which is the use of the money supply to change output.

The modern macroeconomic consensus acknowledges that there is some validity to both viewpoints. In the short run, Keynesian assumptions of sticky prices are probably accurate, and at very low levels of output, there is not likely to be much inflation. In the long run, prices have time to adjust and output beyond the full-employment level of output is not possible. Some textbooks present this synthesis in the AD-AS model as an AS curve that contains three ranges, as shown in Figure 16-3. Here, the aggregate supply curve is split into a Keynesian or short-run range, an intermediate range, and a classical or long-run range. If aggregate demand increases in the Keynesian range, there will be increases in output but not inflation. If the aggregate demand increases in the intermediate range, there will be increases in output but also in price level. However, in the classical range, any increase in aggregate demand will result only in increases in the price level.

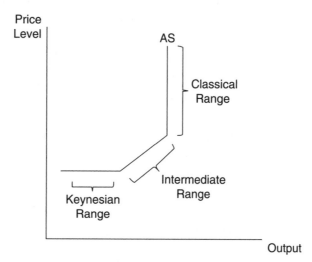

FIGURE 16-3 · Aggregate Supply Curve with Three Ranges

Fiscal Policy

Let's return to the AD-AS model that we introduced in Chapter 14. Recall that aggregate demand is made up of the components of GDP (C, I, G, and $X - M$). Fiscal policy is the use of taxes (which would alter C and I) or government spending (G) to increase or decrease aggregate demand. When a government undertakes *expansionary fiscal policy*, it either increases government spending or decreases taxes to shift aggregate demand to the right. Increasing aggregate demand increases output, which in turn increases employment, both of which are desirable when the economy is below full employment. However, if the price level is able to adjust at all, it will also increase. One consequence of expansionary fiscal policy is a heightened risk of inflation.

There may also be times when the economy is operating above full employment and inflation is the more serious of the two economic problems. In this case, the government can engage in *contractionary fiscal policy* by either reducing government spending or increasing taxes. These policies serve to shift aggregate demand to the left and reduce the price level. The trade-off, of course, is that output will decrease and unemployment may increase.

Let's consider an economy that is initially in long-run equilibrium, but that has a sudden decrease in investor confidence that lowers investment and consumption by $200 billion. If we were to graph this, it would show a decrease in the aggregate demand curve that resulted in an output level that was $200 billion less than the full-employment level, and the economy would have a recessionary gap. If government spending were used to correct this, we could return to our initial equilibrium without causing inflation. However, if we overcorrect, we will go beyond the full-employment level and cause inflation. If we undercorrect, we will fail to return the economy to the full-employment level, and we will have higher rates of unemployment than are ideal.

If we are going to use expansionary fiscal policy, we need to know how much to increase spending or how much to decrease taxes. You might think that this is obvious—if we increase government spending by $200 billion, the aggregate demand curve shifts by that amount, and we are back to equilibrium. However, let's follow the chain of events when that happens.

Suppose the government initiates a $200 billion spending program that involves building and repairing roads and bridges. In order to do that, the government needs to hire construction workers and buy materials and equipment. That $200 billion then becomes income that households and businesses can either spend or save. That rise in spending would then show up in consumption and shift aggregate demand out even further. The degree to which the aggregate demand curve will shift out further will depend on how much of every additional dollar that they receive people tend to spend or save, also known as the *marginal propensity to consume (MPC)* and the *marginal propensity to save (MPS)*. Since a consumer can either spend or save additional dollars of income, it must be true that MPC + MPS = 1.

For instance, if people tend to spend 75 percent of each additional dollar and save 25 percent of each additional dollar, the MPC is equal to 0.75 and the MPS is equal to 0.25. To stimulate the economy, the government decides to spend only $100 billion. Table 16-2 goes through the chain of events for the first few rounds of spending that this will spur.

TABLE 16-2 The Multiplier Effect of Government Spending		
Round	**Increase in Consumption of Goods and Services That Results from This Round (in billions)**	**Total Increase in GDP (in billions) as of This Iteration**
1 (initial government spending)	$100 (75% of this will be spent and become income or wages for someone else)	$100
2	$75 (75% of this will be spent and become income or wages for someone else)	$100 + $75
3	$56.25	$100 + 75 + 56.25

This multiple expansion should look familiar, as it is very similar to the multiple expansion of the money supply from Chapter 15. We calculate the *multiplier (M)*, or the amount of the total change in GDP that results from an autonomous injection of spending, by using a very similar formula for the multiplier:

$$M = \frac{1}{1 - \text{MPC}} = \frac{1}{\text{MPS}}$$

So, in our case, $1/(1 - 0.75) = 1/0.25 = 4$. Thus a $100 billion injection will result in a $400 billion increase in GDP, which would push output beyond the full-employment level. Because every new dollar of government spending is multiplied by a factor of 4, we need only $50 billion of fiscal policy to increase GDP by $200 billion.

TIP *Because* MPS + MPC *must always equal 1, another way to compute the multiplier is M = 1/MPS. Like the reserve requirement that plays a key role in the money multiplier, the* MPS *represents savings that is being pulled out of circulation and is therefore not leading to new spending. Thus a larger* MPS *will reduce the size of the multiplier because more dollars are being saved and fewer are being consumed at each round of spending.*

The Tax Multiplier

The government can also engage in fiscal policy by reducing taxes. Let's assume that changes in taxes come in *lump sums* whereby the government either reduces or increases income taxes by a flat amount. To investigate the impact of this fiscal policy, we need to modify Table 16-2. Instead of the government purchasing $100 billion in labor and materials, the government sends consumers a check (this reduces taxes like receiving a tax rebate) in the amount of $100 billion.

TABLE 16-3 The Multiplier Effect of a Tax Decrease		
Round	Increase in Consumption of Goods and Services That Results from This Round (in billions)	Total Increase in GDP (in billions) as of This Iteration
1 (initial lump sum tax decrease)	$100 × 0.75 = $75 (75% of this will be spent and become income or wages for someone else)	$75
2	$56.25 (75% of this will be spent and become income or wages for someone else)	$75 + $56.25
3	$42.19	$75 + 56.25 + 42.19

These rounds will continue until someone is trying to spend 75 percent of virtually nothing. The only difference between Tables 16-2 and 16-3 is that the lump-sum tax cut doesn't inject the entire $100 billion. The multiplier process is immediately smaller because the first round of spending is 25 percent smaller. Thus the *tax multiplier* (T_m) can be computed as:

$$T_m = \frac{\text{MPC}}{\text{MPS}}$$

In our example, the tax multiplier would be 0.75/0.25 = 3. Thus the $100 billion tax cut will increase GDP by $300 billion.

Difficulties with Fiscal Policy

At first glance, the multiplier effect suggests that fiscal policy is a very promising way to carry out stabilization policy. Unfortunately, that is not the end of the story. Suppose a government has decided to increase government spending to expand output. In order to do that, it must acquire the funds needed to do it in one of three ways: increase taxes, create money, or borrow money. If the government finances an increase in government spending through an equivalent increase in taxes, the net effect on output is going to be much smaller. For example, the previous example showed that a $100 billion increase in government spending will increase GDP by $400 billion. To finance this spending, taxes must be increased by $100 billion, which will reduce GDP by $300 billion. The net effect of this balanced-budget approach to fiscal policy is to increase GDP by only $100 billion. Therefore, there is no net multiplier effect. Some textbooks refer to this as the *balanced-budget multiplier*, and it is always equal to 1.

If the government creates money to finance the spending, this will cause inflation to increase. When inflation goes up, the power of the multiplier decreases. This is because rising prices mean that, at each round of spending, people are simply paying higher prices for the same consumption, not necessarily increasing consumption.

Finally, there is the possibility of borrowing money. If a government spends more than the tax revenue it collects, it runs a *budget deficit*. Over time, deficits accumulate to form *debt*. Just like households and firms, if the government wants to spend more than it earns, it must borrow to do so. This means that deficit spending has an effect on the loanable funds market. Let's start with the loanable funds market in Figure 16-4 before there is a government borrowing, where $\$Q_0$ in funds are loaned out and the market rate of interest is i_0. If the government needs to borrow, it joins the other demanders of savings, and the demand for loanable funds increases from D_0 to D_1. If the original rate of interest remained, the total amount of loanable funds in the economy would be $\$Q_1$ (with the government borrowing $\$Q_1 - \$Q_0$ of those funds). However, there aren't $\$Q_1$ worth of savings being supplied when the interest rate is low. Eventually, the interest rate will increase and the total amount of investment will be $\$Q_T$ in equilibrium. Since the difference $\$Q_1 - \$Q_0$ still represents the amount of government borrowing, this means that the amount of private borrowing has decreased to $\$Q_P$.

In other words, public (government) borrowing has crowded out private investment, which is why this phenomenon is known as the *crowding-out effect*. As a result of the government borrowing, the interest rate increases, which leads to decreased private investment, therefore offsetting some (or all) of the increases in GDP from G by decreasing C and I. The crowding-out effect is illustrated in Figure 16-4.

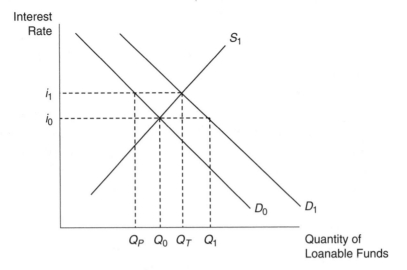

FIGURE 16-4 • Crowding-Out Effect

CAUTION *If you are using this book as a supplement to a textbook, this expla-nation of the crowding-out effect may be slightly different from the one in your textbook. Some economists take the view that rather than increasing the amount of loanable funds demanded, deficits reduce the amount of savings supplied. If this occurs, the supply of loanable funds decreases from S_1 to S_2, as shown in Figure 16-5. In both cases, however, the interest rate increases.*

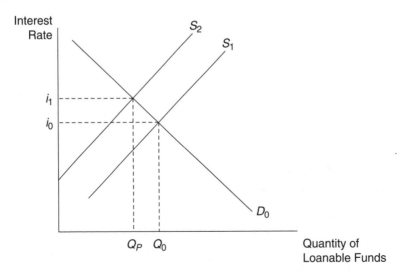

FIGURE 16-5 • Change in the Supply of Loanable Funds

The multiplier effect and the crowding-out effect can have competing impacts on GDP. This raises the question about what the final impact on GDP of an increase in government spending will be. The answer will depend on whether the multiplier effect or the crowding-out effect is stronger. For instance, if the multiplier effect is stronger than the crowding-out effect, the shift outward of aggregate demand will be farther than the shift inward of aggregate demand caused by the crowding-out effect, and the final impact will be an increase in GDP, as shown in panel *a* of Figure 16-6. On the other hand, if the crowding-out effect is strong and the multiplier effect is weak, an increase in government spending can actually wipe out any gains from the government spending, as shown in panel *b* of Figure 16-6.

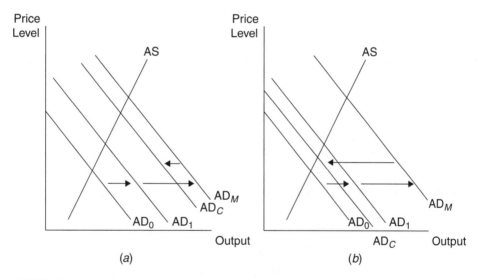

FIGURE 16-6 • (*a*) Multiplier Effect Stronger; (*b*) Crowding-Out Effect Stronger. AD_0 is the initial aggregate demand before government action. AD_1 shows the initial effect of government spending. AD_M shows the effect on aggregate demand as a result of the multiplier effect, and AD_C shows the effect on aggregate demand of the crowding-out effect.

Monetary Policy

The other type of stabilization policy that can be used is *monetary policy*, which is the use of the money supply to affect aggregate demand. In Chapter 14, we introduced the liquidity preference model and the role that the money supply plays in determining interest rates. When a central bank increases the money supply, the interest rate decreases, and when a central bank decreases the money supply, the interest rate increases.

In the United States, the Federal Reserve is the central bank. Changes in the money supply are almost exclusively done by the Federal Open Market Committee (FOMC), which meets at least eight times per year to set an *interest-rate target*. To achieve this target, the Open Market Desk of the Federal Reserve Bank of New York buys or sells Treasury securities in the open market in order to achieve the targeted rate. For instance, if the current rate of interest is 4 percent, but the FOMC has decided on a target rate of 4.25 percent, the Open Market Desk will sell bonds until the market rate of interest adjusts to the higher target rate (if bonds are sold, the Federal Reserve is injecting bonds back into the market and taking money out of the money supply). On the other hand, if the Fed wants to lower the interest rate, it will buy Treasuries from the public. When the Fed is an open market buyer of these securities, money is injected into the economy and the securities are taken out. Thus buying Treasuries increases the money supply and reduces the interest rate.

The Federal Reserve also has other tools at its disposal to change the money supply, including changing the reserve ratio or lending through the discount window (overnight lending to banks). However, these options are seldom used, as they do not allow the same kind of control over the money supply that open market operations allow.

By changing the interest rate, the Federal Reserve can moderate the amount of investment in the economy. If the Federal Reserve is engaging in *expansionary monetary policy*, its goal is to increase aggregate demand by lowering the interest rate, which it does by increasing the money supply. If the interest rate goes down, investment demand goes up, and there is more private investment and consumption. If the Federal Reserve is engaging in *contractionary monetary policy*, its goal is to decrease aggregate demand by increasing the interest rate, which it does by decreasing the money supply. If the interest rate goes up, investment demand goes down, and there is less private investment and consumption.

This latter point might seem strange, as so far a lot of our focus has been on correcting economic downturns. However, central banks such as the Federal Reserve are charged not just with fighting recessions, but also with ensuring price stability. In general, the goal of price stability is a low and positive rate of inflation.

Consider an economy that is operating beyond full employment, as illustrated in Figure 16-7. Output Y_0 is higher than the full-employment level Y_f. We know from our analysis of the Phillips curve in Chapter 13 that if the unemployment rate is below the full-employment rate, as it would be here, this places upward pressure on wages and leads to a wage-price spiral. In fact, at Y_0, the price level PL_0 is higher than it would be if aggregate demand returned to the long-run equilibrium (P_{full}). To correct this, the Federal Reserve could sell bonds, which would decrease the money supply from MS_0 to MS_1, as in panel b of Figure 16-7, and raise interest rates from i_0 to i_1. An increase in interest rates would lower investment and eventually consumption, which would return aggregate demand back to the long-run equilibrium level of output.

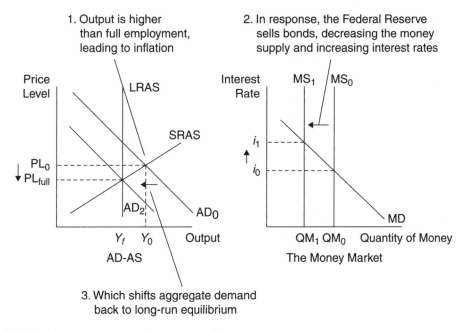

FIGURE 16-7 • Contractionary Monetary Policy

Central banks have a number of criteria for deciding when and why to undertake monetary policy. Some set explicit *inflation targets*, such as 2 percent annual inflation, and engage in monetary policy in order to achieve that regardless of the output level. The downside to this method, however, is that there are situations in which there are both inflation and a recessionary output gap, and inflation targeting restricts the central bank to only one objective. An alternative method that was suggested by the economist John Taylor takes both inflation and output into account using the *Taylor rule*. According to this simple equation, the interest rate that the Federal Reserve targets should be as follows:

Federal funds rate = 1 + (1.5 × inflation rate) + (0.5 × output gap)

For instance, if inflation is currently 2 percent and output is 3 percent less than the full-employment rate:

$$1 + 1.5 \times 2 + 0.5 \times (-3) = 2.5\%$$

Problems with Fiscal and Monetary Policy

Given the fiscal and monetary tools available, it would seem that policy makers should be able to regulate the economy so that severe recessions and excessive booms (and the inevitable busts that follow them) do not occur, or at least do not become severe. Unfortunately, this is not the case. Neither monetary policy nor fiscal policy can be used to fine-tune the economy. In fact, the implementation of either type of stabilization policy is not without problems.

The Taylor rule actually gives us a clue to one of the problems that monetary policy can encounter. According to the Federal Reserve Bank of San Francisco, the output gap in the first quarter of 2009 was −6.2 percent and the inflation rate was −0.4 percent (meaning that there was a brief period of deflation). This would imply that the Federal Reserve should set a target of −2.7 percent, a negative and therefore impossible rate of interest (a real interest rate of zero is loaning money for free; a negative interest rate would be paying somebody to borrow money from you). In fact, the federal funds rate has been between 0 percent and 0.25 percent since early 2009. Even if it wanted to, at this point the Federal Reserve could not use monetary policy to expand aggregate demand, a problem known as a *liquidity trap*. Monetary policy has been rendered ineffective because the interest rate is up against the lower bound of zero.

An additional problem with monetary policy, and with fiscal policy as well, is that both suffer from *lags*. The first category of lags is called *inside lags*, which is the time taken between recognizing a problem and taking action. *Outside lags* are the length of time before an action has its full impact on the economy. While both monetary theory and fiscal policy suffer from policy lags, each is affected differently by different aspects of the lags.

A *recognition lag* is an inside lag that refers to the time it takes to recognize that there is a problem. Unemployment and inflation data that are produced this month are actually a report of what was happening in the previous month. In fact, unemployment data themselves tend to reflect conditions that may have existed for quite some time (for instance, firms may wait to see if a downturn is temporary before laying off workers).

Decision lag refers to the length of time it takes for an action to be chosen. Fiscal policy has a significant disadvantage in terms of this lag. Monetary policy decisions are made routinely, and the FOMC can call special meetings to make changes if the committee agrees on the urgency of a situation. Fiscal policy, however, is subject to the legislative system. If policy makers want to engage in *discretionary fiscal policy* (that is, changes in government spending that require specific action), the wait can be very long indeed as bills are debated in Congress, revised, redebated, and voted on. For this reason, much of the fiscal policy that is used routinely is in the form of *automatic stabilizers*. These are provisions in the tax code and transfer payment systems that change without the need for any additional legislative action. For instance, when the unemployment rate goes up, the amount of transfer payments for unemployment insurance increases and progressive income taxes decrease, which help to offset the effects of a recession.

Finally, the *impact lag* or outside lag is the length of time required for the action to work its way through the economy. For instance, monetary policy may not suffer from as severe a decision lag as fiscal policy, and implementation of monetary policy is fairly rapid (trades usually occur the same day, and the interest rate starts to adjust as soon as this occurs). However, it may take a while to change investment strategies to take the new interest rate into account. Finally, any multiplier effect will also take time to work its way through the economy. These lags are significant drawbacks of any kind of stabilization policy. Because the time between recognition and impact can be significant, economic conditions may improve (or worsen) on their own, making the action chosen inappropriate.

Another important distinction is that these policies are not effective at changing output or unemployment in the long run. Stabilization policy can really only return an economy to the full-employment rate of output, not stimulate *economic growth*. Economic growth is an increase in the ability to produce more goods and services, as reflected by an increase in the long-run aggregate supply curve. The consensus in macroeconomics is that monetary policy and fiscal policy are not very effective at changing this in the long run.

Applying Policy Actions to Economic Fluctuations

Let's walk through a few different scenarios that we might see in our AD-AS model and determine what impact monetary and fiscal policy might have. Before we do, however, we must remember that policy makers always have the option of taking no action at all. An economy may stabilize (that is; return to the full-employment level of output) on its own. However, this may take so long to occur that it is unpleasant or politically destabilizing, such as extended levels of high unemployment. The economist John Maynard Keynes referred to this problem with his statement, "In the long run we are all dead." In each of our scenarios, we start with an economy in long-run equilibrium where our initial aggregate demand AD_0 intersects our initial short-run aggregate supply $SRAS_0$ at the full-employment level of output Y_0 and a price level PL_0.

First, let's consider a familiar example: a recessionary gap caused by a downward shift in aggregate demand from AD_0 to AD_1. This could be caused by declining expectations, declining wealth, a decline in net exports (more on this in the next chapter), or declining investment spending. As a result, output decreases and the price level decreases. If nothing is done, wages will adjust downward, and the short-run aggregate supply curve will shift outward from $SRAS_0$ to $SRAS_1$, returning the economy to full output, but at a permanently lower price level (that is, with deflation, which can be painful), as shown in Figure 16-8a. If policy makers wanted to intervene, they could use fiscal policy by increasing government spending or decreasing taxes. They could also use monetary policy, increasing the money supply, lowering the interest rate, increasing investment, and shifting aggregate demand to the right back to AD_0. They could also use some combination of the two. Figure 16-8b illustrates the result of either fiscal or monetary policy: output returns to the original price level and the original output level.

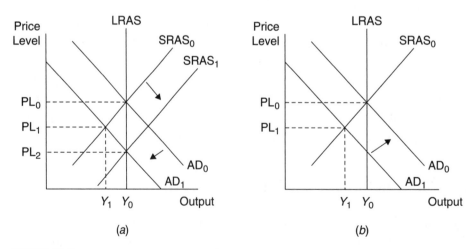

FIGURE 16-8 · (a) No Policy Action Taken; (b) Either Expansionary Monetary Policy or Expansionary Fiscal Policy Used

Next, let's consider an inflationary output gap. Figure 16-9 illustrates an inflationary gap caused by an increase in aggregate demand. Again, policy makers may choose to do nothing. In this case, prices will eventually adjust— for example, the lower rate of unemployment will drives up wages. In the end, SRAS shifts leftward and output returns to the full-employment level, but there is now a permanently higher price level, as shown in Figure 16-9a. Instead, policy makers could undertake contractionary fiscal policy by decreasing spending or raising taxes. The central bank could use contractionary monetary policy by selling bonds, lowering the money supply, raising interest rates, and lowering investment. In either case, aggregate demand will return to AD_0 from AD_1 and there will not be a permanent increase in the price level (see Figure 16-9b).

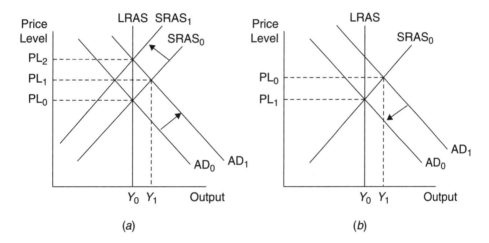

FIGURE 16-9 · (a) No Policy Action Taken; (b) Either Contractionary Monetary Policy or Contractionary Fiscal Policy Used

Finally, let's consider the special case of supply-induced inflation. This can result when there is a sudden increase in the price of inputs, as happened during the recession in the 1970s, or any other negative supply shock. We show the effect of this on the AD-AS model in Figure 16-10. As you can see, we have the worst of all worlds: stagnant GDP and inflation (a combination known as *stagflation*). If policy makers allow the economy to self-adjust, short-run aggregate supply will return to the initial level as price adjusts. However, policy makers face a dilemma—any action that they take to increase output and lower unemployment will result in a permanently higher rate of inflation.

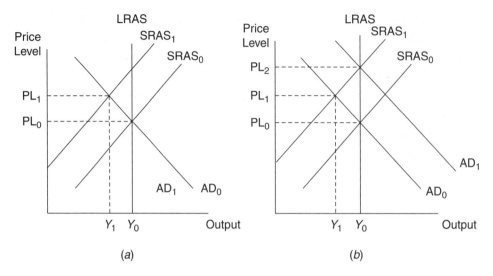

FIGURE 16-10 · (*a*) No Policy Action Taken; (*b*) Either Expansionary Monetary Policy or Expansionary Fiscal Policy

Still Struggling

Questions that ask you to trace the chain of events when monetary policy and fiscal policy are used to stabilize an economy are a favorite of instructors. As you get practice tracing through the process, it will be helpful to always follow these steps:

1. **Start with an initial point.** The question you are given will give you a starting point. There are usually five possibilities for these: long-run equilibrium, an inflationary gap, a recessionary gap, stagflation, or a supply-induced increase in output.

2. **Figure out the key event.** The question might then ask you what kind of policy should be undertaken. For instance, an economy that starts in long-run equilibrium may enter a recession or an inflationary period, or a government may engage in expansionary fiscal policy.

3. **Figure out the effect of the key event on the AD-AS model.** For instance, if the key event is expansionary fiscal policy, you should show that in your AD-AS model and figure out what the effect is on output, employment, and the price level.

4. **Figure out if there are any secondary or long-run effects of the event.** For instance, if the price level changes, this may have an impact on foreign exchange. We examine this possibility in Chapter 17.
5. **Apply the correct fiscal and/or monetary policy to the outcome of the key event.** If you know that inflation is becoming a problem, you would prescribe a contractionary policy to reduce AD and relieve the upward pressure on prices.

Summary

In this chapter, we discussed the important role that private investment plays in the business cycle. Small changes in investment can lead to large changes in output, employment, and the price level. Because of this, macroeconomic stabilization has a lot to do with the interest rate. If fiscal policy is used to stabilize the economy, government spending and tax rates change aggregate demand through a multiplier effect, but this may be offset by the effect that government borrowing has on the loanable funds market. Monetary policy does not suffer from the same problem, as it targets interest rates directly. However, it may face the problem of a liquidity trap. Both monetary and fiscal policies suffer from lags that may lessen their effectiveness in managing economic fluctuations. This does not imply, however, that stabilization policies should never be attempted, as allowing the economy to self-adjust may sometimes be long and painful. We concluded this chapter with examples of how monetary and fiscal policy affects the AD-AS model. In many of our examples so far, we have assumed a closed economy. We drop this assumption in Chapter 17 and explore how these models change when we allow for international trade.

QUIZ

For each of the following, choose the answer that best fits.

1. Although_____makes up the largest category of GDP in the United States, changes in_____are responsible for most recessions and expansions.
   A. investment; net exports
   B. investment, consumption
   C. consumption, investment
   D. government spending, net exports

2. The crowding-out effect refers to:
   A. Decreases in the demand for loanable funds that occur as a result of government deficit spending.
   B. Decreases in the amount of private investment that occur as a result of government deficit spending.
   C. Decreases in the demand for loanable funds that occur as a result of expansionary monetary policy.
   D. Decreases in the amount of private investment that occur as a result of expansionary monetary policy.

3. Which of the following is associated with the classical theory of macroeconomics?
   A. A vertical aggregate supply curve
   B. A horizontal aggregate supply curve
   C. An upward-sloping aggregate supply curve
   D. A role for activist fiscal policy

4. Which of the following is associated with the Keynesian theory of macroeconomics?
   A. Sticky prices below full employment
   B. A horizontal aggregate supply curve below full employment
   C. A role for activist fiscal policy
   D. All of the above

5. Suppose the marginal propensity to save is 0.4. The final impact on GDP of a $100 billion injection of government spending will be:
   A. GDP will increase by $250 billion, regardless of the crowding-out effect.
   B. Less than $250 billion, depending on what the crowding-out effect is.
   C. GDP will increase by about $166 billion, regardless of the crowding-out effect.
   D. Less than $166 billion, depending on what the crowding-out effect is.

Refer to Figure 16-11 for questions 6 through 8.

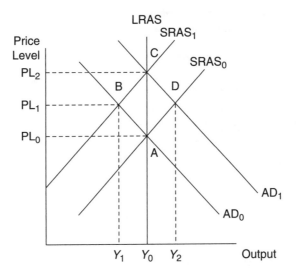

FIGURE 16-11

6. **The movement shown from point A to point B could best be explained by:**
   A. A decrease in wealth
   B. An increase in wages
   C. An increase in investment
   D. An increase in optimism

7. **If an economy moved from point C to point B, which of the following would be an effective method of returning to full employment?**
   A. Decreasing government spending
   B. Selling bonds
   C. Buying bonds
   D. Increasing the tax rate

8. **Suppose the economy moved from point A to point B. If policy makers engage in expansionary fiscal policy, which of the following is likely to occur?**
   A. Output will return to full employment, and the price level will remain unchanged.
   B. Output will return to full employment, and the price level will increase.
   C. Output will increase beyond full employment, and the price level will decrease.
   D. Output will decrease further, and the price level will increase.

Answer questions 9 and 10 as indicated.

9. **Consider the economy of Ame, which is in long-run equilibrium. As a result of a decline in the value of homes, household wealth decreases.**

   I. Indicate the effect of this action on output and price level, using an AD-AS curve.

   II. You are the head of the central bank of this country. Describe what kind of stabilization policy you should pursue. Assuming your job is similar to that of the head of the Federal Reserve, how will you accomplish this?

   III. Show the effect of your action on the appropriate market.

   IV. Show the effect of your action on the AD-AS model.

   V. What situation might make it impossible for you to take any action?

10. **Consider the economy of Ema, which is experiencing stagflation.**

   I. Show the current situation in Ema using an AD-AS model.

   II. What kind of event could have caused this?

   III. Suppose that the government of Ema has determined that the government spending multiplier effect in Ema is 4. What is the marginal propensity to consume in Ema?

   IV. Suppose the government of Ema is studying whether the multiplier effect or the crowding-out effect is stronger. What kind of policy is it contemplating?

   V. The government of Ema has decided to undertake the policy action being considered in part IV. On the AD-AS model, illustrate the impact of the policy on output and price level. State what will happen to the level of unemployment.

chapter **17**

The Global Economy

So far, much of this book has focused on the U.S. economy, but clearly American consumers and American firms buy and sell in the global economy. Consumers enjoy buying products made in other nations, and firms enjoy selling to foreign customers. This chapter explores the concept of comparative advantage and mutually beneficial trade and how trade is facilitated by the foreign currency markets.

CHAPTER OBJECTIVES

After completing this chapter, the student should be able to:

1. Use the production possibilities model to show a nation's capacity to produce two goods and how the production possibilities curve (PPC) can be used to determine comparative advantage in production.

2. Understand how two nations benefit from trade if trade is based on comparative advantage.

3. Use the foreign exchange markets to show how currencies appreciate and depreciate with the flow of trade and with the impact of fiscal and monetary policy, and how this affects the AD-AS model.

4. Understand a nation's balance of payments accounts and how they are affected by trade.

5. Describe how a tariff or quota distorts markets and creates inefficiencies.

Production Possibilities

Economists use a very simple representation of production known as the *production possibilities model* to demonstrate several important concepts, such as scarcity, opportunity cost, economic growth, and the benefits of trade between nations. We begin with two simple assumptions:

- A nation produces only two goods.
- Resources (labor, capital, land, and entrepreneurial talent) and technology are fixed.

Suppose the nation of Elijastan produces only two goods, washing machines and tomatoes. Table 17-1 shows the nation's production possibilities, meaning all the different combinations of washing machines and tomatoes that it can produce given its current stock of resources and technology.

TABLE 17-1 Elijastan Production Possibilities	
Washing Machines (*W*)	Tomatoes (*T*)
100	0
90	30
70	60
40	80
10	95
0	98

Table 17.1 shows that as more tomatoes are produced, fewer washing machines can be produced with the same amount of resources. The data in the table can be converted to a graph, and the downward-sloping curve in Figure 17-1 is called the *production possibilities curve* (PPC).

Note that the PPC is downward-sloping. This is because, as reflected in the table, in order to produce more of one good, Elijastan must give up producing some of the other good. Not only is the PPC downward-sloping, but it gets steeper as more tomatoes are produced. The slope of the PPC also has an intuitive interpretation—the slope of the PPC represents the opportunity cost of producing tomatoes. For instance, if the nation moves from point A to point B,

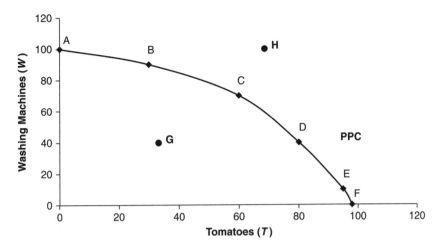

FIGURE 17-1 • Elijastan Production Possibilities

30 tomatoes are gained, but 10 washing machines are lost. Thus the opportunity cost of just 1 tomato is $\frac{1}{3}$ of a washing machine. However, when the nation moves from point E to point F, 3 tomatoes are gained at a cost of 10 washing machines. The opportunity cost of 1 tomato here is 3.33 washing machines. We can see that the opportunity cost of producing tomatoes rises as more are produced.

Why does this opportunity cost rise? It rises because a nation's resources are not perfectly suited to the production of all things. Some land is great for tomatoes and some land is not. Some machines are great for heavy manufacturing but not so good for farming.

Remember that along the PPC, the resources of Elijastan are fully employed. Suppose that the nation is currently producing at point A, with zero resources devoted to tomatoes and all resources devoted to washing machines. If the nation wants to move to point B, resources need to be allocated to tomatoes and away from machines. Of course Elijastan should allocate the *best* agricultural resources to tomatoes, and if those resources are the best for agriculture, they are likely to be the worst for manufacturing. The gain in tomatoes is big, and the loss in machine production is small.

But when the nation gets to point E and wants to move to point F, all of the good agricultural resources have already been devoted to tomatoes, and only the best manufacturing resources remain producing washing machines. When the last move is made to point F, tomato production rises by an insignificant amount at a very high cost in lost washing machines.

TIP *The opportunity cost of the good on the x axis is always the slope of the PPC between two points. The opportunity cost of the good on the y axis is always the inverse of the slope between two points. So if the opportunity cost of moving from point E to point F is 3.33 washing machines to gain 1 tomato, the opportunity cost of moving from point F to point E is 0.33 tomato to get 1 washing machine (10 machines gained and 3 tomatoes lost).*

A point like point G that lies inside the PPC represents a combination of washing machines and tomatoes that doesn't use all the available resources. At this point, there are unemployed and idle resources, which might mean that there is a recession in Elijastan. A point like point H that lies beyond the PPC is a combination of goods that is currently unattainable. Economic growth could allow the nation's production possibilities to expand.

Suppose that Elijastan develops better crop technology that allows it to grow 25 percent more tomatoes with the same quantity of resources. The new PPC shifts outward by 25 percent along the x axis, indicating that the nation's production possibilities have expanded. This won't help the nation produce washing machines, so the PPC still intersects the y axis at 100 machines.

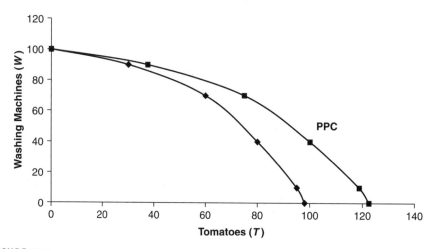

FIGURE 17-2 • Elijastan Production Possibilities with New Technology

TIP *The production possibilities curve is sometimes called the* production possibilities frontier. *This is because the line represents the frontier, or boundary, of what can be produced given a certain level of resources. If a country has more resources or better technology, its production frontier expands, meaning that it can produce more goods.*

Comparative Advantage and Gains from Trade

Now suppose that the nation of Elijastan has a neighboring nation, Maxigania, that can also manufacture washing machines *(W)* and grow tomatoes *(T)*. To keep things slightly simpler, we will assume that the opportunity costs are constant, rather than increasing. This gives production possibility curves that are linear rather than concave. Figure 17-3 shows the PPCs for both nations side by side. Note: For the purposes of this example, the production possibilities of Elijastan are different from those in the earlier example.

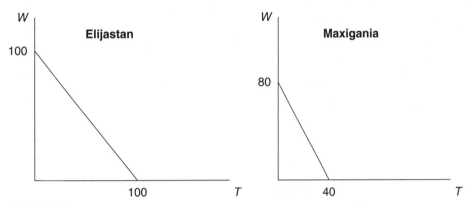

FIGURE 17-3 · Production Possibilities for Elijastan and Maxigania

We can see that Elijastan can produce more washing machines *and* more tomatoes than Maxigania if it focuses all its resources on either of these two goods. In other words, if both countries devoted all of their resources to making washing machines, Elijastan would produce 100 units, but Maxigania would produce only 80, and if instead they devoted all of their resources to growing tomatoes, Elijastan would produce 100 units, but Maxigania would only produce 40. When one nation can produce more of any particular good than another nation, it is said to have an *absolute advantage* in the production of that good. In this case, Elijastan has an absolute advantage in *both* goods.

We also see that the slopes of the PPCs are different for the two nations. The slope of Elijastan's PPC is 1 (we can ignore the negative sign), and the slope of Maxigania's PPC is 2. Recall that the slope tells us the opportunity costs of producing the good graphed on the *x* axis. Table 17-2 shows the opportunity cost of producing tomatoes and washing machines for both nations.

TABLE 17-2 Opportunity Costs for Elijastan and Maxigania

Elijastan		Maxigania	
Opportunity cost of 1 more tomato	Opportunity cost of 1 more washing machine	Opportunity cost of 1 more tomato	Opportunity cost of 1 more washing machine
= 1 washing machine	= 1 tomato	= 2 washing machines	$= \frac{1}{2}$ tomato

Elijastan can produce tomatoes at a cost of one washing machine for each tomato. Maxigania can also produce tomatoes, but at a cost of two washing machines for each tomato. When a nation can produce a good at a lower opportunity cost than another nation, that nation is said to have a *comparative advantage* in that good. Elijastan has a comparative advantage in tomato production. Maxigania has a comparative advantage in the production of washing machines because each washing machine costs it only $\frac{1}{2}$ of a tomato, while a washing machine costs Elijastan one full tomato.

Still Struggling

When we have linear PPCs, another way we can solve for opportunity cost is by using simple algebra. Let's start with Elijastan. Using all its resources (R), it can produce 100 washing machines, so $R = 100W$. If it devotes all its resources to making tomatoes, $R = 100T$. Note that:

$$100W = R = 100T$$

We can simplify this to:

$$100W = 100T$$

To find the opportunity cost of washing machines, we simply solve for W:

$$W = 100T/100 = T$$

so each washing machine costs one tomato. To find the opportunity cost of tomatoes, we solve for T:

$$T = 100W/100 = W$$

so each tomato costs one washing machine.

We can do the same for Maxigania:

$$80W = 40T$$

$$W = 40T/80 = \frac{1}{2}T$$

so one washing machine costs $\frac{1}{2}$ of a tomato. To find the opportunity cost of a tomato, we solve for T:

$$2W = T$$

so one tomato costs two washing machines.

How is this information about opportunity costs and comparative advantage useful? Suppose that each nation is currently producing at the midpoint (points M) of its PPC. Figure 17-4 shows this point of production.

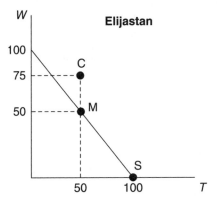 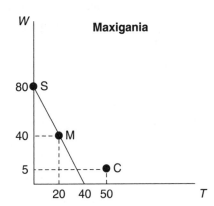

FIGURE 17-4 • Specialization and Gains from Trade

We have already seen that a nation's economy can grow with technological progress, but in 1817 David Ricardo wrote in his book *On the Principles of Political Economy and Taxation* that trade based upon specialization and comparative advantage can also allow a nation to consume beyond its PPC. To see how this works, we imagine that Elijastan *specializes* in producing tomatoes because it has a comparative advantage in that good. Maxigania specializes in producing washing machines because it has a comparative advantage in that good. These decisions to specialize are seen as points S in Figure 17-4.

TIP *The gains from trade come from comparative advantage, not absolute advantage. It is possible for a country to have an absolute advantage in producing both goods, as Elijastan does. It is not possible, however, for a country to have* *a comparative advantage in both goods. This means that as long as there are differences in opportunity costs (that is, the slopes of the two PPCs are not identical), there is* always *the possibility for gains from trade.*

The two specializing nations would then sit down to negotiate *terms of trade* that are mutually beneficial. Suppose we are trade representatives for Elijastan. Elijastan wants washing machines and can produce them without trade by giving up one tomato for each machine. If Elijastan is going to receive washing machines from Maxigania, each machine must cost less than one tomato or the deal doesn't benefit Elijastan.

Maxigania must also find acceptable terms of trade. Maxigania wants tomatoes and can produce them without trade by giving up two washing machines. If Maxigania is going to receive a tomato from Elijastan, it must cost less than two washing machines or it will not make the trade.

Suppose that these nations negotiate a trade such that, for every tomato that Elijastan sends to Maxigania, Maxigania will send 1.5 washing machines to Elijastan. Will this be mutually beneficial? Well, suppose that Elijastan sends half of its tomatoes (50) to Maxigania. According to the terms of trade, Maxigania will send 75 (1.5 × 50) washing machines to Elijastan. Without trade, Elijastan would have only 50 washing machines if it gave up 50 tomatoes. Now it has 75 washing machines and 50 tomatoes. That's better because it can now consume beyond its PPC, at point C in the graph.

What about Maxigania? It sent 75 washing machines to Elijastan, which seems like a lot, because it now has only 5 washing machines left. But it received 50 tomatoes in return. Given its resources and technology, 50 tomatoes weren't even possible without trade. That's better for Maxigania too, and we see that point C is beyond its PPC.

Still Struggling

At first it can be difficult to see where mutually beneficial terms of trade must be negotiated. One quick way to find the terms of trade is to go back to the opportunity cost of the good on the *x* axis. It costs Maxigania two washing machines for each tomato produced. It costs Elijastan one washing machine for each tomato produced. Elijastan has a comparative advantage in tomatoes, and the terms of trade must be somewhere between one and two washing machines for each tomato traded.

In other words, mutually beneficial terms of trade will exist when the exchange price is somewhere between the two countries' opportunity costs. Recall from our mathematical example that for Maxigania, $W = \frac{1}{2}T$, and for Elijastan, $W = 1T$. Therefore, a mutually beneficial trading price for washing machines would be between $\frac{1}{2}T$ and $1T$. Similarly, for Maxigania, $T = 2W$, and for Elijastan, $T = W$. Therefore, a mutually beneficial trading price for tomatoes would be between 1 and 2 washing machines. In our example, the price of tomatoes was $T = 1.5W$ (which is between the two countries' opportunity costs), and the price of washing machines was $W = 0.75T$ (which is between the two countries' opportunity costs).

Foreign Exchange Markets

When nations trade goods as in the example just given, they must also trade currencies. After all, the tomato growers in Elijastan want to be paid in their own currency so that they can spend the money in their own nation. When American companies sell products to European consumers, they don't want to be paid in euros, they want to be paid in dollars. And when Mexican firms sell their products to Americans, they want to be paid in pesos, not in dollars. This implies that the flow of goods and services is associated with a flow of currencies. The flow of currencies is facilitated by *currency markets*.

Suppose we focus on the trade between Mexico and the United States. The market for the U.S. dollar is priced in how many pesos it takes to buy a dollar. The supply of dollars $(S_\$)$ comes from Americans or anyone else who has dollars in his possession. The demand for dollars $(D_\$)$ comes from those who wish to buy goods made in America because they are priced in dollars. Figure 17-5 shows the market for U.S. dollars. At the equilibrium in the market, the current price of a U.S. dollar is 10 Mexican pesos. This is often called the *exchange rate*.

Of course, there is also a market for Mexican pesos. The market for pesos is the mirror image of the market for dollars. If it takes 10 pesos to get one dollar, it takes $\frac{1}{10}$ of a dollar to get one peso. Figure 17-6 shows the market for pesos.

Currency Appreciation and Depreciation

Just as market forces cause the prices of gasoline and clothing to change, market forces cause the price of a currency to change. We look at how the price of

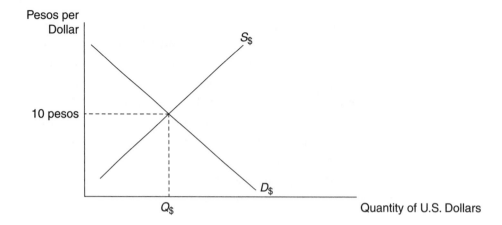

FIGURE 17-5 • The Market for U.S. Dollars

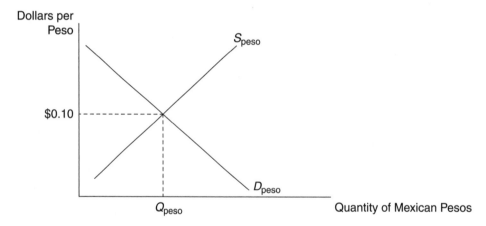

FIGURE 17-6 • The Market for Mexican Pesos

dollars and pesos can be affected by market forces and how rising and falling exchange rates affect the flow of trade between nations. Continuing the previous example, the market for the U.S. dollar is currently in equilibrium, and the exchange rate is 10 pesos to the dollar.

Suppose that the Mexican economy is experiencing a very strong recovery from a recession. Incomes are rising, and Mexican consumers are increasing their consumption of goods imported from the United States. If Mexican consumers want to buy American-made products, they are going to need dollars. And in order to get those dollars, they are going to need to supply their pesos in the market for pesos at the going exchange rate. Simultaneously, these transactions cause an increase in the supply of pesos and an increase in the demand for dollars. Suppose that when each market reaches a new equilibrium, the new price of a dollar is 12.5 pesos. This implies that the new price of a peso is $0.08. These shifts are seen in Figure 17-7.

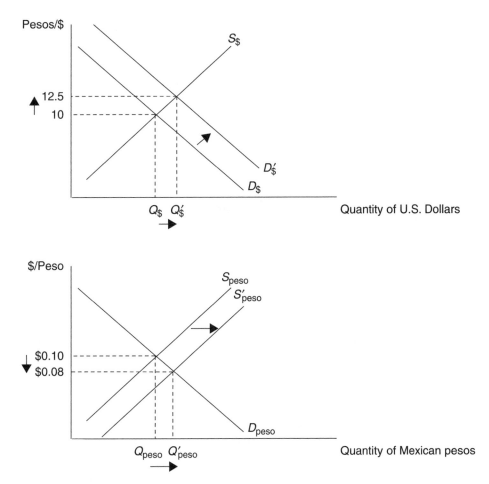

FIGURE 17-7 • Changes in Exchange Rates

Because it now takes more pesos to buy a U.S. dollar, the dollar is said to have *appreciated* in value. And because it now takes fewer dollars to buy a peso, the peso is said to have *depreciated* in value. There are several general reasons why demand for a currency may increase or decrease:

1. **Incomes in one nation are rising faster than incomes in other nations.** When a nation's economy is booming relative to those of its trading partners, that nation will import more goods from the other nations.

2. **Inflation is more rapid in one nation than in others.** If prices in Mexico are rising rapidly, but prices in the United States are stable, Mexican consumers will increase their demand for American-made goods and thus increase their demand for dollars. This is because American goods are now relatively cheaper to Mexican consumers.

3. **Interest rates are higher in one nation than in others.** If interest rates in the United States are higher than they are in Mexico, Mexicans will want to save their money in American financial assets like Treasury bonds. To do this, these savers increase their demand for dollars.

4. **Stronger preferences for goods made in one nation over others.** If Mexican consumers find American goods to be of higher quality, or more fashionable or trendy, then the demand for those goods, and the dollars needed to buy them, will increase.

How Do Exchange Rates Affect Aggregate Demand?

So how do exchange rates affect us on a daily basis? Suppose that you are an American who is planning a vacation in Mexico. When the exchange rate is 10 pesos to the dollar (or $0.10 dollar to the peso), your research discovers that you can reserve a hotel room that is priced at 1,000 pesos per night. If that exchange rate stays constant, this room will cost you $100 per night (1,000 pesos divided by 10 pesos per dollar). But suppose that the peso depreciates, and now each dollar can be exchanged at the rate of 12.5 pesos. The price of the hotel room for an American traveling to Mexico is now $80 (1,000 pesos divided by 12.5 pesos per dollar). So an appreciating dollar (each dollar buys more pesos) is good news for those who have dollars, like American consumers and firms that are looking to buy things in Mexico.

An appreciating dollar is also good for Mexico because more tourists will come from the United States to spend their new "stronger" dollars, and even those who stay home will purchase more goods produced in Mexico. Mexican vegetables will be less expensive in American grocery stores, for example. So when the dollar is appreciating against the peso, we expect to see more dollars flow to Mexico as Americans import more products from Mexico.

On the other hand, the Mexican peso is depreciating when the dollar is appreciating. Each peso now buys only $0.08, so Mexican consumers will find American-made products more expensive. They will reduce their imports from the United States, and they will find it more expensive to travel to the

United States for business or pleasure. Therefore, a depreciating peso causes fewer pesos to flow from Mexico into the United States as Mexicans import fewer products from the United States.

From Chapter 14, we know that when net exports decline, aggregate demand in the United States will shift to the left, reducing GDP and the price level, and increasing unemployment. A stronger dollar (and a weaker peso) reduces exports from the United States to Mexico and increases imports from Mexico into the United States. All else equal, this falling component of aggregate demand can weaken the U.S. economy. On the other hand, net exports in Mexico are rising because of a weaker peso, which, all else equal, should boost this component of the Mexican economy. Panel *a* of Figure 17-8 shows the negative impact that the stronger dollar has on aggregate demand in the U.S. economy, and panel *b* shows the positive impact that the weaker peso has on aggregate demand in the Mexican economy.

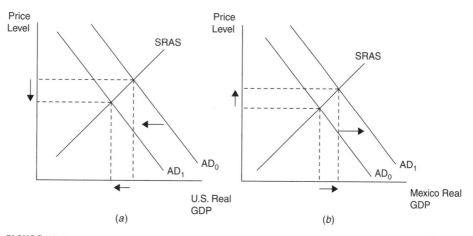

FIGURE 17-8 · Effect of a Stronger Dollar and Weaker Peso on (*a*) the U.S. Economy and (*b*) the Mexican Economy

Balance of Payments

Nations track the international flow of currency, goods and services, and physical and financial assets in their *balance of payments accounts*. Money from other nations can flow into the United States in several different ways:

- An American firm sells a foreigner a good or service.
- An American receives a foreign payment for her labor.
- An American company is sold to a foreign buyer.

- An American firm sells a financial asset to a foreign buyer.
- The U.S. government sells either financial assets or physical assets to foreigners.

We can think of transactions between nations as either those that are of a short-term nature or those that are more long-term investments. Table 17-3 shows a simplified and very hypothetical balance of payments for the United States for 2010.

TABLE 17-3 Hypothetical Balance of Payments for the United States

	Cash Flow from Foreigners	Cash Flow to Foreigners	Inflow – Outflow	
Current Account				
Exported goods and services	$15			
Imported goods and services		$30		
Balance on goods and services			$15 – $30 = –$15	
Factor income	$ 8	$ 6	$8 – $ 6 = $2	
Cash transfers	$10	$12	$10 – $12 = –$2	**Balance in current account = –$15**
Financial Account				
U.S. sale of assets to foreigners	$25			
U.S. purchase of foreign assets		$10		**Balance in financial account = $15**

Short-term transactions are included in the *current account* and include the import and export of goods and services and the flow of money as income for foreign and domestic labor. For example, in the table, the United States exports $15 worth of goods and services to other nations and imports $30 worth of goods and services from other nations. This reflects a *trade deficit in goods and services* and is a typical result in the U.S. balance of payments. If exports had exceeded imports, there would have been a *trade surplus*.

The current account also includes factor income that flows across borders. For example, if a British publisher pays an American author to write a book, this will show up as money that flows into the United States. Of course, companies in the United States also make factor payments to foreign workers.

The table indicates that $2 more money flowed into the United States than flowed out for factor payments.

The final entry in the current account is the transfer of cash across borders, called *remittances*. For example, a person from Guatemala may come to the United States and take a construction job. If he sends some of his wage dollars back to Guatemala, it would be recorded as dollars flowing out of the United States.

The *balance of payments on the financial account* tracks the flow of cash across borders for long-term assets, both physical and financial. For example, if an American company buys a building in Japan, this is a purchase of a physical asset and an outflow of dollars to Japan. If a Chinese bank buys a U.S. Treasury bond, this is a foreign purchase of a financial asset and an inflow of dollars into the United States. The Federal Reserve Bank and foreign central banks also engage in the buying and selling of U.S. financial assets, so this flow of dollars is not limited to private firms and individuals. Table 17-3 shows that the balance of payments on the financial account is positive.

It is no coincidence that the deficit in the current account is offset by the surplus in the financial account. For the most part, this is true of the actual balance of payments accounts. Why? The answer lies in the fact that U.S. dollars are really most useful when they are being used to either consume U.S. goods or invest in U.S. assets, including financial assets. Suppose that the United States has a trade deficit in goods and services. This means that foreign nations have sold Americans more goods and services than America has sold to them. Those foreign firms, citizens, and governments have a surplus of dollars on their hands. What will they do with the dollars? They will seek to invest them in physical assets, perhaps buying a company or a building, or financial assets, perhaps buying shares of stock in a U.S. company, saving their dollars in a U.S. bank, or purchasing U.S. Treasury bonds. If the United States had a current account surplus, the opposite would occur; Americans would have a surplus of foreign currencies, and they would find ways to invest those currencies back in those nations.

Foreign Currency and Economic Policy

The flow of cash between nations can also be influenced by domestic policies, particularly monetary policy. For example, suppose the Federal Reserve has used expansionary monetary policy to fight fears of higher unemployment. The effect of the monetary policy is to decrease interest rates and increase aggregate demand, but it also affects the international flow of dollars.

As interest rates in the United States begin to fall, the return on financial investments in the United States is less attractive to foreign investors. If we return to the example of the dollar and the Mexican peso, this would imply that Mexican investors would decrease their demand for dollars and decrease their supply of pesos to these financial markets.

Figure 17-9 below shows the impact of this monetary policy in the market for the dollar. The decreased demand for dollars causes the value of the dollar to depreciate. The peso is simultaneously appreciating. Because the peso is appreciating against the dollar, Mexican consumers will find American goods to be less expensive, thus increasing imports from America. This should cause net exports in the United States to rise, and this will also help to increase aggregate demand in the United States.

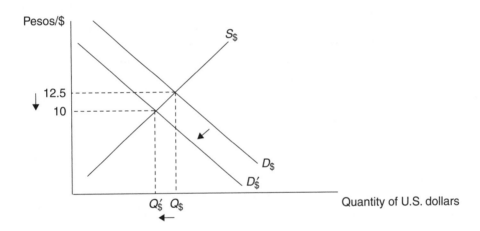

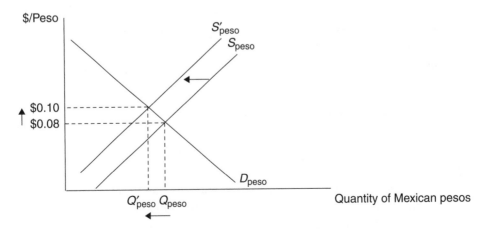

FIGURE 17-9 • Effect of Expansionary Monetary Policy on the Dollar-Peso Exchange Rate

Trade Barriers

So far in this chapter, we have discussed the benefits of free trade and the impact that trade has on the flow of currency across international borders. The final topic of this chapter is trade barriers.

The United States and many other nations grow sugar cane to make sugar. Suppose that in the domestic U.S. market for sugar, when trade does not exist, the price is $800 per ton, and 100,000 tons are consumed in equilibrium. Figure 17-10 shows the U.S. sugar market. If the price on the world market is $700 per ton, U.S. consumers would increase the quantity demanded to 120,000, but U.S. sugar producers would reduce their production to 80,000 tons. The difference between the domestic quantity supplied and the domestic quantity demanded (40,000 tons) is the amount of sugar that would be imported into the U.S. market.

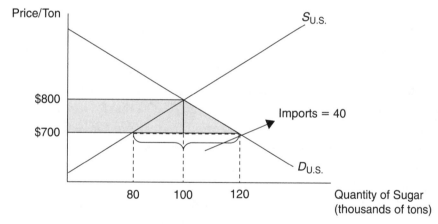

FIGURE 17-10 • The U.S. Sugar Market

Consumers definitely benefit from imported sugar at the lower price because their area of consumer surplus increases by the trapezoidal area shaded in Figure 17-10. Foreign suppliers of sugar benefit because they are able to expand their exports to the U.S. market. American sugar producers are not pleased because they have lost producer surplus and market share to the foreign competition.

Suppose sugar producers in the United States ask the government to protect them from foreign sugar imports by levying a *tariff* on imported sugar. A tariff is like an excise tax that is applied only to imported sugar and increases the U.S. price in Figure 17-11 to $750. At this higher price, quantity demanded falls

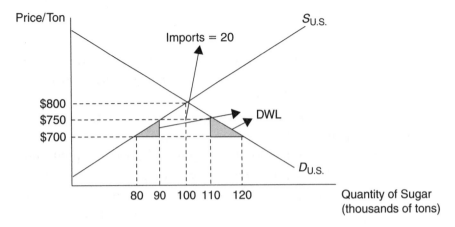

FIGURE 17-11 • Effect of a Tariff on the U.S. Sugar Market

to 110,000 tons, and domestic quantity supplied rises to 90,000 tons. After the tariff, only 20,000 tons of sugar are imported.

There are clear winners and losers from this tariff policy. Consumers lose some consumer surplus, while domestic producers gain back some producer surplus because the price has risen. Foreign sugar producers lose some customers and market share in the United States, and the U.S. government collects tariff revenue equal to $1,000,000 ($50 × 20,000 tons). Deadweight loss also exists because part of the gray trapezoid from Figure 17-10 doesn't go to anybody. This is seen as two small triangles in Figure 17-11.

Governments also use import *quotas* to reduce the quantity of a good that is allowed into the domestic market from foreign producers. Suppose in Figure 17-10 that the U.S. government had chosen to reduce the quantity of imported sugar from 40,000 tons to 20,000 tons. The impact of the quota would have been identical to the impact of the tariff, with one exception: there would have been no government tariff revenue.

In addition to the negative consequence of deadweight loss, economists generally disapprove of tariffs and quotas because they protect inefficient domestic producers at the expense of consumers and more efficient foreign producers. Foreign competition gives domestic producers a big incentive to produce their goods as efficiently as possible and to engage in research and development to improve their production technology. These improvements provide opportunities for long-run economic growth in the domestic economy.

Summary

This chapter began by introducing the production possibilities model and using it to show how nations can mutually gain from trade based upon comparative advantage. We then introduced the market for foreign currency and used that market to explain how and why currencies appreciate and depreciate and how changes in the value of a currency affect net exports. Next, we discussed the balance of payments statement, which tracks the flow of dollars to and from foreigners. A connection was made between monetary policy, the interest rate, and foreign exchange markets. Finally, the impact of tariffs and quotas was presented to show that these forms of trade barriers create inefficiencies.

QUIZ

Is each of the following statements *true* or *false*? Explain.

1. Nations that trade on the basis of comparative advantage can consume beyond their production possibilities curve.

2. If a large nation can outproduce a small nation in all goods and services, there is no way that the large nation can benefit by trading with the small nation.

3. Tariffs and quotas both create deadweight loss, but quotas lower the price of an imported product, while tariffs increase the price of that product.

4. If the dollar has appreciated against the euro, we know that the demand for the dollar has increased.

5. A trade deficit occurs when a nation imports more goods and services than it exports.

For each of the following, choose the answer that best fits.

Use Table 17-4 to answer questions 6 and 7.

TABLE 17-4

		Wine	Cheese			Wine	Cheese
Spain	All resources used to produce wine	30	0	**Portugal**	All resources used to produce wine	10	0
	All resources used to produce cheese	0	30		All resources used to produce cheese	0	20

6. Suppose that Spain and Portugal can both produce wine and cheese. The production possibilities are given in Table 17-4. If Spain uses all its resources to produce wine, it can produce 30 units of wine. If it uses all its resources to produce cheese, it can produce 30 units of cheese. Likewise, if Portugal uses all its resources to produce wine, it can produce 10 units of wine. If it uses all its resources to produce cheese, it can produce 20 units of cheese. We know that:
   A. Spain has an absolute advantage in both wine and cheese.
   B. Spain has an absolute advantage in wine, and Portugal has an absolute advantage in cheese.
   C. Portugal has a comparative advantage in both wine and cheese.
   D. Spain has a comparative advantage in wine, and Portugal has an absolute advantage in cheese.

7. Suppose that Spain and Portugal can both produce wine and cheese. The production possibilities are given in Table 17-4. If these nations trade based on comparative advantage,
   A. Both nations will consume inside their production possibilities curve.
   B. Spain should trade cheese to Portugal in exchange for wine.
   C. Portugal should trade cheese to Spain in exchange for wine.
   D. There is no trade that can allow these nations to consume beyond their PPCs.

8. The United States and Japan engage in trade with each other. Suppose that the Federal Reserve increases interest rates through monetary policy. Given this, how would the demand for the dollar, the value of the dollar against the Japanese yen, and the supply of the yen change?

Demand for Dollar	Value of Dollar	Supply of Yen
A. Increase	Increase	Decrease
B. Decrease	Decrease	Decrease
C. Increase	Decrease	Increase
D. Increase	Increase	Increase

9. Suppose the United States trades with the nation of Ame. The currency of Ame is the quid. If American consumers become infatuated with all products made by Ame, we would expect the _____ dollars to _____ and the quid to _____ against the dollar.
   A. demand for; increase; appreciate
   B. supply of; increase; appreciate
   C. demand for; decrease; depreciate
   D. supply of; decrease; depreciate

10. Which of the following would *not* be a typical consequence of an import tariff?
   A. Producer surplus increases in the domestic market.
   B. Consumer surplus increases in the domestic market.
   C. Deadweight loss is created.
   D. Government revenue is created.

chapter **18**

Public Goods and the Environment

Up to this point, in both micro and macro chapters, we have focused on goods and services that are easily (and often efficiently) exchanged in markets. These are referred to as *private goods*. However, there are some goods and services, called *public goods*, that cannot be efficiently exchanged in markets. In this chapter, we return our focus to micro product markets and explore the difference between private goods and public goods, and develop the concept of positive and negative externalities. Because public goods and externalities represent *market failures*, we also discuss ways in which government can attempt to remedy these market failures and provide goods that markets cannot provide.

CHAPTER OBJECTIVES

After completing this chapter, the student should be able to:

1. Explain the difference between private and public goods.

2. Understand the free-rider problem and why it prevents markets from providing public goods efficiently.

3. Construct a graph that shows the impact that negative and positive externalities have on the market for some goods and services.

4. Explain how policies can remedy these externalities and provide more efficient outcomes in those markets.

Private and Public Goods

Up to now, when we have discussed goods and services, we have used examples of *private goods*—markets for chicken nuggets, gasoline, bicycles, maps, and other such things. These are private goods because they share two important characteristics:

- **They are *excludable*.** Those who do not pay to consume a box of chicken nuggets are excluded from consuming that box of chicken nuggets.
- **They are *rival in consumption*.** The same gallon of gasoline that I purchase and burn in my car cannot also be purchased by you and burned in your car.

Examples of *public goods* include national defense, street lamps, disease prevention, and fire protection. Why are these not private goods? Because these goods and services have neither of these characteristics; in fact, they are:

- **Nonexcludable.** I cannot be excluded from the benefits of national defense even if I strongly believe that the military is a poor use of taxpayers' money.
- **Nonrival.** If I walk beneath a street lamp and use that benefit, I do not deprive the next person of the same illumination.

NOTE   *Private goods and public goods are polar opposites because they either do or do not have these two characteristics. However, there are goods that fall between these two extremes. For example, there are artificially scarce (or club) goods that are excludable but nonrival. A pay-per-view sporting event is such a good. It is excludable because the event is available only to those homes that are willing and able to pay the fee. However, it is nonrival because millions of homes can watch the same event simultaneously. Because it is more efficient for these types of goods to be produced by natural monopolies, some economists refer to these goods as "natural monopoly goods."*

There are also common resources that are rival but nonexcludable. A school of bluefin tuna in the ocean is an example. Those fish are rival because once I have harvested a fish, it cannot be harvested again. They are nonexcludable because anyone with a boat can go on the open seas and fish for tuna. Because nobody owns the common resource and everyone has an interest in harvesting it, such resources tend to be overharvested. Written descriptions of the problem with commonly held resources have been traced as far back as the Greek philosophers Thucydides and Aristotle. In 1968, ecologist Garrett Hardin published a more contemporary and often-cited article, "The Tragedy of the Commons," that has become a foundation of the argument for sustainably harvesting such resources so that they are not made extinct. Policies such as limited seasons and expensive licenses to fish have helped, but not solved, this problem with ocean fisheries.

Providing Public Goods

Markets can provide private goods fairly effectively. These markets may not always be competitive and efficient (monopoly, for example), but at least the goods are provided for sale to consumers. But if a good is nonexcludable and nonrival, why won't a market also provide it? Suppose that there were a producer of milk in the community and the milk was nonexcludable. This means that the producer would provide milk to everyone who wanted milk, even if she didn't pay for it. It's highly unlikely that the milk would ever be produced by a private firm whose objective is to maximize profits. The same would be true of a privately owned firm that sought to profit from installing street lamps around town. If a person could benefit from the light without having to pay, there's no way for the firm to earn profit from it.

The nonexcludability of the street lamps and other public goods means that their provision suffers from the *free-rider problem*. There are many individuals who benefit from the public good, but will not pay for it, even though they still hope to enjoy it. In other words, they want to take a free ride. If there are sufficient benefits to be gained, and yet no private firm can emerge to sell the good, the government must provide it. So if government is required to provide a public good like fire protection services and national defense, how much of that good should be provided? Once again, it should depend upon the additional benefit that society would receive and the additional cost that society would incur.

Still Struggling

It's helpful to arrange the different types of goods in a table, as in Table 18-1.

TABLE 18-1 Characteristics and Types of Goods		
	Excludable?	
	Yes	**No**
Rival? **Yes**	*Private Goods* Chicken nuggets Gasoline	*Common Resources* Fish in the ocean Special problem: tragedy of the commons
No	*Artificially Scarce Goods* Cable television Phone service	*Public Goods* National defense Street lamps Special problem: free–rider problem

Note that the two types of goods with a special problem have something in common: they are nonexcludable. This is because a nonexcludable good has no price. Price is an important concept in economics because it serves the purpose of indicating the value of something to a buyer and its value to a seller. Recall that it is price that adjusts to bring quantity supplied and quantity demanded together. In other words, for nonexcludable goods, the rationing function of a price has failed, leading to a market failure.

Suppose Madisonville is trying to determine the number of police officers to employ to protect its citizens and enforce the laws. Each officer will cost the city $50,000. To gauge the benefit each citizen believes he will receive from an additional officer, the city surveys Average Joe, who represents each of the 1,000 people in Madisonville. Joe is asked, "How much would you be willing to pay for one police officer? How much for the second officer?" until he responds that he will not pay anything for more than eight officers. Joe's *willingness to pay* is also his individual marginal benefit for additional officers. If we multiply Joe's own marginal benefit by 1,000 citizens in town, we get the *marginal social benefit* that the town places upon each additional officer. Table 18-2 compares the marginal benefit, the marginal social benefit, and the marginal cost of each police officer.

TABLE 18-2 Marginal Benefit, Marginal Social Benefit, and Marginal Cost of a Police Officer

Number of Police Officers	Average Joe's Marginal Benefit	Madisonville's Marginal Social Benefit (MSB)	Marginal Cost of an Officer
1	$150	1,000 × $150 = $150,000	$50,000
2	$130	$130,000	$50,000
3	$110	$110,000	$50,000
4	$ 90	$ 90,000	$50,000
5	$ 70	$ 70,000	$50,000
6	$ 50	$ 50,000	$50,000
7	$ 30	$ 30,000	$50,000
8	$ 10	$ 10,000	$50,000

The results of this survey show that the marginal social benefit of hiring police officers is exactly equal to the marginal cost when six officers are hired. Figure 18-1 converts this analysis into graphical form. Beyond six officers, there is still marginal social benefit; it's just not enough to justify the marginal cost. The area of the triangle below MSB and above MC gives the total value of the social surplus (TS) earned from the efficient hiring of six officers.

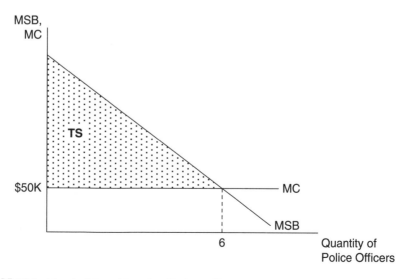

FIGURE 18-1 • Marginal Social Benefit of Police Officers

TIP   *Many citizens, and all politicians, believe that when it comes to police protection and crime prevention, there is never too much. Many people feel the same way about public education, scientific research, national defense, and environmental protection. These are all public goods, but as the hypothetical example just given shows, there is an efficient amount of a public good. If government provides more than this amount, it is devoting resources to a good for which the marginal cost exceeds the marginal benefit. For example, if Madisonville had employed a seventh police officer, the city would have received marginal social benefit of $30,000, but that officer would have cost the city $50,000. From a social welfare perspective, this is wasteful because it generates a negative net benefit of $20,000. There is probably another project that could benefit from the $50,000. Maybe Madisonville has hired so many police officers that it doesn't have any parks. If the first public park had an MSB greater than $50,000, the city should eliminate the seventh officer and build a park.*

The moral of this example is that, even with public goods, it is possible to "have too much of a good thing"!

Positive Externalities

Suppose you live in an apartment building or dorm and someone next door plays music that you really enjoy. You don't have to pay for that person's music, but you receive benefit from it. This is a *positive externality*. If your roommate gets a flu shot and you do not, you are receiving benefit from your roommate's vaccination, but you don't have to pay for it. And when your next door neighbors spend lots of money to keep their house and yard beautiful, it not only improves the value of their home but also improves the value of yours. As we have seen throughout much of this book, when people consume goods and services, they receive individual benefit from that consumption, and that *private benefit* is reflected in the price that they are willing to pay for it. These examples demonstrate that sometimes third parties receive *spillover benefits* when others consume goods and services. Most of the time these spillover benefits are not reflected in the price of the good, and this leads to a failure of the market to provide the socially optimal quantity of that good.

Suppose that when a homeowner purchases landscaping services (either through his own efforts or with a paid service), it provides a positive externality to the rest of the community by raising property values. The *marginal private benefit* (MPB) of consuming the landscaping is enjoyed by those who actually purchase it; this is reflected in the market demand curve for it. When there are positive spillover benefits to neighbors, the *marginal social benefit* (MSB) from landscaping is greater than the marginal private benefit. In Figure 18-2, this is seen as a MSB curve that lies above the MPB = *D* curve. The vertical distance between the two curves is the amount of the spillover benefit.

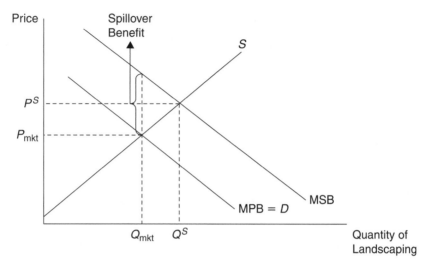

FIGURE 18-2 • Spillover Benefit

Figure 18-2 shows two important intersections. The market for landscaping services will come to equilibrium at the intersection of the demand and supply curves. The equilibrium price will be P_{mkt} and the quantity will be Q_{mkt}. But the demand curve reflects only the marginal private benefits of this good. If we acknowledge the spillover benefits to society, then the socially desirable quantity is Q^S at a price of P^S. We see that the market will underproduce this good relative to the quantity that is socially efficient. This is why economists call it a market failure.

Negative Externalities

If you have ever driven past a smelly factory, paper mill, meatpacking plant, or large livestock operation, you have experienced a *negative externality*. As we have seen in Chapter 5, when goods are produced, the firms producing them incur costs. The costs to these producers can be described as *marginal private costs*. But if the production of these goods creates a bad smell, a plume of smoke, a discharge of foul liquid, harm to humans or wildlife, reduced property values, or anything else that might cause harm to the broader society, there are also *spillover costs* that should be acknowledged. The market price of the product almost never reflects spillover costs, and thus the market fails to produce the socially optimal quantity of the product.

Suppose that the production of chickens in large, confined feeding operations creates a "fowl" odor that drifts downwind to a small village. The smell makes it difficult for homeowners to sell their property, and so property values fall. This is a spillover cost to society that is not included in the *marginal private cost* (MPC) of producing chicken. The MPC reflects only the production costs incurred by the producers and, as we saw in Chapter 5, is also the market supply curve. Figure 18-3 shows that the *marginal social cost* (MSC) curve lies above the MPC = S curve. The vertical distance between the two curves is the amount of the spillover cost.

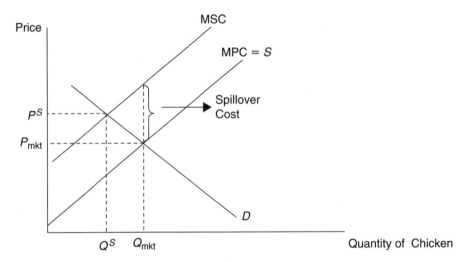

FIGURE 18-3 • Spillover Cost

Equilibrium in the chicken market happens at the quantity Q_{mkt} and the price P_{mkt}. But the supply curve reflects only the marginal private costs of this good. When we acknowledge the spillover costs to society, then the socially desirable quantity is Q^S at a price of P^S. Left to the market, chickens will be overproduced relative to the socially optimal quantity. Again, this is a market failure. We next discuss how government might design a policy to achieve the optimal quantity and eliminate the market failures of both positive and negative externalities.

TIP *When we are dealing with externalities, it is important for us to be able to distinguish between what the market* actually *does and what it* should *do if the social costs and benefits are taken into account. The market considers only* inter-nal *costs and benefits, but external costs and benefits (that is, costs and benefits that affect someone other than the buyer and the seller) also matter. This gives us a hint at how to solve the problems of externalities: find a way to make the market internalize them.*

Government Remedies for Externalities

If the market underproduces goods that generate positive externalities and overproduces goods that generate negative externalities, it makes sense to some that the government should try to promote consumption of the former and deter consumption of the latter.

First we look at the market for landscaping services that were generating spillover benefits to the neighborhood. One way we can prompt more consumption of a good is to provide consumers a subsidy. If the subsidy is exactly equal to the spillover benefit, the MPB curve will shift upward to the MSB curve.

Figure 18-4 shows how a government subsidy of S dollars could work to increase the quantity of landscaping services from Q_{mkt} to Q^S. The price that sellers of landscaping services receive increases to P^S, which is good for the

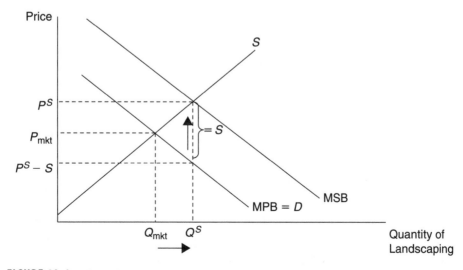

FIGURE 18-4 • Effect of a Government Subsidy on a Positive Externality

firms, and the price paid by the consumers is S dollars lower ($P^S - S$). As a result, both sellers and buyers benefit from the subsidy.

TIP *From Figure 18-4, it appears that the price of landscaping has risen. So then how can we say that the price paid by consumers has actually fallen? The subsidy creates a gap between the price that sellers receive at the cash register (P^S) and the price that consumers eventually pay ($P^S - S$). Try to think of the subsidy as something that works like a coupon. Suppose you have a coupon that says "$1 off your next Sno Cone." When you take the coupon to the Sno Cone shack, the seller tells you that a Sno Cone costs $3, but you hand over the "$1 off" coupon and only $2 cash. The subsidy works the same way, except that it's the government giving you a coupon that you can redeem for landscaping services.*

Next we look at the market for chicken that was generating spillover costs to the downwind village. If there is too much production of a good, the government can tax that good to reduce the production of it. If the tax is exactly equal to the spillover cost, the MPC curve will shift upward to the MSC curve.

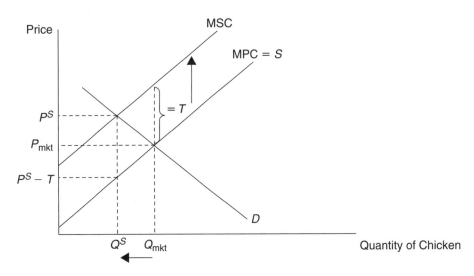

FIGURE 18-5 • Effect of a Tax on a Negative Externality

Figure 18-5 shows how a government tax of T dollars could work to reduce the quantity of chicken being produced from Q_{mkt} to Q^S. Consumers pay a higher price P^S than before, and sellers receive a lower price equal to ($P^S - T$). Like the excise taxes discussed in Chapter 6, this means that both buyers and sellers share in the burden of the tax.

Still Struggling

If the production of chicken (to continue with the example) generates pollution that is harmful to others, why isn't the best strategy to simply outlaw the production of chicken and anything else that creates a negative externality? Remember that, although the chicken producers are polluting the air, the market for chicken is creating social welfare in the form of consumer and producer surplus. The point of the tax is to *internalize* the externality. By requiring the consumers and producers of chicken to pay a tax on this item, we reduce output to the level that maximizes social welfare. It does *not* eliminate the pollution; it reduces it to an efficient level. We discuss the economic approach to designing effective policies for reducing pollution in the next section of the chapter.

NOTE   *The per-unit subsidies and taxes just described to fix the market failures of externalities are often called* Pigouvian subsidies and taxes *after the English economist Arthur Pigou. Pigou did some early work on the topic of externalities and their effects on economic efficiency. One of the difficulties with these remedies, a difficulty that Pigou himself noted, is that it is difficult to precisely measure the exact size of the subsidy or tax necessary to eliminate the market failure. Some economists argue that if this is miscalculated, the policy may even worsen the problem rather than fixing it.*

How Can Economics Reduce Pollution?

Some people argue that the efficient level of pollution is *zero* pollution, but this would require the elimination of the entire chicken market (and many other markets). Consumers would lose all of their consumer surplus and producers their producer surplus. Reducing pollution to zero levels would have significant opportunity costs. Despite the significant benefits to our health and the environment, society would be worse off. Remember from our discussion of public goods that there are people who also claim that there can never be too much law enforcement, national defense, or public education. If there can be too much of a bad thing (pollution), it makes sense that there can also be too much of a good thing (pollution reduction).

We all consume goods and services, and we enjoy the benefits from those goods. Unfortunately, when those goods are produced, pollution is created. Thus, there is a benefit (the goods and services) to pollution. Of course there are very real costs to pollution. Likewise, there are benefits from reducing pollution and costs of reducing pollution. Economists argue that we need to strike a balance between society's gains from reducing pollution and society's costs of doing so. Let's use our finely honed skills of marginal analysis to figure out how much pollution is efficient.

Figure 18-6 shows an upward-sloping *marginal social cost* of pollution curve. As more tons of pollution are emitted, the pollution does more and more damage to our buildings, our health, our atmosphere, and the rest of our natural environment.

There is also a downward-sloping *marginal social benefit* of pollution curve. How can there be additional benefit from more tons of pollution? Imagine what we would need to do to reduce pollution by one ton. Suppose we would need to spend $5 million of society's scarce resources to install special air or water filters to clean a factory's emissions. If we *allow* that ton of pollutants, it frees up that $5 million to be spent on something else that has value.

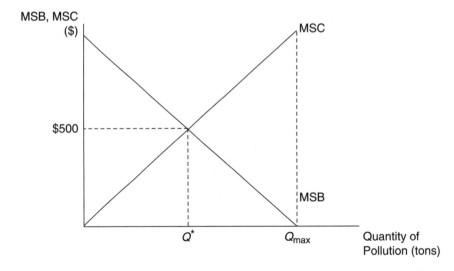

FIGURE 18-6 • Costs and Benefits of Pollution

In Figure 18-6, we see that if unregulated polluters are allowed to emit until the marginal social benefit equals zero, they will emit a maximum quantity of pollution at Q_{max}. At this point, the MSC would be extremely high, and we can imagine a very dirty environment in which to live! The efficient level of pollution is Q^*, where the MSB = MSC at $500. The big question is, how can we best get to Q^* rather than Q_{max}?

Command-and-Control Standards

Let's begin with the premise that the government could dictate either that pollution be abolished, a policy that would deprive us of most of the goods and services that make up modern society, or that there be strict limits on the pollution that each firm can produce. This latter approach has been called *command-and-control* policies. For example, the government might say that every plastics factory, whether it is old and rusty or new and shiny, must reduce pollution by the same amount. Economists don't favor this type of policy because it is inefficient, inasmuch as there is a less costly way to achieve the same goal. Let's see why.

Suppose that there are two plastics factories: Dusty Rusty (DR) and Fancy Schmancy (FS) Plastics. The DR firm has been around for nearly 70 years and uses old technology to control emissions. The FS firm has just recently begun operations and uses state-of-the-industry pollution controls. Because it is more costly for DR to reduce emissions, it has a higher marginal benefit (MB_{DR}) curve to pollute in Figure 18-7. In an unregulated market, each firm would emit to the point where MB = 0, and this would occur at 1,000 tons each.

Now suppose the government said that each producer must reduce its emissions by half, to 500 tons each. Both firms can achieve this standard, but economists see this as inefficient. Why? Because the same result could be achieved at

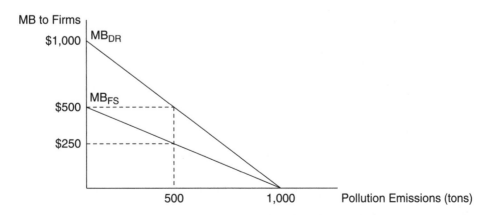

FIGURE 18-7 • Marginal Benefit to Pollute for Two Firms

lower cost. For example, suppose FS Plastics reduced its emissions by one more ton. It would cost the firm slightly more than $250 to do so. This would allow DR Plastics to increase pollution by one ton at a benefit of slightly less than $500. Society would gain nearly $250 of additional benefit ($500 of benefit – $250 of cost), and pollution would be the same as it would be if each reduced emissions by half. If we can keep pollution at the same level *and lower the cost of doing so*, then the standard is inefficient. So long as the cost of reducing the next ton of emissions differs for any two polluters, the cost of reducing pollution could be lower and more efficient.

Pollution Taxes

Economists love efficient solutions to a problem. Pollution standards, or command-and-control policies, are inefficient because the costs differ for our two plastics companies. One way to achieve efficiency is to levy an emissions tax on each ton of pollution and to set that tax so that the cost of reducing pollution is the same and the pollution is reduced to a safe level.

If we revisit the previous example, we begin with the goal of reducing pollution by half, to a total of 1,000 tons. If we set an emissions tax of $400 per ton, each firm will emit pollution up to the point where its MB curve intersects the $400 tax (see Figure 18-8). For FS plastics, this happens more quickly, at 400 tons, because it is more efficient. The inefficient polluting firm, DR Plastics, continues to emit 600 tons of pollution. Because the MB of polluting is $400 for each firm, there is no opportunity for the firms to "trade" tons of pollution to lower total cost. This is an efficient outcome.

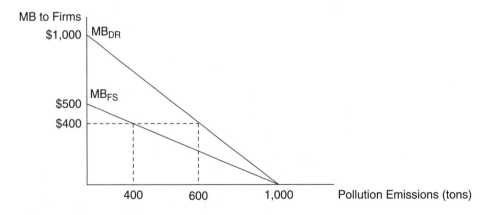

FIGURE 18-8 · Effects of a Pollution Tax

Not only is the pollution tax efficient, but it also generates tax revenue for the government and provides an incentive for both firms to become more efficient in their emissions control. For example, FS Plastics is currently sending $160,000 ($400 × 400 tons) to the government, and DR Plastics is sending $240,000. Over time, if these firms can improve their pollution control technology, their MB curves will shift downward, fewer tons will be emitted, and smaller checks will be sent to the government.

Tradable Pollution Permits

A chief concern with a Pigouvian tax on a negative externality like pollution is that it can be difficult to measure the precise size of the tax that will lead to the socially efficient level of output being produced. One way to get around that is to create a market for the right to emit pollution and then let the market determine the price necessary to reduce pollution to the desired amount. Most of these policies are referred to under the name *cap and trade*. How do they work?

Again suppose that the government has decided that a total of 1,000 tons of pollution from our plastics industry is an acceptable amount for society. Each firm is allocated 500 pollution permits that give it the right to emit 500 tons into the environment. This initial situation (Figure 18-9) looks quite similar to Figure 18-7, except that the vertical line represents the number of permits allocated to each firm.

Suppose that our clean firm, FS Plastics, doesn't need one of its permits. It could put that permit in the drawer and reduce pollution by one ton at a

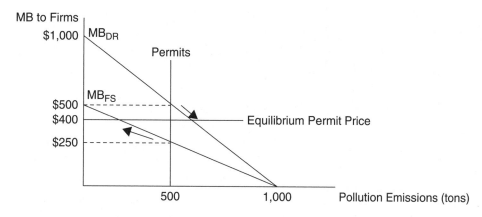

FIGURE 18-9 · Initial Effect of a Cap-and-Trade Policy

marginal cost of about $250, or it could look for a buyer for the permit. Would DR Plastics buy the permit? Sure! If DR Plastics emits one more ton of pollution, it will receive a marginal benefit of just under $500, so if it can buy a permit at a price lower than $500, it will do so. Somewhere between $250 and $500, FS Plastics will sell this one permit to DR Plastics, and a market for pollution permits has been established. DR Plastics will buy permits from FS Plastics and increase its pollution along its MB_{DR} curve. As FS Plastics has fewer permits, it will reduce pollution along its MB_{FS} curve. Negotiations like this will take place until there are no more gains to be made from trading permits in this market. The only place where this occurs is where the MB of the next ton of pollution, and thus the price of pollution permits, is the same for both firms. Just as with the pollution tax, this occurs at a price of $400 per ton.

Another way to see what is happening is to draw a market for the permits like the one in Figure 18-10. The supply is vertical and fixed at 1,000 tons, and the demand for a permit is downward-sloping because the MB for pollution is downward-sloping. The equilibrium price of a permit is $400. Over time, the government can reduce the emissions that go into our environment by issuing fewer pollution permits. If firms continue to use the same emissions control technology, the price of a permit will begin to rise. Because firms have an incentive to clean up their emissions (they can sell permits rather than buy them), the demand for permits will gradually decrease. In either case, we clean up our environment.

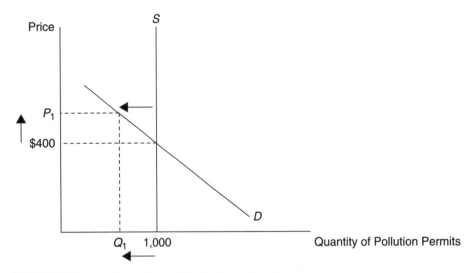

FIGURE 18-10 · Supply and Demand for Pollution Permits

The Coase Theorem

Suppose that you live in a building of condominiums and your neighbor plays his heavy metal music very loudly. Every day the music shakes your walls so much that a drinking glass falls off the shelf and shatters. When you replace the glass, it costs you $5, so his negative externality costs you $5 per day. Economist Ronald Coase, in his 1960 article "The Problem of Social Cost," proposed that negative externalities between two parties could be remedied without government intervention so long as property rights were clear and transaction costs between the parties were low. Transaction costs refer to the costs of the two parties negotiating an agreement. Property rights identify whether the polluter, in this case your neighbor, has the right to pollute (play loud music), or whether the victim (you) has the right to have intact drinking glasses.

Let's say that your neighbor has the right to play his music as loud as he wants, but his music costs you $5 each day. The Coase theorem implies that you could approach your neighbor and offer him up to $5 to not play his music. If he agrees, the externality is removed. You get to keep your drinking glasses intact, and he gets cash to forgo the music that he loves, or to turn down the volume.

Another possibility is that your neighbor loves his loud music, so he approaches you and offers you at least $5 to compensate you for the inevitable damage to your property. You're both happy because he pays for the right to play the music and you are compensated for the damage.

In the real world, the Coase theorem is often difficult to implement because transaction costs, such as negotiating compensation or enforcing an agreement, are not small. In our neighbor example, if your neighbor agrees to pay you $6 per day for the damage, but then never does, your only recourse may be to take him to small claims court, a costly and probably fruitless endeavor. If the pollution from a large factory is injuring thousands of people, there is no practical way for those victims to negotiate with the factory to find a mutually satisfactory agreement on compensation. In this case, the courts or the Environmental Protection Agency must become involved.

Summary

This chapter began by addressing the difference between private goods and public goods and explained why public goods cannot be efficiently produced in the market; the government must usually produce such goods. Positive externalities exist in markets when the exchanges of some good convey spillover benefits to third parties. The market fails because it underproduces the good, producing less than the socially efficient quantity. Per-unit subsidies can attempt to fix the market failure of a positive externality. Negative externalities, like pollution, exist when the market for a good imposes spillover costs on third parties. In this case, the market fails because it overproduces the good, producing more than the efficient quantity. Government can attempt to lessen the damage caused by pollution with environmental standards, emission taxes, or creating a market for tradable permits. The Coase theorem is also a way to eliminate a negative externality if the property rights are clear and the transaction costs are low. In the next chapter, we address a type of good that also seems to not "play by the rules" when it comes to markets—healthcare.

QUIZ

Is each of the following statements *true* or *false*? Explain.

1. **The presence of free riders prevents the market from producing cheeseburgers effectively.**

2. **One reason why public education is subsidized by the government is that education creates a positive externality.**

3. **Negative externalities create market failure, but positive externalities do not.**

4. **Command-and-control pollution standards tend to be more efficient than taxes on pollution.**

5. **If the consumption of a good creates a positive externality, it is true that the marginal social benefit exceeds the marginal social cost at the market equilibrium quantity.**

For each of the following, choose the answer that best fits.

6. **Which of the following is the best example of a public good?**
   A. Mountain bikes
   B. Cable TV
   C. Electricity
   D. Scientific research

7. **Suppose the market for gleeks generates a negative externality. At the market equilibrium, which of the following is true?**
   A. $MSC > MPC = MSB$
   B. $MSC = MPC = MSB$
   C. $MSC = MPC > MSB$
   D. $MSC > MPC > MSB$

8. **Which of the following would *not* be an appropriate policy to reduce pollution caused by power plants?**
   A. Issue a fixed quantity of pollution permits to power plants so that they can be traded in a market.
   B. Provide a subsidy to households for each unit of electricity consumed.
   C. Impose a tax on power plants for each unit of pollution emitted.
   D. Impose a tax on power plants for each unit of electricity produced.

Use Figure 18-11 to respond to questions 9 and 10.

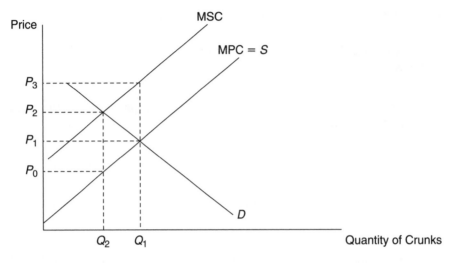

FIGURE 18-11

9. **Figure 18-11 shows the market for crunks. From the graph, we can see that crunks are a:**
   A. Private good that generates a positive externality
   B. Public good
   C. Private good that generates a negative externality
   D. Normal good

10. **Figure 18-11 shows the market for crunks. The unregulated crunk market will produce an equilibrium price of _____ and an equilibrium quantity of _____.**
    A. $P_2; Q_2$
    B. $P_3; Q_1$
    C. $P_0; Q_2$
    D. $P_1; Q_1$

chapter 19

Health Economics and the Market for Health Insurance

The healthcare industry has recently garnered a great deal of attention during the debates leading up to the passage of the Patient Protection and Affordable Care Act of 2010 (PPACA 2010, but sometimes also just called the Affordable Care Act). However, much of the debate and public discourse on this act indicates that, by and large, the public does not understand how this industry works. In this chapter, we examine the markets for health and healthcare. We start by discussing why healthcare in the United States is financed differently from the way it is financed in any other country. We continue by explaining why we have to reexamine our assumptions about markets and the consequences of healthcare markets being fundamentally different, and the difficulties this presents for a healthcare financing system. Finally, we discuss the demand for health insurance and the challenges of setting health insurance premiums.

CHAPTER OBJECTIVES

After completing this chapter, the student should be able to:

1. Briefly describe the historical development of the U.S. healthcare financing system.

2. Describe why healthcare is fundamentally different from other goods and how increasing competition may have unintended consequences in healthcare markets.

3. Define asymmetric information and moral hazard, and describe how these affect healthcare markets.

4. Explain the premium death spiral and the benefits and drawbacks of insurance mandates.

Introduction to Health Economics

The largest industry in the United States in terms of share of GDP is government (including federal, state, and local governments). Many people would be surprised to learn that the second-largest industry in the United States is not the automotive industry or steel, but healthcare. In fact, according to most estimates, healthcare makes up around 17 percent of GDP and is growing much faster than any other industry.

Given the size of this industry, it might be also be surprising that the field of health economics is somewhat new. The academic journal of health economics research, the *Journal of Health Economics*, did not begin publishing until 1982. In fact, a paper that is considered to be the seminal (beginning) work in health economics, "Uncertainty and the Welfare Economics of Medical Care," by a Nobel Prize–winning economist named Kenneth Arrow, was not published until 1963. Why did healthcare as an industry suddenly start to attract attention? To answer this question, we have to start with a brief history of how *healthcare financing*, or the way healthcare is paid for, has changed in the United States over the past 100 years. As with so much else in economics, the changes began around the time of the Great Depression.

Prior to 1900, healthcare was still fairly primitive. Germ theory was relatively new, and the introduction of anesthesia during the Victorian era had just made surgery a less barbaric option. In the early 1900s, there was a radical alteration in medical education that changed physicians from a hodgepodge group of variously qualified tradesmen into a profession with a set of standards for education, training, and ethics. However, the technology available was still fairly simple—x-rays were not used therapeutically until 1908, and even though it was discovered in 1928, penicillin wasn't in widespread use until the 1940s.

When it came to financing, this was also fairly simple. The health insurance that we are familiar with today simply did not exist. While *casualty* insurance, or insurance to cover a defined loss, had been in existence since antiquity, commercial insurers were not interested in insuring healthcare because of the difficulty in defining a loss (in other words, how can you really insure "health"?). If you needed healthcare, either you paid for it out of your own pocket, you received charity care, or you simply went without it.

Even though most hospitals were not-for-profit entities, their revenues were severely affected by the Great Depression. Take, for example, Baylor University Hospital (BUH) in Dallas, Texas. In 1929, hospital receipts (that is, money received from patients) were $236 per patient, but in 1930, those receipts were a mere $56 per patient. Meanwhile, charity care had increased 400 percent. As bad as this sounds, BUH was doing better than many other hospitals at the time, and many closed. This was obviously not sustainable, however, and a BUH hospital administrator came up with a plan. The hospital approached the Dallas Independent School District and offered it a hospital plan—if every single teacher in the system enrolled and paid 50 cents per month, each teacher would be guaranteed to have up to 21 days of hospital care covered (not physician services, however—physician charges are different from hospital charges, and physicians were largely opposed to any kind of insurance system). The steady stream of income from a group, or *pool*, of relatively healthy and young people provided guaranteed revenue for the hospital, and individuals in the plan had the peace of mind that it provided at a relatively low cost.

Similar hospital plans became more common, and hospitals began asking their trade association, the American Hospital Association (AHA), to develop a systematic way to implement them. In 1936, the AHA developed the AHA Service Plan. In 1946, the committee overseeing this plan became the AHA Blue Cross Commission. As physicians began to accept the idea of such insurance plans, a partner commission, Blue Shield, was formed, giving rise to the now familiar Blue Cross/Blue Shield, a nonprofit health insurance company.

The real spread of health insurance, however, occurred during the next great crisis in the United States—World War II. During World War II, price controls were implemented as a way to control the inflation that often occurs during wars (when an economy is trying to produce beyond its full-employment level of output). Firms faced labor shortages, but they could not use higher wages to attract more workers because of the wage controls that were in place to prevent the type of inflation that is common during wars. However, a ruling by the Internal Revenue Service allowed benefits such as health insurance to not be subject to price controls, and employers began offering health insurance plans as part of their benefits packages.

Not long after this, the Internal Revenue Service decision meant that such benefits were also not subject to income tax. This has an important implication from the employee's point of view—more benefits become more attractive than more salary. Consider a worker who has a marginal tax rate of 20 percent. If the worker is offered $1 more in salary, she takes home 80 cents. However, if the worker is offered $1 in health insurance, she gets the full $1 worth of insurance. These two events lead to a peculiar feature of the U.S. health financing system: employer-based health insurance.

The next major change in healthcare financing in the United States came in the 1960s. Titles XVIII and XIX were added to the Social Security Act in 1965, creating the *social insurance* programs Medicare and Medicaid. Social insurance is a type of insurance in which a government becomes the payer, as opposed to *private insurance*, where a private entity such as an insurance firm pays for healthcare. Medicare covers the elderly (those over age 65) and was modeled after the Blue Cross/Blue Shield system. Medicaid covers certain low-income individuals and is a joint federal and state program.

The end result is that the United States has a mixed system. Figure 19-1 breaks down the percentage of individuals in the United States that fall into different healthcare financing categories, using data from the Kaiser Family Foundation, a nonprofit, nonpartisan organization that tracks healthcare issues and statistics. We have private employer-based insurance, which covers about half of all individuals (most individuals who have any form of health insurance are covered through their employer), and a very small market for individual insurance. For those without health insurance, the final safety net for healthcare financing is receiving healthcare through emergency rooms (which cannot legally turn individuals away) or government-funded programs that reimburse hospitals for some of the amount of unfunded care they provide.

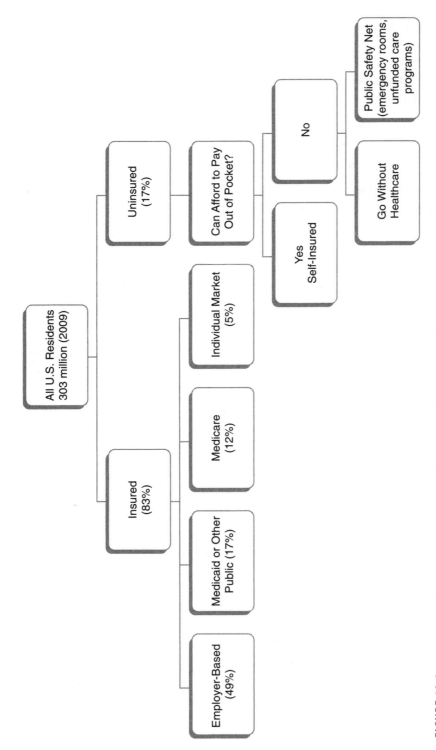

FIGURE 19-1 • Breakdown of U.S. Healthcare Coverage by Financing Categories
Source: Kaiser Family Foundation

Healthcare Markets

Healthcare is a good that is fundamentally different from other goods. To see why, let's review some of the assumptions of a competitive market and see how well they apply to healthcare.

1. **Free entry and exit of firms.** Sellers of healthcare, such as hospitals and physicians, do not have free entry and exit. We require licensing and certification to ensure quality.

2. **Perfect information and no uncertainty.** Healthcare markets are fraught with uncertainty. We do not know if we will need healthcare tomorrow or next year. We don't always know that a particular treatment will work. Our physicians have a better idea than we do, but this means that there is asymmetry between what the buyer (the patient) knows and what the seller (the doctor or hospital) knows. Moreover, because of health insurance, we frequently don't even know what a particular treatment costs.

3. **A homogeneous product.** Physicians and other healthcare professionals aren't alike. All else equal, we would prefer higher quality to lower quality. However, quality can be expensive. If we are insulated from the true price of a good—for instance, if it is covered by insurance—we may look for the best quality possible. This means that firms are competing on the basis of quality rather than price.

4. **Buyers and sellers are price takers.** Sellers negotiate prices with insurance companies, and buyers are frequently unaware of prices.

5. **Utility maximization/profit maximization.** Individual physicians have more than just a profit motive—while they are certainly interested in creating an income, they also have an altruistic motive. In the United States, the dominant business form of hospitals is not-for-profit, which means that profit maximization must not be their goal.

6. **No externalities.** Vaccines, as we mentioned in the previous chapter, are just one example of the positive externalities that healthcare exhibits.

7. **Price rationing.** Recall from the discussion on externalities that price serves an important function—it brings supply and demand into equilibrium. If there is no price, or if price is effectively hidden, as it is in any system with a *third-party payer* (a payer that is not the patient or provider), then price has no ability to perform its rationing function.

The net effect is that the market for healthcare does not function in accordance with our traditional competitive market assumptions. In particular, healthcare that is financed through a third-party-payer system may lead to a situation in which increased competition actually drives up costs. Consider an individual who is covered by insurance, be it social insurance or private insurance, and who is looking for a hospital in which to have a baby. If she is covered by insurance, she is not concerned with costs. She is, however, concerned with whether or not she gets a private room, whether or not there will be an assigned nurse for her, how nice the meals are, or even whether there is a "gift box" for the new parents. All of these things would drive up the costs. The more hospitals there are in the market, the more each individual hospital would have to do to "one-up" another hospital in order to attract patients. This can lead to a *medical arms race*, a term that describes how quality and cost continue to escalate as hospitals compete with one another.

As in the case of externalities, the key here to bringing the costs back down is to bring some sort of rationing back to the system, whether price rationing or some other form. This might be done by reintroducing some sort of price sensitivity. Insurance companies accomplish this with the use of *cost sharing* tools such as *copayments* and *deductibles*. For instance, if a family has to consider that it will pay 10 percent of a hospital bill, known as *coinsurance*, it will be more sensitive to price and limit its consumption of high-quality (in other words, expensive) services. This can also be done by creating *provider networks*. When insurance companies limit individuals to certain providers, they have negotiated lower payments to these providers in exchange for guaranteeing a certain volume of patients. Finally, private and public insurers alike can limit what services they will pay for. Each of these is a form of rationing that is implemented to replace the rationing function of price.

The Market for Insurance

The primary healthcare financing mechanism for most individuals is private insurance. In order to understand the market for healthcare, one needs to understand how the supply and demand for health insurance are determined. For this, we will move away from a supply and demand diagram briefly and look at each analytically.

Let's consider a group, or *pool*, of 100 people. In any given year, each of these people has a 5 percent risk of having a health issue that entails a cost of $20,000. To find the amount that the insurance company expects it will have to pay in a given year, we need to find the *expected value* of the loss that the insurance company will incur. If 5 percent of the people in the pool will lose $20,000 each, with a pool of 100 people, the insurance company will expect to pay 5 × $20,000 + 95 × 0 = $100,000. If the insurance company divides this up among all the people in the pool, we get what is called an *actuarially fair premium*—in other words, a premium that accurately reflects the probability of a loss. Here, the actuarially fair premium would be $100,000/100 = $1,000 per person. However, administering the plan is not costless for the insurance company—it must hire workers to make sure the providers get paid, rent offices, incur other administrative costs, and possibly even make profit—the company passes these costs along to the buyers of insurance in the form of a *loading fee*. Let's suppose that a particular insurance company charges a loading fee of $200. Therefore, the amount of the insurance premium that the insurance company charges would be $1,200.

Now let's consider this from the individual's side. The individual knows that she has a 5 percent risk of losing $20,000 and a 95 percent risk of losing nothing. To the individual, her expected loss is a probability weight of these two potentials: 5 percent × $20,000 + 95 percent × $0 = 0.05 × $20,000 + 0.95 × $0 = $1,000. This means that, on average, the individual can expect to lose $1,000 and so would be willing to pay at least this much. However, the possibility of losing much more is daunting to anyone who is *risk averse*. Because of this, a person would be willing to pay an amount greater than the actuarially fair premium just to avoid that possibility. Suppose that an individual was willing to pay a *risk premium* of $200 on top of any actuarially fair premium, meaning that the individual was willing to pay a total premium of $1,200.

At first this seems perfect—the price that buyers are willing to pay is exactly the price at which sellers are willing to sell. However, there are two characteristics of healthcare markets that will alter this. The first is *moral hazard*. The underlying idea of moral hazard is that, once they are insulated from the financial impact, people will alter their behavior. For instance, they will consume more healthcare than they otherwise would, or they will engage in riskier behavior. Our family looking for a hospital would choose services that it otherwise would not, or one of our 100 people might do things that would make his risk of loss increase from 5 percent.

To understand the other issue, *adverse selection*, let's consider what would happen to our insurance market if one more person entered this pool. This person, however, has a 100 percent risk of losing $20,000, but the insurance company cannot distinguish him from anyone else. Now, the insurance company has a pool of 101 people and an expected loss of $120,000, yielding an actuarially fair premium of $1,188 and a total premium of $1,388. This is more than anyone other than the person who has a guaranteed loss is willing to pay, and people elect not to buy insurance.

This is a very simple illustration of a problem called the *premium death spiral*. If premiums increase, people with lower expected losses will drop out of an insurance pool when the premiums increase beyond the amount that they are willing to pay. As healthier people drop out of the pool, the expected loss goes up, and insurance companies will be forced to raise the premium again. Eventually, the only people left in the pool will be those who have guaranteed losses. In other words, it leads to a complete failure of insurance. This is why it is called adverse selection. When insurance companies charge more, they are less likely to attract the people they want most—the healthy—because those people are willing to pay less.

TIP   *To see the math of the premium death spiral, let's assume that only 20 healthy people drop out of the insurance pool. Now we have 80 people that each have a 5 percent chance (or 4 people) of a $20,000 medical loss and a 95 percent chance (or 76 people) of no loss, and one "sick" person who knows that he will have a $20,000 loss.*

The insurance company expects to lose:

$$4 \times \$20,000 + 76 \times \$0 + \$20,000 = \$100,000$$

And since we have a pool of 81 people, the actuarially fair premium is $100,000/81 = $1,235, and when we add the $200 of overhead, the insurance company needs to have each person pay $1,435.

Still Struggling

The idea of expected value can be tricky. To understand what an expected value of loss is, consider a gamble that forces you to flip a coin 100 times, and any time tails comes up, you must pay $3. You know that, on average, heads will come up as often as tails, so 50 percent of the time you will pay $0 and 50 percent of the time you will pay $3. This means that you should expect to lose about $150 from having to play this gamble.

You could then extend that to having to play the game just once. You know you will have a 50 percent chance of losing $3 and a 50 percent chance of losing nothing. Mathematically, then:

$$EV = 0.5 \times (-\$3) + 0.5 \times \$0 = -\$1.50$$

Healthcare Policy Reform

The goal of a healthcare system is to make healthcare affordable and high-quality, and to have wide access to it. Unfortunately, the problems of moral hazard and adverse selection make this trinity difficult to achieve. Healthcare reform has tried to tackle these issues in a variety of ways and with varying success.

If the focus of a system is on cost alone, in an attempt to make healthcare more affordable, then this can be accomplished by limiting access to care or reducing quality. Consider the issue of access. From an equity point of view, it would be ideal if anyone who needed healthcare could obtain it. There are various financing systems that could accomplish this. For instance, there could be a private, *multipayer* system in which people who could not easily get insurance were assisted in obtaining it. The PPACA provides for subsidies for those who cannot afford private health insurance and the creation of systems to match up insurance with people who cannot obtain it through their employer. Other countries, such as Canada, have used a *single-payer* system, in which there is essentially a single insurance company (the government) that provides health insurance.

Unfortunately, *universal coverage* of any kind would worsen the problem of moral hazard. Universal coverage describes the situation in which every single person in a healthcare system is covered by insurance, and if everyone has coverage, then everyone has insulation against cost. Because of this, the cost of healthcare could increase, making it less affordable. Moreover, if people have the option of opting out of a system, they might do so if the cost exceeded their perceived risk. On the other hand, universal coverage may lead to lower costs if it encourages prevention of disease. Without more information about the problems a healthcare system is facing, it is not possible to say which is likely to have a greater effect on overall spending.

The problem of people choosing to opt out of a system (and still having a safety net) is one of the reasons that the PPACA required an insurance *mandate*, meaning that people are required to have health insurance: to prevent the problem of adverse selection. Insurance mandates are controversial, at least in the United States. Many people object to the idea of being required to purchase something that they may never need. However, the problem arises when someone does need it. In essence, healthcare in the United States could be considered a common resource. It is rival in the sense that healthcare resources are finite and need to be used effectively. It is also nonexcludable, as our current system has safety nets such as emergency rooms to enable people to get care regardless of their insurance coverage or their ability to pay. Because of this nonexcludability, when people are uninsured, whether by choice or by constraint, there is an opportunity to free-ride off the payments made by private insurance companies and government resources. In fact, the lack of an insurance mandate makes the U.S. healthcare system unique among those of other industrialized nations, as other countries with a variety of different systems all require individuals to be covered by either public or private insurance.

Summary

Healthcare is a good that is fundamentally different from other goods because almost none of the assumptions of a competitive market hold for healthcare. Issues such as asymmetric information, moral hazard, and adverse selection make the functioning of a private health insurance system somewhat problematic and may lead to market failures. Given that this is the primary financing system for healthcare in the United States, recent healthcare reform could actually be considered health insurance reform. Whether or not this reform effort will achieve the three goals of a healthcare system remains to be seen, and much research on the issue is likely to be done in the near future. In our final chapter, we turn our attention to this research process, and how economists develop and test ideas and disseminate information to arrive at the ideas and conclusions that we discuss in this book.

QUIZ

Is each of the following statements *true* or *false*? Explain.

1. Healthcare is the second-largest industry in the United States.

2. Given the U.S. tax system, an additional $1 worth of health insurance is worth less than an additional $1 in income.

3. The largest number of Americans get health insurance through individual markets.

4. The U.S. healthcare system could be considered a private system.

5. It would be appropriate to use a traditional competitive market model to analyze healthcare markets.

6. If all healthcare were self-financed, moral hazard would not be an issue.

7. Insurance mandates would solve the problem of moral hazard, but would worsen adverse selection.

8. A risk premium reflects the potential risk of a loss.

9. Healthcare is not rationed in the United States.

10. Coinsurance can mitigate the problem of moral hazard.

Economic Research

The bulk of this book has discussed the basic toolkit of economics—the theory and tools that make up the body of economic knowledge. We now turn our attention to how such knowledge is created. In this chapter, we introduce the research process in economics. We begin with an overview of what is meant by research in economics and how this differs from what many people assume. Next, we outline a typical research process. Finally, we conclude with how economists share new knowledge.

CHAPTER OBJECTIVES

After completing this chapter, the student should be able to:

1. Describe what economic research is and what it is not.

2. Outline a typical research process in economics.

3. Understand how economists share information.

4. Describe the peer-review process of an academic economics journal.

Introduction to Research in Economics

Up to now, we have focused exclusively on what might be called *pure content*, that is, the facts and pronouncements of the discipline of economics. At this point, an attentive reader will know a fair amount about the basics of economics. Knowing, however, is quite different from doing. *Research* is the process of "doing" by creating, evaluating, and confirming knowledge.

The field of economics is somewhat different from other disciplines studied in college in that many of the other physical and social sciences give a great deal of attention to research at this level. The professional consensus in economics has long been that the degree of content knowledge and, more important, analytical skills that a typical undergraduate student possesses is inadequate to truly add to the body of knowledge in economics. However, there is growing recognition of the value of learning economics by doing economics. For this reason, many economics majors either have the option or are required to complete a research project or similar capstone experience.

Research is, in fact, what economists do that makes them economists. This might seem obvious, but if you think about the economists that you are most likely to be exposed to in the media or on the Internet, such as the chairman of the Federal Reserve or a guest columnist for a nationally renowned newspaper, they will rarely (if ever) talk about the work they do on a day-to-day basis. This chapter gives you some insight into how those people got to their positions of influence and authority—by creating knowledge and disseminating it to the greater economics community.

Before we move on, however, it is probably as useful for the reader to understand what economics research *isn't* as to understand what it is. Common misperceptions about doing economics research usually fall into the following categories:

1. **Summarizing previous research.** Students will sometimes approach us and ask if they can do a "research paper" in order to earn extra credit. However, such students usually don't actually mean that they want to engage in research; instead, they want to read up on some topic and summarize what they read. This is not economics research. In some fields, particularly in humanities subjects such as history or English, research is almost exclusively the review and synthesis of existing works. In economics, however, this is just one step in the research process (which we outline in the next section). Remember that research creates *new* knowledge. If research were simply the rehashing of what already exists, new knowledge would never be created.

2. **Collecting data.** First and foremost, economics research revolves around answering questions. The data that are used in the vast majority of today's research are merely the bricks that are used to construct the ideas. Collecting data is akin to gathering up the bricks needed for a building, but not yet building anything.

Even if you aren't required to do research as part of a degree plan or a course of self-study, you should still be familiar with how and why research is done. Doing research in economics is valuable and constructive for a number of reasons. First of all, it helps you summarize what is already known, and what is not, in a field. For instance, if you are interested in international trade, conducting a research project on a trade-related issue will more firmly cement the questions whose answers are known and help you understand what still is not known in that field. Second, research makes *you* an economist by contributing to the field, by solving a puzzle or problem, or perhaps just by testing existing knowledge in a new way. Finally, it allows you to weigh in on a debate in a meaningful way.

The Research Process

There is a temptation to think about the goal of research as being an end product such as a paper or an article. The correct way to approach research is to think about that product as a step toward the ultimate goal of building knowledge. For this reason, research is really a *process* rather than a product. In economics, the research process is a series of stages that the researcher will go through to create new knowledge. Moreover, it is important to keep in mind that the research process is iterative. You may have to go through some of the steps several times before you get to a product.

The basic pattern in economic research is that first an idea or argument is created that takes a particular stance. Evidence for that stance is then gathered, analyzed, and presented to the community. The community gives feedback on the argument and ways to improve the analysis, and frequently other scholars develop competing ideas or approaches. Over time, the most credible arguments that stand up to scrutiny survive and become part of the body of economic knowledge.

The first step is to develop a question. Research in economics, like other formal research, is based on the scientific method. This means that you must develop a testable *hypothesis*, meaning that you must come up with a question that is answerable. For instance, let's suppose that you are interested in health economics and the role of insurance in the healthcare decisions that physicians make. This is not a research question because it is not a question. Narrowing down your ideas further might yield something that is testable, such as, "Do people with insurance have an easier time getting doctor's appointments than people without insurance?" Usually, you will have an idea of what you expect to find as an answer to this question. This is your hypothesis. For instance, your research question would be to determine whether this statement is true or false: "People with insurance have an easier time getting doctor's appointments than people without insurance."

Research ideas typically fall into three broad categories:

- **Proposing a new theory.** This is research that develops a new way of explaining an observed phenomenon. For instance, when it was observed that in the short run, an increase in the money supply led to an increase in prices but not in output, the quantity theory of money was developed (a very simplified version of which appears in our chapter on money). Theoretical papers are usually very mathematically complicated, and are rarely seen at the undergraduate level.

- **Testing an existing theory with data.** This is *empirical* (meaning "to measure") research that tests a theory numerically. For instance, if we were to test the theory that as wages increase, workers supply more labor, we could find data on wages and see if as wages increased, people indeed supplied more labor. If we got a different result, we would first want to make sure that something else wasn't going on—the *ceteris paribus* assumption. If something else was going on, such as an increased marginal product of labor, we would need to find a way to account for that in our empirical test. If there wasn't something else going on, we might suggest that our theory is incorrect or needs revision (such as revising the law of supply when it applies to labor to allow for backward-bending supply curves).

- **Prediction.** In this type of research, we might try to model what may happen in the future based on some change. For instance, if we were interested in economic growth, what might happen to our full-employment level of output if savings rates increased? We could also predict a future situation based on past trends or a policy change.

TIP *Many students have trouble narrowing down very broad ideas that they are interested in to a question form. When you are trying to form a research question, use a postcard. If you can narrow your research idea down to a few simple lines, you are getting closer to a single, answerable question. Don't confuse the motivation for your question with the question itself.*

The second step is to determine what the existing literature says on the topic. This is a process known as a *literature review*. Your goal at this point is to review *primary sources*, such as peer-reviewed academic journals whose audience is professional or scholarly, for what is known about your question and what still remains unknown. *Secondary sources*, which include sources like news outlets (such as the magazine the *Economist* or the *Wall Street Journal*) that summarize primary sources, are a great starting point for ideas to form your original question, but your literature review should be made up of primary sources. Your goal with your literature review is to summarize the existing work, determine what has been done, and determine what questions remain or what inconsistencies may exist. During this process, you may find that your original question has already been answered, and students sometimes get discouraged by this. The good news is that your literature review helps point you toward a new question.

Still Struggling

Reading a professional, peer-reviewed journal can be daunting. There is likely to be a great deal of theory or a mathematical process that seems "over your head." The key to understanding an article is to tackle it in a methodical and critical way. When students are struggling with an article, we suggest that they attack it this way:

1. Read it in the following order: abstract, introduction, conclusion, background, results. If the way the researcher got the results is of particular interest, then pay as much attention to the methodology as to the results.
2. Try to answer the following questions:
   a. What is the author (or authors) trying to say? What is the fundamental question that he is trying to answer?
   b. What answer did he come up with?
   c. What did the author say in the article about what other people had written on the question or the general subject? Did this author's findings differ from this, reinforce this, or build on this?
   d. What evidence did the author provide?

By breaking the process down into steps, getting to the bottom of what the article is saying is much more manageable.

Next, you need to develop a conceptual framework for your question. What is the appropriate theory for your question? How should it be answered? For instance, if you are interested in the question presented earlier, you should examine how the subfield of health economics approaches similar questions. Once you have set up your concept of the question, collect and analyze the appropriate data. If you are doing an *empirical study*, that is, a project that examines observations in a mathematical way, you will probably need a background in statistics or even *econometrics*.

In our example hypothesis, we can use publicly available data that have been previously collected that have information on a patient's ability to get the appointment that she desires and her insurance status. We can then see if the patient's insurance status is a good predictor of whether or not the patient got the appointment she wanted. After we have *analyzed the data* in this manner, we then interpret our findings.

The final step is to disseminate the findings. The most common way of doing this is by writing a research paper or research article. In economics, researchers will usually first prepare what is called a *working paper*. This is a polished draft (that is, not a rough draft) of a paper that is shared with other researchers for feedback. Usually, a researcher will present this at a conference, where other researchers will attack various points and methods used in the paper. The purpose of this is not to destroy, however, but to build up. By having its weaknesses and strengths pointed out, and its flaws corrected, the evidence presented becomes more credible and the findings more sound.

Finally, the researcher will usually submit the paper to one of the many peer-reviewed economics journals to be considered for publication. In the *peer-review* process, the journal will remove identifying information about the author and send the article to other knowledgeable researchers in the field. They will review the paper and determine whether the findings are credible enough to share broadly through publication. Usually, the reviewers will request changes to strengthen the paper before it is published. The time between the first preparation of a manuscript in working paper form and its publication in a peer-reviewed journal can be quite long. A five-year time span is not unusual. For this reason, economists who are interested in staying abreast of the latest research will attend conferences where new research is being presented.

The process, however, doesn't end at this point. Later, when another researcher is going through this same process, someone else who is doing his own literature review may come along and find a way to challenge or strengthen the hypothesis. Recall that research is the building of knowledge. It is a constant, continuing enterprise.

Summary

In this chapter, we presented an outline of what economists actually do to generate the ideas that are contained in the rest of this book. Economic ideas are hypothesized, tested, challenged, and improved through a continual process of economic research. The research process involves developing a research idea and plan, checking the existing literature for what has been said about the research idea, testing the question that was formed, and sharing the results. Even if you are not planning to do economic research yourself, it is helpful to know the process through which economic knowledge is formed in order to have confidence that the ideas presented in this book are being vetted, being tested, and under continuous scrutiny to improve what we know about the economic world in which we live.

QUIZ

Is each of the following statements *true* or *false*? Explain.

1. A book report is an example of economic research.

2. Primary sources such as Wikipedia, an encyclopedia, and news outlets should be used in doing a literature review.

3. Collecting data on inflation between 2000 and 2011 and presenting it in a table would be considered research.

4. An individual researcher must collect her own data.

5. Research in peer-reviewed journals may be several years old.

6. When forming a research question, you should conceptualize it in the broadest possible terms.

7. A published finding is unassailable.

8. The goal of economic research is to produce a journal article.

9. Theoretical research tests ideas, while empirical research creates ideas.

10. Economic research uses the scientific method.

Final Exam

1. A nation has a productive lobster fishery off the coast. Which of the nation's economic resources do the lobsters represent?

   A. Labor   B. Land   C. Capital   D. Food

2. Kelly has a difficult decision to make concerning how she should spend two hours this evening. She can study for her economics exam, she can babysit and earn $10 per hour, or she can work at the campus library and earn $7 per hour. The opportunity cost of studying for her economics exam is:

   A. $20   B. $17   C. $14   D. $34

3. When a consumer weighs the additional benefit of doing something against the additional cost of doing it, it is said that she is engaging in:

   A. Resource analysis   B. Consumer analysis

   C. Marginal analysis   D. Profit analysis

4. Which of the following headlines is best classified as a macroeconomic topic?

   A. "The Ford plant in Louisville will rehire 100 production workers."

   B. "The price of gasoline has fallen by 10 percent since the weekend."

   C. "Motorola plans to introduce a new phone by Christmas."

   D. "The unemployment rate in the United States was reported to be 9.1 percent last month."

Use Table 1 to answer question 5.

TABLE 1	
Cans of Soda (per day)	Marginal Benefit
1	$7
2	$5
3	$3
4	$1
5	–$1

5. Sherman enjoys buying cans of soda from the vending machine at his office. Cans of soda from the machine cost $1.50. Given Sherman's daily marginal benefit for cans of soda, he will buy _____ each day.

A. 5   B. 4   C. 3   D. 2

6. Josh purchases cans of soup (*S*) and video games (*V*) with his income of $100. His budget constraint can be written as:

$$\$100 = \$4 \times S + \$20 \times V$$

Given this information, the most soup that Josh could buy with his income is:

A. 25 cans   B. 100 cans   C. 5 cans   D. 4 cans

7. Josh purchases cans of soup (*S*) and video games (*V*) with his income of $100. His budget constraint can be written as:

$$\$100 = \$4 \times S + \$20 \times V$$

Given this information, which of the following combinations would lie on Josh's budget constraint?

A. 50*S* and 2*V*   B. 10*S* and 10*V*
C. 20*S* and 2*V*   D. 10*S* and 3*V*

Use Table 2 for questions 8 and 9.

TABLE 2	
Slices of Pizza	**Marginal Utility (utils)**
1	18
2	15
3	12
4	9
5	6
6	3
7	0
8	−3

8. Table 2 shows a consumer's marginal utility from consuming additional slices of pizza. If this consumer eats 3 slices of pizza, how many utils of total utility will he enjoy?

A. 3   B. 45   C. 12   D. 30

9. Table 2 shows a consumer's marginal utility from consuming additional slices of pizza. If there is no price for buying a slice of pizza, how many slices of pizza will maximize his total utility?

A. 6   B. 3   C. 7   D. 1

10. Brody is currently spending all of his income on coffee and bagels. The price of coffee is $2 per cup, and the price of bagels is $3 each. Suppose that Brody's current marginal utility for a cup of coffee is 10 utils and his marginal utility for a bagel is 15 utils. Is there a way for Brody to adjust his consumption to increase his utility?

A. Yes. He should consume more bagels and less coffee.

B. Yes. He should consume more coffee and less bagels.

C. No. He has already maximized his utility.

D. Yes. He should consume more coffee and more bagels.

11. **The demand for gasoline has decreased. Which of the following could have caused this to occur?**

A. The price of gasoline increased.

B. Income increased, and gasoline is a normal good.

C. The price of cars and trucks increased.

D. Consumers expect the price of gasoline to rise in the future.

12. **Which of the following best reflects the law of demand?**

A. The price of gasoline increased, and Stan reduced his driving for a week.

B. Stan received a pay raise and bought a new bike.

C. The price of apples increased, and Stan bought a pound of oranges.

D. Stan saw a commercial for a new kind of frozen pizza and went to the store and bought one.

13. **Suppose the price elasticity of demand for good X is 1.5. If the price of X falls by 5 percent, we expect quantity demanded to rise by:**

A. 5 percent   B. 7.5 percent

C. 15 percent   D. 3.33 percent

14. **When the price of carrots increases by 2 percent, suppose the quantity of peas demanded rises by 4 percent. Given this, we can say that:**

A. Carrots and peas are normal goods, and the income elasticity is equal to 2.

B. Carrots and peas are complementary goods, and the cross-price elasticity is equal to 2.

C. Carrots and peas are substitute goods, and the cross-price elasticity is equal to $\frac{1}{2}$.

D. Carrots and peas are substitute goods, and the cross-price elasticity is equal to 2.

15. **All else equal, when the price of laptop computers falls by 5 percent, we observe that computer manufacturers see total revenues increase. What explains this?**

A. The demand for laptop computers is price-elastic.

B. The demand for laptop computers is price-inelastic.

C. Laptop computers and desktop computers are substitute goods.

D. Laptop computers are normal goods.

16. **Mr. Funelli has a pizza restaurant. Which of the following is most likely a fixed input in his short-run production of pizzas?**

A. The cans of tomato sauce that he buys from a supplier.

B. The number of students from the high school that he employs.

C. The electricity that he uses to operate the appliances.

D. The size of the kitchen and dining room.

Use Table 3 to answer questions 17 and 18.

TABLE 3	
Total Output (Q)	Total Cost
0	$100
8	$150
18	$200
26	$250
32	$300
36	$350
38	$400
39	$450

17. Given the short-run cost data in Table 3, what is the total fixed cost associated with producing 36 units of output?
    A. $350   B. $100   C. $250   D. $50

18. Given the short-run cost data in Table 3, which of the following choices best describes the shape of the marginal cost curve?
    A. Vertical   B. Upward-sloping
    C. Downward-sloping   D. Horizontal

19. Which of the following production or cost equations is correctly stated?
    A. $TVC = TC - TFC$ B. $AP_L = L \times TP_L$

    C. $MP_L = \left(\dfrac{\Delta TP_L}{\Delta Q} \right)$ D. $MC = \left(\dfrac{\Delta TC}{\Delta L} \right)$

20. Which of the following statements *incorrectly* describes short-run production and cost relationships?
    A. When the marginal product of labor is falling, the marginal cost is rising.
    B. When the marginal product of labor is less than the average product of labor, the average product is falling.
    C. The vertical distance between the total cost and total variable cost curves is equal to total fixed cost.
    D. When the marginal product of labor is falling, the total product of labor is falling.

21. Which of the following would cause the supply of carrot cake to increase?
    A. Several suppliers of carrot cake have recently gone out of business.
    B. The price of carrot cake has increased.
    C. The price of raw carrots has decreased.
    D. Consumer income has increased, and carrot cake is a normal good.

22. Suppose the price elasticity of supply of good Y is 2. If we observe that the quantity of good Y supplied has decreased by 6 percent, we can conclude that:

   A. The price of good Y has decreased by 3 percent.

   B. The price of good Y has increased by 2 percent

   C. The price of good Y has decreased by 0.33 percent.

   D. The price of good Y has decreased by 12 percent.

23. The law of supply is consistent with the notion that:

   A. Supply curves are upward-sloping in both the short run and the long run.

   B. Supply curves are horizontal in the short run and upward-sloping in the long run.

   C. Supply curves are upward-sloping in the short run and vertical in the long run.

   D. Supply curves are horizontal in the short run and vertical in the long run.

24. Last month the price of coffee was $2 per pound and 1,000 tons were supplied by producers. This month the price remained at $2, but 1,200 tons were supplied. It is most likely that:

   A. The supply of coffee decreased.

   B. The supply of coffee increased.

   C. There was an upward movement along the fixed supply curve.

   D. There was a downward movement along the fixed supply curve.

Use Figure 1 to answer question 25.

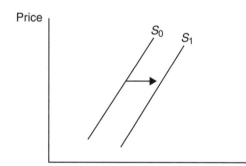

FIGURE 1

25. What may have caused the change seen in Figure 1?

   A. The price of fertilizer increased.

   B. The price of lettuce increased.

   C. Workers conducted a labor stoppage to protest working conditions in the lettuce fields.

   D. The price of cabbage, an alternative crop, decreased.

Use Figure 2 to answer questions 26 to 28.

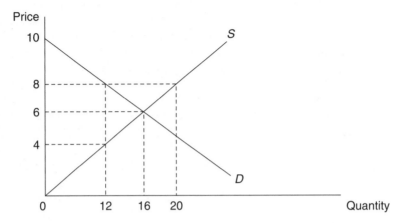

FIGURE 2

26. This market will come to equilibrium at a price of _____ and a quantity of _____.
    A. $8; 16   B. $6; 16   C. $4; 12   D. $16; 6

27. In equilibrium, producer surplus is equal to:
    A. $48   B. $24
    C. $32   D. 16 units of output

28. Suppose the market in the graph is in equilibrium. What could cause the equilibrium price to rise to $8 and the quantity to rise to 20 units?
    A. The price of a substitute good falls.
    B. The price of an input used in producing this good falls.
    C. Consumers' preferences for this good weaken.
    D. Consumer income rises, and this is a normal good.

29. The market for gasoline in the city of Smoggybottom is in equilibrium. Which of the following policies would create deadweight loss in the gasoline market?
    A. A price floor
    B. A price ceiling
    C. An excise tax on each gallon supplied
    D. All of the above

30. Assume the market for bread is in equilibrium. If the demand for bread increases and the supply of bread decreases, how will the price and quantity of bread change in the market?

	Price of Bread	Quantity of Bread
A.	Ambiguous	Ambiguous
B.	Increases	Decreases
C.	Increases	Ambiguous
D.	Ambiguous	Increases

31. A perfectly competitive firm is producing where profit is maximized and the price is below the average total cost. In the long run, what do we expect to happen to the number of firms in the industry, the market price of the product, and the firm's level of output?

	Number of Firms	Market Price	Firm's Output
A.	Rising	Falling	Falling
B.	Falling	Rising	Falling
C.	Falling	Falling	Rising
D.	Falling	Rising	Rising

32. The perfectly competitive price of a grunk is $10. A profit-maximizing grunk producer calculates that the average total cost of making grunks is $7 and the average variable cost is $4. If the firm is producing 20 units, how much economic profit or loss is being made?

A. $60

B. $3

C. $200

D. −$20

Use Figure 3 for question 33.

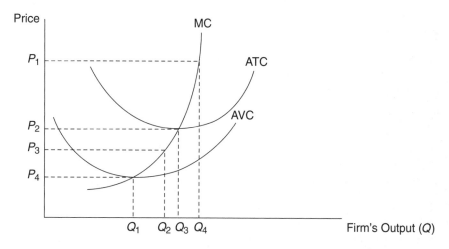

FIGURE 3

33. The long-run price and quantity for this perfectly competitive firm are:

A. P_1 and Q_4

B. P_2 and Q_3

C. P_4 and Q_1

D. P_3 and Q_3

34. Which of the following is *not* a long-run outcome of perfectly competitive markets?

A. Total welfare is maximized.

B. Average total costs are minimized.

C. Deadweight loss occurs.

D. Allocative efficiency is achieved.

Use Table 4 to complete question 35.

TABLE 4			
Q	TFC	TVC	TC
0	$20.00	$ 0.00	$ 20.00
1	$20.00	$ 1.50	$ 21.50
2	$20.00	$ 6.00	$ 26.00
3	$20.00	$ 13.50	$ 33.50
4	$20.00	$ 24.00	$ 44.00
5	$20.00	$ 37.50	$ 57.50
6	$20.00	$ 54.00	$ 74.00
7	$20.00	$ 73.50	$ 93.50
8	$20.00	$ 96.00	$116.00
9	$20.00	$121.50	$141.50
10	$20.00	$150.00	$170.00

35. If the market price is $7.50, what are the profit-maximizing level of output and the total economic profit or loss?

	Output	Economic Profit
A.	3	−$11
B.	2	$1.50
C.	0	−$20
D.	3	$9

36. Which of the following choices correctly describes a monopolist?

   A. Deadweight loss exists because the marginal cost exceeds the price of the last unit sold.

   B. Rivals are blocked from entering the market in the short run, but entry is possible in the long run.

   C. The marginal revenue earned from the next unit sold is less than the price at which it was sold.

   D. Economic profits are not possible in the long run.

37. In the long run, the monopoly outcome is where:

   A. $P > MR > MC$ B. $P > MR = MC$

   C. $P = MR = MC$ D. $P = MR > MC$

38. If a profit-maximizing monopolist can engage in perfect price discrimination, _____.

   A. consumer surplus will equal producer surplus.

   B. economic profit will equal zero.

   C. deadweight loss will exist.

   D. all consumer surplus will be transferred to the firm.

Use Figure 4 to answer questions 39 and 40.

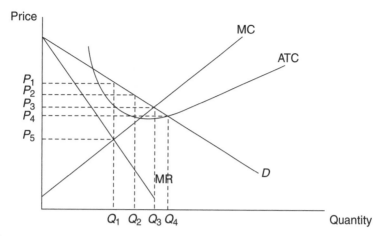

FIGURE 4

39. **In Figure 4, the profit-maximizing output and price are:**
    A. Q_3 and P_3 B. Q_1 and P_5
    C. Q_1 and P_1 D. Q_4 and P_4

40. **Suppose the government wishes to regulate this monopolist so that profits are equal to zero. In this case, output is _____ and price is _____.**
    A. Q_3; P_3 B. Q_1; P_5
    C. Q_1; P_1 D. Q_4; P_4

41. **The grocery market in the city of Mossy Bottom is monopolistically competitive. Frannie's Fresh Foods is currently maximizing her profit, and she is earning an economic profit. Given this, firms will _____ the Mossy Bottom grocery market, causing the demand for Frannie's Fresh Foods to _____ and causing the price to _____ until profits are _____.**
    A. enter; decrease; increase; zero
    B. exit; increase; decrease; zero
    C. exit; decrease; increase; zero
    D. enter; decrease; decrease; zero

42. **Select the choice that is *not* consistent with the model of monopolistic competition.**
    A. Barriers to entry exist in the long run.
    B. Product differentiation exists.
    C. Economic profits are equal to zero in the long run.
    D. Deadweight loss exists.

43. **Suppose the grocery giants Kroger and Safeway are independently deciding whether to build a new store in Mexico City. The game matrix shown here gives the choices**

and payoffs of this game (in millions of dollars). If the game is played only once, are there any dominant strategies?

| | | Kroger's Choices | |
		Expand	Don't Expand
Safeway's Choices	Expand	Safeway: $5 Kroger: $6	Safeway: $10 Kroger: $ 3
	Don't Expand	Safeway: $3 Kroger: $3	Safeway: $ 4 Kroger: $ 1

   A. Yes. Choosing expand is the dominant strategy for both firms.
   B. Yes. Choosing don't expand is the dominant strategy for only Kroger.
   C. Yes. Choosing expand is the dominant strategy for only Safeway.
   D. No. Neither firm has a dominant strategy.

44. Suppose the grocery giants Kroger and Safeway are independently deciding whether to build a new store in Mexico City. The game matrix shown here gives the choices and payoffs of this game (in millions of dollars). If the game is played only once, what is the outcome?

| | | Kroger's Choices | |
		Expand	Don't Expand
Safeway's Choices	Expand	Safeway: $2 Kroger: $6	Safeway: $10 Kroger: $ 3
	Don't Expand	Safeway: $3 Kroger: $3	Safeway: $ 4 Kroger: $ 1

   A. Both firms expand.
   B. Kroger expands and Safeway does not expand.
   C. Safeway expands and Kroger does not expand.
   D. Both firms choose to not expand.

45. Which of the following scenarios best describes an oligopoly?
   A. There is only one bank in a small town.
   B. Thousands of small soybean farmers offer their output to the global market.
   C. The firms Coca-Cola and PepsiCo sell more than 70 percent of the carbonated soft drinks in North America.
   D. The restaurant industry in a city is very diverse, and firms struggle to break even in the long run.

Use Table 5 to respond to questions 46 and 47.

| TABLE 5 | |
# of Employees	Total Product of Labor
1	14
2	36
3	46
4	54
5	60
6	64
7	66

46. The firm in Table 5 sells each unit of output in a perfectly competitive product market at a price of $4. The value of the marginal product of labor for the fourth worker is equal to:

A. $54   B. $216   C. $32   D. $4

47. In Table 5, if the competitive market wage is equal to $30 per employee and the competitive price of the output is $3, how many workers will be employed to maximize profit?

A. 3   B. 4   C. 5   D. 6

48. Rebecca is currently employing labor at a wage of $12 per unit, and capital at a rate of $25 per unit. The marginal product of labor is currently equal to 48 units, and the marginal product of capital is equal to 125 units. Rebecca should:

A. Increase hiring of both labor and capital.

B. Increase hiring of labor and decrease hiring of capital.

C. Do nothing; she has already hired the least-cost combination of labor and capital.

D. Decrease hiring of labor and increase hiring of capital.

49. The labor market for carpenters is in equilibrium. If interest rates are very low and this prompts a boom in new home construction, how is the market for carpenters affected?

A. Demand for carpenters increases, increasing the wage and decreasing employment.

B. Demand for carpenters increases, increasing the wage and increasing employment.

C. Supply of carpenters increases, increasing the wage and increasing employment.

D. Supply of carpenters increases, decreasing the wage and decreasing employment.

50. The demand for factors of production like labor is referred to as a(n) _____ demand because the demand for the factor is partly determined by the demand for the product that the factor produces.

A. backward-bending

B. elastic

C. derived

D. inelastic

51. Nations use _____ to measure the value of all goods and services produced within the nation.
    A. gross domestic product
    B. macroeconomics
    C. gross national product
    D. government spending

52. In the circular flow diagram, households _____ their inputs in _____ markets and _____ goods and services in _____ markets.
    A. buy; factor; buy; product
    B. sell; factor; buy; product
    C. buy; factor; sell; product
    D. sell; product; buy; factor

53. An American consumer buys a stereo made in Japan. This purchase would enter the calculation of GDP in Japan as:
    A. Import spending
    B. Government spending
    C. Consumer spending
    D. Export spending

54. If GDP is calculated using the expenditures approach, the following formula would be used:
    A. $GDP = C - I - G + (X - M)$
    B. $GDP = C + I + G + (M - X)$
    C. $GDP = C + I + G + (X - M)$
    D. $GDP = W + R + I + PR$

55. Which component of the economy fluctuates the most from year to year?
    A. Consumption spending
    B. Government spending
    C. Investment spending
    D. Export spending

56. When the number of unemployed persons is divided by the number of persons in the labor force, we calculate the:
    A. Export-import rate
    B. Discouraged worker rate
    C. Labor force participation rate
    D. Unemployment rate

57. Sharon was recently fired from her only job and last week had a job interview. Sharon is classified as:
    A. Employed
    B. Unemployed
    C. Out of the labor force
    D. Retired

58. The theory that firms pay workers a wage that exceeds the market wage in an effort to increase the productivity of workers is known as the _____ theory.
    A. discouraged worker
    B. minimum wage
    C. underemployment
    D. efficiency wage

59. In the town of Hickory, population 1,200 citizens, there are 1,000 people above the age of 16. Of those 16 years old or older, 200 people are out of the labor force and 600 are working at least one hour each week. What is the unemployment rate in Hickory?
    A. 50 percent
    B. 25 percent
    C. 75 percent
    D. 20 percent

60. In the town of Hickory, population 1,200 citizens, there are 1,000 people above the age of 16. Of those 16 years old or older, 200 people are out of the labor force and 600 are working at least one hour each week. What is the labor force participation rate in Hickory?
    A. 50 percent
    B. 67 percent
    C. 75 percent
    D. 80 percent

61. In the United States, the most widely used measure of price inflation is the:
    A. Wage index
    B. Consumer Price Index
    C. Unemployment index
    D. Producer Price Index

62. Suppose the Consumer Price Index is 105 in 2009, 108 in 2010, and 113 in 2011. The inflation rate from the base year to 2011 was:
    A. 8 percent
    B. 13 percent
    C. 5 percent
    D. 113 percent

63. Cartman's annual salary increased by 3 percent from 2010 to 2011. Over the same period of time, the Consumer Price Index increased from 100 to 102. Given this, we can say that:
    A. Cartman's nominal income increased by 3 percent and his real income increased by about 5 percent.
    B. Cartman's nominal income increased by 3 percent and his real income stayed constant.
    C. Cartman's nominal income increased by 2 percent and his real income increased by 3 percent.
    D. Cartman's nominal income increased by 3 percent and his real income increased by about 1 percent.

64. Which of the following groups are likely to *not* be hurt by rapid, unexpected inflation?
    A. Workers paid a salary that is fixed by a long-term contract
    B. Retired autoworkers receiving a fixed pension every month
    C. Banks that have lent money to homeowners at a fixed rate
    D. Borrowers that are repaying their loans at a fixed rate

Use Figure 5 to answer question 65.

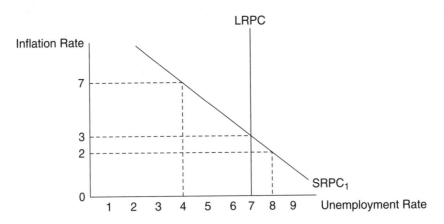

FIGURE 5

65. **Figure 5 shows the macroeconomy in both the short run and the long run. In the long run, the unemployment rate will be _____ and the inflation rate will be _____.**
    A. 4 percent; 7 percent
    B. 8 percent; 2 percent
    C. 7 percent; 0 percent
    D. 7 percent; 3 percent

66. **Aggregate demand in the macroeconomy will shift to the right with:**
    A. An increase in household wealth
    B. An increase in interest rates
    C. A decrease in consumer optimism
    D. A decrease in government spending

67. **Which of the following statements are accurate?**
    I. The aggregate demand curve is downward-sloping because of the interest-rate effect.
    II. The aggregate demand curve is downward-sloping because of the wealth effect.
    III. The aggregate demand curve is downward-sloping because of the exchange-rate effect.
    A. I only
    B. I and II only
    C. I, II, and III
    D. II only

68. **If the economy is in short-run equilibrium, what is the expected short-run impact of an increase in consumer optimism?**
    A. Aggregate demand increases, increasing the price level and increasing real output.
    B. Aggregate demand increases, decreasing the price level and increasing real output.
    C. Aggregate demand increases, increasing the price level and decreasing real output.
    D. Short-run aggregate supply increases, decreasing the price level and increasing real output.

Use Figure 6 to answer questions 69 and 70.

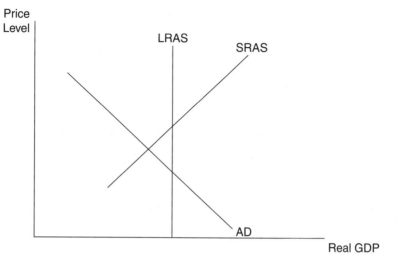

FIGURE 6

69. **The economy depicted in the graph is currently in short-run equilibrium. What must be true of this economic situation?**

    A. The economy is currently at full employment.

    B. The unemployment rate is higher than the natural rate of unemployment.

    C. The economy is experiencing rapid inflation.

    D. The economy is producing beyond the level that corresponds to full employment.

70. **If the SRAS in the economy depicted in the graph is allowed to adjust to a long-run equilibrium, what would happen to factor prices, the SRAS curve, the unemployment rate, and the price level?**

	Factor Prices	SRAS Curve	Unemployment Rate	Price Level
A.	Increases	Decreases	Increases	Increases
B.	Decreases	Increases	Decreases	Decreases
C.	Decreases	Increases	Increases	Decreases
D.	Decreases	Increases	Increases	Increases

71. **The paper currency that nations use today (like U.S. dollars and Mexican pesos) is referred to as _____ money. It can be used to purchase goods and services because the government declares that it is legal tender.**

    A. commodity

    B. gold standard

    C. barter

    D. fiat

72. Suppose that Patrick takes $100 from his piggy bank and puts it into his checking account. How will this affect the M1 and M2 measures of money supply?

	Change in M1	Change in M2
A.	No change	Decreases
B.	Increases	No change
C.	No change	No change
D.	Increases	Increases

73. After Aunt Thelma passes away, the members of her family find $1,000 that has been hidden in the toaster for many years. They deposit the $1,000 into a new checking account. If banks have a reserve requirement of 0.05, the money multiplier is equal to:

A. 20
C. 1,000

B. 5
D. 10

74. After Aunt Thelma passes away, the members of her family find $1,000 that has been hidden in the toaster for many years. They deposit the $1,000 into a new checking account. If banks have a reserve requirement of 0.05, this deposit of $1,000 could eventually increase demand deposits by:

A. $20,000
C. $10,000

B. $5,000
D. $1,000

75. Suppose the demand for money increases. According to the liquidity preference theory, this will increase the _____ in the money market.

A. real GDP
B. Consumer Price Index
C. unemployment rate
D. interest rate

76. The _____ theory of macroeconomics believes that the _____ curve is vertical at full employment GDP.

A. classical; aggregate supply
B. classical; aggregate demand
C. Keynesian; short-run aggregate supply
D. Keynesian; long-run aggregate supply

77. If the economy is in a recession, the best fiscal policy would be to:

A. Increase taxes with no change in government spending.
B. Increase the money supply.
C. Increase government spending with no change in taxes.
D. Decrease the demand for loanable funds.

78. The marginal propensity to consume is 0.90. If government spending were to increase by $5 billion, this spending would multiply to a total of:

A. $500 billion
C. $15 billion

B. $40 billion
D. $50 billion

79. If the ecoppnomy is experiencing very low unemployment but a high inflation rate, the appropriate open market operation would be to:
    A. Raise taxes
    B. Lower government spending
    C. Sell Treasury bonds
    D. Raise the federal funds rate

80. Suppose the economy is currently in a recession as a result of weak aggregate demand. If policy makers take no action, we expect long-run economic output to _____ and the price level to _____.
    A. return to full employment; decrease
    B. continue to decrease; decrease
    C. return to full employment; increase
    D. increase beyond full employment; decrease

81. Suppose the produpction possibilities curve for a nation is linear. If all of the nation's resources are used to produce cars, 1,000 cars can be produced. If all of the nation's resources are used to produce candy, 5,000 candies can be produced. The opportunity cost of 1 car is equal to:
    A. 1 candy
    B. 5 candies
    C. 5,000 candies
    D. 20 candies

Use Table 6 to answer questions 82 and 83.

TABLE 6		Bread	Butter			Bread	Butter
England	All resources used to produce bread	30	0	Ireland	All resources used to produce bread	10	0
	All resources used to produce butter	0	30		All resources used to produce butter	0	20

82. Suppose that England and Ireland can both produce bread and butter. The production possibilities are given in Table 6. If England uses all its resources to produce bread, it can produce 30 units of bread. If it uses all its resources to produce butter, it can produce 30 units of butter. Likewise, if Ireland uses all its resources to produce bread, it can produce 10 units of bread. If it uses all its resources to produce butter, it can produce 20 units of butter. We know that:
    A. Ireland has an absolute advantage in both bread and butter.
    B. England has an absolute advantage in bread, and Ireland has an absolute advantage in butter.
    C. Ireland has a comparative advantage in both bread and butter.
    D. England has a comparative advantage in bread, and Ireland has a comparative advantage in butter.

83. Suppose that England and Ireland can both produce bread and butter. The production possibilities are given in Table 6. Given these production possibilities:
    A. England will export butter to Ireland.
    B. England will import bread from Ireland.
    C. Ireland will import bread from England.
    D. Ireland will export bread to England.

84. If goods produced in America become more popular in foreign countries, all else equal, we would expect:
    A. Demand for the U.S. dollar to decrease, appreciating the dollar against other currencies
    B. Demand for the U.S. dollar to increase, depreciating the dollar against other currencies
    C. Demand for the U.S. dollar to increase, appreciating the dollar against other currencies
    D. Supply of the U.S. dollar to increase, appreciating the dollar against other currencies

85. An American clothing company sells a T-shirt to a consumer in Canada. This transaction would show up as _____ in the U.S. _____ account.
    A. an increase; current   B. a decrease; current
    C. an increase; financial   D. a decrease; financial

86. Of the following choices, the best example of a public good is:
    A. A cell phone   B. The local police department
    C. A bottle of aspirin   D. A ticket to the opera

Use Figure 7 for questions 87 and 88.

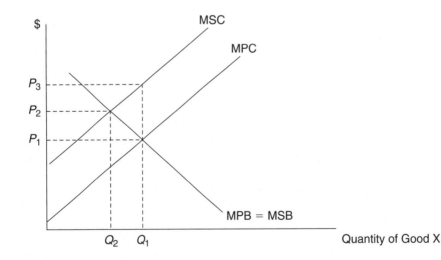

FIGURE 7

87. According to Figure 7, the market for good X exhibits a _____ externality because, at the market equilibrium quantity, the _____ is greater than the _____.
    A. negative; MSB; MPB
    B. negative; MSC; MSB
    C. positive; MSC; MPC
    D. negative; MPC; MPB

88. According to Figure 7, which of the following policies would remedy the externality in the market for good X?
    A. Impose a per-unit tax equal to $(P_2 - P_1)$.
    B. Impose a per-unit subsidy equal to $(P_3 - P_1)$.
    C. Impose a per-unit tax equal to $(P_3 - P_1)$.
    D. Impose a per-unit tax equal to $(P_3 - P_2)$.

89. Which of the following best describes a situation that generates a positive externality?
    A. A trash incinerator is located in your neighborhood.
    B. A farmer spreads chemical pesticides that leak into your drinking water.
    C. A beekeeper lives down the street, and his honeybees fly to your yard and pollinate your cherry trees.
    D. A neighbor has a swampy pond, and mosquitoes are often flying into your patio.

90. The socially efficient quantity of pollution is the quantity where:
    A. The MSB = 0 for the last ton of pollution emitted.
    B. The MSC = 0 for the last ton of pollution emitted.
    C. Zero tons of pollution are emitted.
    D. The MSB = MSC for the last ton of pollution emitted.

91. Mr. Pham receives health insurance from his employer that will pay nearly 100 percent of any illness or injury that he may suffer, after he pays a small deductible. Suppose Mr. Pham, now that he has health insurance, decides to train to climb Mount Everest. This kind of behavior is an example of:
    A. Pooling behavior
    B. Moral hazard
    C. Symmetric information
    D. The premium death spiral

92. When Betty was hospitalized for pneumonia, she was responsible for paying the first $1,000 of her bill, and her health insurance company paid the rest. This $1,000 payment represents Betty's:
    A. Deductible
    B. Asymmetric information
    C. Copayment
    D. Actuarially fair premium

93. Suppose there is a health insurance pool of 1,000 people. Within the pool, 1 percent of the people will get very sick and suffer $200,000 in medical bills, while the other 99 percent of the people will remain healthy and have no medical bills. The health insurance firm must also charge each person in the pool a loading fee of $100. Including the loading fee, what is the premium that each person will be charged?
    A. $2 million
    B. $1,200
    C. $2,100
    D. $4,200

94. The problem of _____ affects the market for health insurance because the sickest people would be the most willing to pay for insurance.

   A. insurance mandates

   B. asymmetric information

   C. adverse selection

   D. copayments and deductibles

95. One way for a health insurance company to reduce the problem of moral hazard is to increase each policyholder's:

   A. Coverage   B. Copayment

   C. Monthly premium   D. Loading fee

96. Samuel is a graduate student in economics and is beginning the research for his thesis. He is reading and summarizing what previous economists have discovered about his topic. At this stage in the research process, Samuel is said to be conducting:

   A. A testable hypothesis

   B. A data-gathering experiment

   C. An empirical analysis

   D. A literature review

97. Economic research is said to follow the scientific method because:

   A. A hypothesis is statistically tested with available data and either confirmed or refuted.

   B. A theory is confirmed with anecdotal evidence.

   C. Past economic behavior is believed to predict future economic behavior.

   D. Economic forecasts are made from the results of an empirical model.

98. Terrence owns a chain of convenience stores. He notices that when the weather is hot, he sells more cold fountain drinks. Terrence believes that there is a direct relationship between the high temperature on a given day and the quantity of cold fountain drinks that he sells on that day. This is an example of:

   A. Empirical analysis   B. An economic theory

   C. A literature review   D. A testable hypothesis

99. Raquel is working on her term paper in her economics class. She has gathered years of data and has begun to statistically measure the impact that a higher minimum wage has on teenage employment. In which stage of the research process is Raquel?

   A. The literature review stage   B. The forecasting stage

   C. The peer review stage   D. The empirical analysis stage

100. Most current economic research involves collecting data to statistically test hypotheses on how some economic variables affect other variables. This type of research is broadly known as:

   A. Empirical economics   B. Literature reviews

   C. Theoretical economics   D. The peer review process

Answers to Quizzes and Final Exam

Answers to Quizzes

Chapter 1

1. False. Economic resources include land (actual land or other natural resources, such as energy or timber), labor (people's work), capital (tools and other things that are produced and used to produce goods and services), and entrepreneurship/technology (the know-how to combine these resources to produce goods and services). Money is not actually an economic resource; it is merely used to facilitate the exchange of these resources.

2. True. Opportunity cost, or the cost of the next best alternative or what is given up to get something, may be different from the monetary price. For instance, if you had to wait in line for five hours to buy a Ferb, the true cost of a Ferb would be $100 *plus* the value of the time spent waiting.

3. False. Rational agents think *marginally*. If a producer is thinking rationally, he will focus on the marginal cost of a good, rather than its average cost.

4. False. Both of these are examples of microeconomics. Microeconomics focuses on the allocation of scarce resources by individual agents (individual people, households, and firms). Macroeconomics focuses on entire economies.

5. False.   Recall that a rational decision maker thinks about the marginal benefit in relation to the marginal cost of the next unit. If the price of the next purplett is $9 (the marginal cost to the consumer) and he or she will receive $10 in marginal benefit from purchasing it, the consumer will purchase it.

6. B.   *Ceteris paribus* is Latin for "with other things the same." Economists make the *ceteris paribus* assumption because many things may be changing at the same time, but when we model something, we are trying to isolate what the effect of a particular thing is, so we assume that nothing else is changing at the same time.

7. D.   Recall that a rational decision maker will take an action if the marginal benefit exceeds the marginal cost. The total cost of producing 36 units is $45 and the total cost of producing 35 units is $40, so the marginal cost of producing the thirty-sixth unit is $45 − $40 = $5. Therefore, a rational decision maker will sell the thirty-sixth T-shirt only if she can get at least $5 for it.

8. B.   Capital is something that is made (built or produced) and that is used to produce other things, such as a factory that is built and used to produce other things. Money that is raised to start a business is what is used to purchase capital, labor, and land/natural resources. Electricity and other forms of energy are natural resources.

9. A.   A rational consumer can make mistakes if the information that she has is inaccurate. However, consumers don't intentionally make themselves worse off.

10. C.   Society is faced with scarcity because we have unlimited economic wants, yet we have only a limited quantity of resources that we can use to satisfy those wants.

Chapter 2

1. False.   The law of diminishing marginal utility says that as you consume more and more of a good, you get less and less utility from each additional unit. While you may be better off with each additional unit of consumption (total utility increases), you are not as much better off from that last unit of consumption as you were from the previous unit (marginal utility decreases).

2. False.   Utility is the way in which economists measure the usefulness or happiness that consumers get from consumption. However, it is measured in terms of a fictional unit, "utils," not dollars (or any other currency).

3. True.   The consumer is getting 80/4 = 20 marginal utils per dollar from Gams, but is getting 100/4 = 25 marginal utils per dollar from Ferbs. According to the utility maximization rule, the consumer should consume at the point all marginal utilities per dollar are equal. If the consumer increases his consumption of Ferbs, the marginal utility from consuming Ferbs will decrease.

4. True.   If the marginal utility of the next unit is negative, that unit actually reduces total utility. This unit should definitely not be consumed!

5. C.   The marginal utility of the fourth chicken liver is the difference between the total utility from four chicken livers and the total utility from three chicken livers. Thus the marginal utility of the fourth chicken liver is 28 − 24 = 4 utils.

6. A.   To maximize utility across two goods, the marginal utility per dollar must be the same for both soda and chicken livers. We are told that marginal utility per dollar for sodas is six. The table informs us that the marginal utility of the third chicken

liver is 6 utils. The only way that Sissy can be maximizing utility is if the price of fried chicken livers is $1.

7. A.   The marginal utility per dollar for doughnuts is 3 (9 utils/$3), and the marginal utility per dollar for coffee is 2.5 (5 utils/$2). Since Jamaal is already spending all of his income, he can increase his total utility by spending more of his income on the good that provides the greater "bang for the buck."

8. D.   Calculating, 10 units of good X would use $4 × 10 = $40 of the budget, and 12 units of good Y would use the remaining $5 × 12 = $60 of the budget.

9. B.   Calculating, 6 units of good X would use $10 × 6 = $60 of the budget, and 25 units of good Y would use $2 × 25 = $50. This would overspend the budget by $10.

10. C.   If Grace's total utility rises by 5 utils for each cupcake she eats and never diminishes, the marginal utility is constant (drawn horizontal) at 5 utils.

Chapter 3

1. True.   The theory of utility-maximizing behavior presumes that marginal utility diminishes with more consumption. As the price of a good falls, this allows the consumer to increase utility by consuming more of the good along the downward-sloping marginal utility curve. This gives us the basis for the downward-sloping demand curve.

2. False.   A lower price of oranges will increase quantity demanded along the demand curve, but will not shift the demand curve. The demand for oranges will shift only if one of the determinants changes.

3. False.   If a good is normal, an increase in income causes an increase in demand. Thus, the income elasticity for a normal good will be a positive number.

4. True.   Complementary goods are those that consumers enjoy together. When the price of one increases, it makes it difficult for consumers to afford both of them, thus decreasing the demand for the complementary good.

5. C.   For normal goods, income and demand move in the same direction. When one increases, the other increases.

6. A.   A careful inspection of the table allows you to determine what Melanie will do when the price falls from $3 to $1.

7. C.   Using the midpoint formula:

$$E_d = \left(\frac{6-10}{140-100} \right) \times \left(\frac{120}{8} \right) = 1.5$$

And any value greater than 1 is elastic.

8. C.   These are complementary goods, so a lower price for one good causes an increase in the demand for the other.

9. A.   Normal goods will have an income elasticity that is positive. If the response to a change in income is inelastic, it will be less than 1.

10. B.   If Mr. Pietro lowers the price by 1 percent, he will see a 3 percent increase in pizzas sold. This upward impact on total revenue will more than offset the downward impact of the lower price, and total revenue will rise.

Chapter 4

1. False. Even if marginal product is falling, so long as the marginal product is still positive, the contribution of the next unit of labor adds to the total product.

2. True. Only in the short run are there fixed inputs because the short run is a period of time that is too brief to change a certain input. This fixed input is usually assumed to be capital.

3. True. Because there is a fixed input in the short run, adding more and more units of a variable input (like labor) causes the marginal product to fall.

4. False. By the very nature of fixed costs in the short run, they neither rise nor fall as more output is produced.

5. True. Marginal cost and marginal product of labor are inversely related.

6. D. If the marginal product is rising, it must be positive, and therefore total product must also be rising. In fact, total product would be rising at an increasing rate.

7. A. The marginal product for the second unit of labor is 8 units of output, but the marginal product for the third unit of labor is 7 units of output.

8. C. Average product is calculated by dividing total output by the units of labor employed.

9. B. Marginal cost and marginal product are inversely related. Choice D is not always true because the marginal product can be falling while average product is still rising. This occurs in the range where marginal product still exceeds average product.

10. D. The rent will have to be paid no matter how much business Haley has during the month. All the other choices describe costs that would rise if she were producing more units of output, and would fall if she were producing fewer units of output.

Chapter 5

1. True. Diminishing marginal product leads to a marginal cost curve with a positive slope. This upward-sloping marginal cost curve is behind the upward-sloping supply curve.

2. False. The law of supply predicts that the price of corn chips and the quantity of chips supplied will move in the same direction. If one falls, the other falls.

3. True. This is precisely what an increase (or rightward shift) in supply means.

4. False. When the price of a product rises, the producer may not be able to increase the quantity supplied by a large amount in the short run. However, in the long run, producers have much more flexibility to adjust to the higher price, and thus the response will be more elastic in the long run.

5. Use the midpoint formula:

$$E_s = \frac{\%\Delta Q_s}{\%\Delta P} = \left(\frac{Q_1 - Q_0}{P_1 - P_0} \right) \times \left(\frac{\bar{P}}{\bar{Q}} \right) = \left(\frac{200 - 300}{\$2 - \$3} \right) \times \left(\frac{\$2.5}{250} \right) = 1$$

Note that when you use the midpoint formula, you are actually finding the price elasticity of supply at the price midway between the two points on your curve.

6.   When a production input becomes less expensive, the supply of autos shifts to the right, as shown in Figure A5-1.

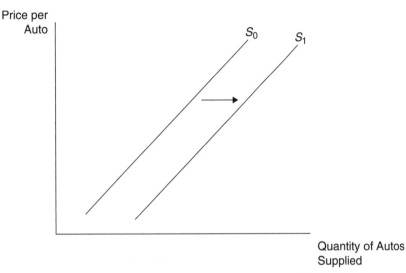

FIGURE A5-1

7. C.   When the price of TVs increases, the supply curve will not shift; there will only be an increase in the quantity of TVs supplied along the supply curve.

8. B.   Since apples are a critical input to apple pies, more expensive apples make it more costly and difficult to supply the pies. Thus the supply curve shifts to the left.

9. A.   The shape of the supply curve comes from the shape of the marginal cost curve. If the marginal cost curve is constant at $80 for each textbook, then the supply curve is also horizontal at $80.

10. C.   If the cookie producers cannot acquire a critical input like the chocolate chips, the supply response to a higher price will be very inelastic.

Chapter 6

1. True.   When the demand curve shifts, it changes both the price and the quantity in the same direction. So a decrease in demand will cause both price and quantity to decrease. This effect can be seen in a graph like Figure 6-5 earlier in the chapter.

2. False.   A price ceiling must be set *below* the equilibrium price if it is to be effective. If the ceiling is set above the market price, market forces will continue to operate, and there will be no surplus or shortage.

3. True.   Total surplus is maximized when the competitive market is in equilibrium. Thus, any sort of price control will necessarily decrease the total surplus.

4. D.   Leather is a key input in the production of basketballs, so the supply curve will shift to the left. Such a shift will cause the price to rise and the quantity to fall.

5. A.   A rightward shift of the supply curve is the only choice that will produce both a lower price of coffee and a higher quantity in the market.

6. B.   The area of consumer surplus is the triangle below the demand curve and above the price. This area is equal to $\frac{1}{2}$($4)(16) = $32.

7. C.   A price floor creates a surplus in the amount of the difference between the units supplied (20) and the units demanded (12). The deadweight loss is the area of a triangle below the demand curve and above the supply curve and between the new quantity of 12 and the equilibrium quantity of 16 units. This area is equal to $\frac{1}{2}$($4)(4) = $8.

8. D.   If both the price and the quantity are falling, the only shift that will produce this outcome is a decrease in demand.

9. A.   A perfectly inelastic demand curve is vertical. When the supply curve shifts upward by T, the new equilibrium price will be exactly T higher.

10. D.   All of these policies will reduce the quantity of chocolate produced in the market away from the equilibrium quantity. When this occurs, deadweight loss is the result.

TIP   *When in doubt, graph it out. If you find yourself in the middle of an exam or trying to complete a homework assignment, do a quick sketch of a supply and demand graph so that you can visualize the shifting curves and the impact on price and quantity.*

Chapter 7

1. True.   Economic profit subtracts opportunity costs from accounting profit, so economic profit is smaller than accounting profit. Therefore, if economic profit is zero, accounting profit must be positive.

2. False.   The firm shuts down if the price falls below average variable cost, not when it falls below average total cost.

3. False.   Perfectly competitive firms are price takers and must accept the market price and use it to maximize profit.

4. True.   In the short run, it is always true that $P = MR = MC$, but only in the long run is it also true that we can include ATC in this equalwwity.

5. B.   This is a key assumption of perfect competition; it ensures that economic profit will be driven to zero in the long run.

6. C.   The absence of entry barriers ensures that short-run profits will be driven to zero by the entry of new firms in the long run.

7. A.   Josie is experiencing the shutdown condition. Every bushel that she produces brings only $50 of revenue but costs an additional $60 to produce.

8. D.   At the price P_1, MR = MC at Q_4 units of output. Because P_1 lies above the ATC curve, there will be positive profits in the short run.

9. B.   The long-run price is where profits are zero, and this occurs at the minimum of the ATC curve.

10. D.   The shutdown point is the minimum of the AVC curve, so prices below P_4 would prompt the shutdown decision.

Chapter 8

1. True.   Because the marginal revenue lies below the price, the profit-maximizing output is less than it would be under perfect competition. The price set by the monopolist is therefore going to be higher than the price under perfect competition.

2. False.   A very important characteristic of monopoly is the presence of barriers to entry. Because new firms cannot enter the market, the short-run profits last into the long run.

3. False.   In perfect competition, the price is equal to the marginal revenue. In monopoly, price exceeds marginal revenue. In neither case does marginal revenue exceed price.

4. False.   If price equals average total cost, profit will be eliminated, but deadweight loss will remain.

5. D.   Because there is only one seller in the market, demand for that firm's product is the entire market demand for the good or service.

6. A.   Joe and Susan are not buying the same product at different prices. Susan is paying a higher price because she has chosen a different (larger) apartment.

7. A.   Whenever price exceeds marginal cost, deadweight loss is the result.

8.   The graph should look something like Figure A8-1.

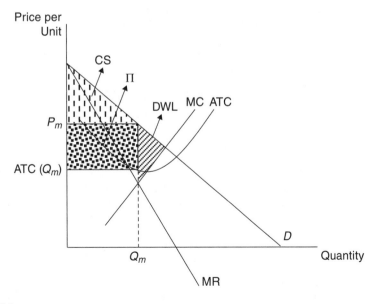

FIGURE A8-1

9.   Unless the government regulated the monopolist to produce output greater than Q_m, there would be no impact on the deadweight loss. The government would simply transfer the area of profit to the consumers, increasing consumer surplus.

10.   The completed table should appear as Table A8-1. MC = MR = $5 at an output of 2 units. The price needed to sell 2 units is $6. Profit is calculated as 2 units × ($6 − $5) = $2.

TABLE A8-1			
Price	Quantity Demanded	Total Revenue	Marginal Revenue
$8	0	$0	
7	1	7	$7
6	2	12	5
5	3	15	3
4	4	16	1
3	5	15	−1
2	6	12	−3
1	7	7	−5
0	8	0	−7

Chapter 9

1. True.   As the name suggests, monopolistic competition shares the characteristics and outcomes of both perfect competition and monopoly.

2. False.   It is true that MR = MC, but price is set higher, at the demand curve. In the long run, it is true that $P = ATC > MR = MC$.

3. False.   There are barriers in oligopoly, and those facilitate long-run economic profits.

4. False.   The Nash equilibrium means that each firm earns the highest payoff possible, *given* the rival's choice.

5. C.   This is a key assumption, and implication, of monopolistic competition.

6. A.   The long-run adjustment to short-run losses would first involve the exit of some firms. Demand for the remaining firms would begin to increase, increasing the price along with it. When all firms are breaking even, exit will stop.

7. C.   Some oligopolies, like the computer and beer industries, have differentiated products. Others, like the oil and gas industries, have identical products.

8. B.   Coke does not have a dominant strategy, as its best choice depends upon what Pepsi is doing. Pepsi will always choose P_L because no matter what choice is made by Coke, choosing P_L always produces the highest payoff.

9. C.   Pepsi has a dominant strategy to always choose P_L. Because Coke knows that Pepsi will choose P_L, Coke will choose P_H to earn the highest payoff.

10. D.   This is really the essence of mutual interdependence.

Chapter 10

1. False.   A downward-sloping labor supply function can happen if the substitution effect of a wage increase is smaller than the income effect of the wage increase. If this is the case, a consumer has a much stronger desire to consume more hours of leisure, and this reduces the number of hours of work supplied.

2. True.   When we compute $VMP_L = P \times MP_L$, we assume that the price is constant and is given by the competitive product market. Thus it is a diminishing marginal product of labor curve that provides the downward-sloping VMP_L curve.

3. True.   The VMP_L curve serves as the firm's labor demand curve. At any wage, if the VMP_L curve shifts to the right, profits will rise if more units of labor are employed.

4. True.   When the demand for labor shifts to the right, wage and employment both rise. When the supply of labor shifts to the left, wage rises and employment falls. So both shifts cause the wage to rise.

5. False.   The least-cost combination occurs when the marginal products *per dollar* are equal. This statement would be true only if both factor prices were equal to $1.

6. A.   The falling wage causes a substitution effect that predicts less labor and more leisure. The falling wage also creates an income effect that predicts less leisure and more labor. So if Eric is to decrease his labor supply at a lower wage, it must be true that the income effect is smaller than the substitution effect.

7. C.   The $VMP_L = \$10 \times MP_L$, so the sixth worker has $VMP_L = \$10 \times 4 = \$40$.

8. C.   The firm hires where $VMP_L = P \times MP_L = $ wage. Since the wage is $30, we look for the $VMP_L = \$3 \times MP_L = \$30$, and this happens at the third worker.

9. B.   The demand for fast food workers falls if the equipment and workers are substitutes. The falling demand will reduce both wage and employment of these workers.

10. D.   Stanley has already found the combination of labor and capital where the marginal products per dollar are equal.

Chapter 11

1. False.   Microeconomics is the study of households, firms, and individuals. Macroeconomics is the study of entire economies as a whole.

2. False.   Consumption makes up the largest percentage of U.S. GDP.

3. True.   The most dramatic changes in GDP occur in investment spending.

4. False.   Gross national product is an indication of what is produced by resources owned by a particular country, whereas GDP is what is produced within a country's borders.

5. False. Gross domestic product counts only final goods produced and sold within a country. It doesn't count used goods or goods sold outside of traditional markets. It also doesn't include things like produce from home gardens that is grown and consumed by households without ever being sold.

6. The grogs are counted in 2009 GDP as additions to inventory. Therefore, this action would add $200 in inventory to 2009 GDP. The grogs were sold in 2010, so inventory would be reduced by the same $200, and $300 would instead appear in consumption, for a total change of +$100 in 2010 GDP. Note that this means that GDP includes the value added from the service of selling the grogs.

7. Durable goods: C
New homes: I
Used homes: not counted in GDP
Inventories: I
Nondurable goods: C
Government purchases: G
Imports: M
Exports: X

8. GDP = $C + I + G + (X - M)$
GDP = ($500 + $900) + ($1,000 + $300) + ($400) + ($280 - $150)
= $1,400 + $1,300 + $400 + $130
= $3,230

9. Used houses aren't counted. The goal of GDP is to capture new production of goods and services. These used homes were already produced in another year. Counting them in this year's GDP would overstate the production this year and double-count them.

10. Maxistan is a net exporter, because it exports more goods than it imports. This means that its net exports add to GDP, rather than reduce GDP.

Chapter 12

1. C. To be counted as unemployed, you must be not working even a single hour, and you must be actively looking for work.

2. A. The efficiency wage theory states that firms pay an efficiency wage, a wage that is higher than the market-clearing wage, in order to generate greater work effort in their employees.

3. D. The labor force includes only civilian working-age people who are not institutionalized.

4. D. When people stop looking for work, they are no longer counted as being in the labor force. However, they are also no longer counted as being unemployed, so the official unemployment rate decreases.

5. B. Frictional unemployment occurs when job placement is costly. If we eliminated frictional unemployment, we would no longer be placing people in jobs that were not necessarily appropriate for them. This would be more efficient for the nation's economy.

6.

TABLE A12-1		
Name	**Category**	**Explanation**
All of the nine children aged 15 and under	Not in the labor force	Nobody under the age of 16 is counted in the labor force, regardless of his or her employment status
Maggie	Not in the labor force	Not looking for work
Grace	In the labor force, employed	Even though she is looking for work, she worked at least 1 hour in the previous week
Owen	In the labor force, employed	Worked more than 1 hour
Erin	In the labor force, employed	Worked more than 1 hour
Bridgette	In the labor force, employed	Worked more than 1 hour
Luke	In the labor force, employed	Worked more than 1 hour
Andrew	In the labor force, employed	Worked more than 1 hour
Jude	In the labor force, unemployed	Because he is actively looking and is not employed, he is counted as unemployed
Alex	In the labor force, unemployed	Because he is actively looking and is not employed, he is counted as unemployed
Max	Not in the labor force	Not looking for work
Ella	Not in the labor force	Only civilian, noninstitutionalized people count in unemployment data
Jack	Not in the labor force	Discouraged workers are not in the labor force because they have stopped looking for work

7. Totals:
    Civilian, noninstitutionalized population = 20
    Civilian labor force = 8
    Unemployed = 2
    Employed = 6

8. Labor force participation rate = LF/civilian working-age population = 8/12 = 66.7%

9. Unemployment rate = 2/8 = 25%

10. Note that if we counted Jack, who is a person that economists call a discouraged worker, then our labor force would be 9 and there would be 3 unemployed, so our unemployment rate would be 3/9 = 33 percent. This illustrates the discouraged worker effect. So if Jack suddenly got more optimistic about his job prospects and started to look for work, we would see a spike in the unemployment rate. If economists were looking only at the unemployment rate, they might draw the opposite conclusion—that all of a sudden jobs prospects were worse!

However, if we also noticed that when Jack reenters the workforce, the LFPR also changes (now you would calculate 9/13 = 69.2 percent), we get a better, more complete picture of the labor market.

Chapter 13

1. False.   Deflation is the opposite of inflation, but it is associated with falling wages, weak spending, and ultimately severe recessions and depressions.

2. False.   The CPI measures the prices that are paid by a typical household for the goods and services that are typically bought. For instance, a typical urban household is not likely to purchase a farm tractor, so increases in the price of tractors would not be reflected in the CPI.

3. False.   This works only if you are comparing the rate of inflation between a year and the base year. For any other two years, you subtract the new CPI from the old CPI and divide that number by the old CPI.

4. True.   If the base year changes, the CPI for any given year will also change. However, the rate of inflation will not change.

5. True.   If the rate of inflation was underestimated, the real interest rate will be lower than expected. This means that the lender will get a lower return then it anticipated and that the real value of the borrower's loan has decreased.

6.   See Table A13-1.

7.   See Table A13-1.

8.   See Table A13-1.

TABLE A13-1							
Year	Price of Ham (per pound)	Price of Bottled Water	Price of Magazines	Hourly Wage of Babysitters	Price of Basket	CPI	Rate of Inflation
1990	$2.00 × 2	$10.00 × 1	$1.00 × 6	$6.00 × 4	$44.00	100.0	—
1991	$2.00 × 2	$11.00 × 1	$1.50 × 6	$6.00 × 4	$48.00	109.1	9.1%
1992	$2.50 × 2	$12.00 × 1	$1.75 × 6	$7.00 × 4	$55.50	126.1	15.6%
1993	$2.75 × 2	$13.00 × 1	$2.50 × 6	$8.00 × 4	$65.50	148.9	18.1%

9.   5 percent. The natural rate of unemployment (NAIRU) is found at the vertical long-run Phillips curve. This is the rate of unemployment that occurs once all expectations have had time to adjust to the actual inflation in the economy.

10.   4 percent inflation and 4 percent unemployment. When the nation experiences unexpected inflation, the SRPC shifts upward by the amount of unexpected inflation.

Chapter 14

1. False.   Although most economies have seen an upward trend in output, which occurs when the LRAS curve shifts to the right, it is entirely possible for an economy to experience a decrease in LRAS. For instance, an economy may not invest a sufficient amount to maintain its stock of capital, or a natural disaster or war may destroy a country's resources.

2. True.   Inflation occurs when AD shifts to the right. Increased consumer confidence shifts AD to the right.

3. False.   Long-run equilibrium is associated with an employment rate equal to the NAIRU, or natural rate of unemployment.

4. False.   It is possible for an economy to produce above the full potential output. However, when it does so, it is straining its resources. For instance, if the unemployment rate is very low and firms have difficulty finding workers, they may have to increase wages to their workers in the form of overtime.

5. False.   Though there is no specific "rule" for defining a recession, a recession is broadly defined as two or more quarters (that is, six months or more) of declining output.

6. D.   The bottom point in the business cycle is the trough. The expansion is when output is increasing, the peak is when expansion hits its maximum, and contraction is when output is falling.

7. C.   Investment is a component of aggregate demand. Whenever a component of AD increases, AD increases as well. Choices A and D would cause SRAS to decrease, and choice B would cause AD to decrease.

8. A.   Each of the others is a potential reason that the AD curve is downward-sloping.

9. B.   Improvement in education would increase the quality of the labor force, which would affect the LRAS. Each of the others would have an impact on short-run variables only.

10. D.   Each of the others would cause a recessionary gap, as they would all decrease SRAS.

Chapter 15

1. True.   If something failed at performing one of the functions, it would end up failing at performing the other functions. For instance, if something could not hold a store of value for long enough, people would be unwilling to accept it as a medium of exchange because they would have to rush to spend it themselves before it lost its value.

2. False.   Fiat money has no intrinsic value, yet most money used is fiat money (such as paper dollars).

3. True.   As long as we believe that something can be used to perform all three functions of money, it is money. In essence, money is a social contract.

4. True.   This is because the things that are included in M2 cannot be used directly to purchase goods and services. They can, however, be converted to money with relative ease, so they are nearly money.

5. False.   If the reserve requirement is 5 percent, the money multiplier is $1/0.05 = 20$. This means that an injection of $1,000 will lead to an increase in the money supply of $20,000 *at most*. The key here is whether or not banks keep excess reserves and people deposit money in the bank.

6. False.   The Federal Reserve sets interest-rate targets, but it achieves those targets by setting the money supply.

7. False.   The Federal Reserve was created in response to economic and banking crises in the late 1800s and early 1900s.

8. False.   According to liquidity preference theory, people have a preference about the amount of liquidity (that is, cash) that they have on hand that will change depending on the interest rate. This means that the interest rate will adjust to changes in either the supply of or the demand for money.

9. False.   If all of a sudden debit cards were made illegal, people would need to keep more cash on hand rather than less, which means that the demand for money would increase.

10. False.   If the Federal Reserve increased the money supply, the money supply curve would shift out, which would lead to a new lower interest rate.

Chapter 16

1. C.   Consumption makes up the largest proportion of GDP, but during recessions and expansions, investment changes by a much larger percentage, which eventually affects consumption.

2. B.   The crowding-out effect occurs when the government's borrowing drives up interest rates.

3. A.   The classical theory assumes that prices will adjust and output will return to full employment.

4. D.   All of these concepts are associated with Keynesian theory.

5. B.   The multiplier = $1/(1 - MPC)$, which is the same as $1/MPS$. The multiplier here is 2.5. However, the actual increase in GDP will depend on the crowding-out effect.

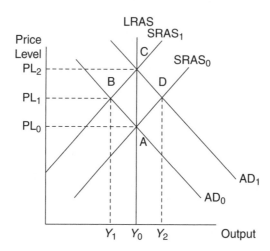

FIGURE A16-1

Refer to Figure A16-1 for the answers to questions 6 through 8.

6. B.   An increase in the price of inputs, such as labor, would cause the SRAS to shift, as illustrated by a movement from A to B.

7. C.   A movement from point C to point B represents a decrease in output as a result of a decrease in aggregate demand. To increase aggregate demand, one could

engage in expansionary monetary policy, which would mean buying bonds to increase the money supply.

8. B.   A movement from point A to point B represents stagflation. Expansionary fiscal policy will increase the aggregate demand curve, which will result in a return to full employment but will embed inflation in the economy.

9.   I.   See Figure A16-2.

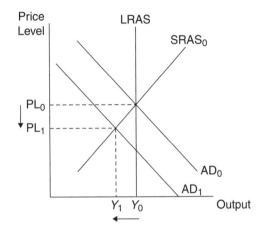

FIGURE A16-2

II.   I would pursue expansionary monetary policy. I would achieve this by buying bonds to increase the money supply, which would lower interest rates and increase aggregate demand.

III. Figure A16-3 shows the effect of my action on the appropriate market.

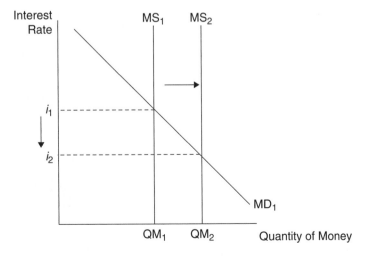

FIGURE A16-3

IV.   Figure A16-4 shows the effect of my action on the AD-AS model.

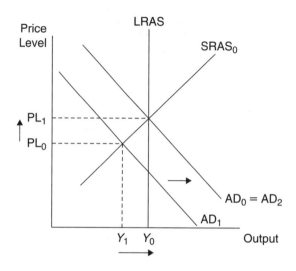

FIGURE A16-4

V.   The liquidity trap. If interest rates are already at zero or close to it, monetary policy cannot stimulate investment and aggregate demand. See Figure A16.5.

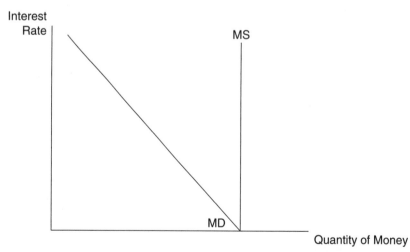

FIGURE A16-5

10.   I.   Figure A16.6 shows the current situation in Ema.

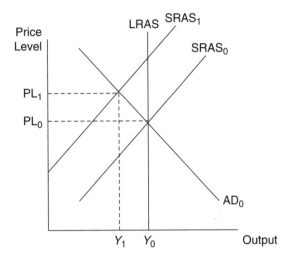

FIGURE A16-6

II.   An increase in the cost of production inputs, such as land, labor, and capital.

III.   Multiplier $= 4 = 1/(1 - MPC)$. MPC $= 0.75$.

IV.   Fiscal policy.

V.   The impact of expansionary fiscal policy is seen in Figure A16-7 as an increase in aggregate demand from AD_0 to AD_1. Unemployment will decrease.

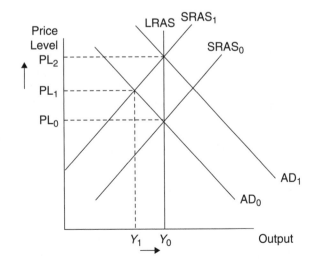

FIGURE A16-7

Chapter 17

1. True. This is precisely the benefit of trade based on comparative advantage.

2. False. Mutually beneficial trade is based upon comparative advantage, not absolute advantage. Even large nations can benefit from trade because the large nation will be able to focus on producing the goods that it can make at the lowest opportunity cost.

3. False. Both tariffs and quotas increase the price of the product. A tariff does it by taxing the imported products. The quota does it by reducing the quantity supplied by the foreign suppliers.

4. False. A currency can appreciate if either the demand for it increases or the supply of it decreases.

5. True. A trade surplus exists if exports exceed imports, and a trade deficit exists if the imports exceed the imports.

6. A. Spain can produce more of both goods, so it has an absolute advantage.

7. C. For Spain, the opportunity cost of each good is 1 unit of the other. For Portugal, the opportunity cost of one unit of cheese is 1/2 unit of wine. This means that Portugal has a comparative advantage in cheese, so it will trade cheese to Spain in exchange for wine.

8. D. Because interest rates are rising in the United States, Japanese investors will increase their demand for U.S. dollars so that they can purchase financial assets. This increase in the demand for dollars is matched with an increased supply of yen. The price of the dollar rises against the yen.

9. B. Americans will need to supply more dollars to increase their demand for the quid. This will lead the quid to appreciate and the dollar to depreciate.

10. B. Consumers lose some surplus when the price rises after trade restrictions are imposed.

Chapter 18

1. False. Cheeseburgers are a private good, and free riding is a problem only for public goods. Free riders enjoy the benefits of something without paying for it. Because public goods are nonexcludable, they suffer from this problem.

2. True. Among the many positive externalities created by education, when more children receive an education, this improves the quality and productivity of the future workforce. These more productive workers will earn more money and pay higher taxes, start successful businesses, and employ more people. All of these benefits spill over to the rest of society and are justly subsidized by the government.

3. False. Both create market failures, but in different ways. A negative externality causes the market to produce too much of a bad thing. A positive externality causes the market to produce too little of a good thing.

4. False. Command-and-control policies can reduce pollution, but at a much higher cost than other policies, such as emissions taxes. If we are going to achieve a cleaner environment, economists prefer to do so at the lowest possible cost.

5. True.   At the market equilibrium, the MPB = MSC. But with a positive externality, there are spillover benefits to society, so the MSB > MPB.

6. D.   The fruits of the research (a cure for a disease, maybe) benefit everybody, even those who do not ever contract that disease. And if the cure is used for one person, it can also be used for another person. Scientific knowledge is nonrival and nonexcludable.

7. A.   At the market equilibrium, the MPB = MPC. With a negative externality, there are spillover costs to society, so the MSC > MPC.

8. B.   When a market produces a negative externality like pollution, the market quantity of the good (electricity in this case) exceeds the socially efficient quantity, so the last thing we should do is make it easier to consume or produce that good. A subsidy would worsen the situation.

9. C.   When Figure 18-11 shows a MSC curve that lies above the MPC curve, it's a clear indication that a negative externality exists in the market for a private good.

10. D.   The unregulated market will come to equilibrium where the MPC = S curve intersects the demand curve.

Chapter 19

1. True.   Healthcare is second behind government.

2. False.   The dollar in income will be taxed, and therefore the actual worth of an additional dollar in income will depend on the marginal tax rate. A dollar in health insurance benefits, however, will be worth a dollar because these benefits are not taxed.

3. False.   The largest number of Americans get health insurance through their employer, meaning that most people with health insurance obtain it outside of an insurance market.

4. False.   The U.S. healthcare system is a mix of private and public financing mechanisms.

5. False.   Healthcare violates many of the conditions of a competitive market, including the fact that there are barriers to entry, imperfect information, and uncertainty.

6. True.   Moral hazard results from insulation against the full financial impact of a loss. If people paid entirely out of pocket, there would be no opportunity for moral hazard.

7. False.   This should be the other way around. Insurance mandates solve the problem of adverse selection, but could make moral hazard a bigger problem.

8. False.   Risk premiums reflect the amount that individuals are willing to pay to avoid the potential of a loss. Actuarially fair premiums accurately reflect the probability of a loss. Thus the total premium that a person is willing to pay for insurance is Total willingness to pay = risk premium + actuarially fair premium.

9. False.   Healthcare is rationed based on price if one is not insured and by policies of insurance companies such as coverage limits, provider limits, and cost sharing if one is insured.

10. True.   Coinsurance and other forms of cost sharing return some price sensitivity to the consumption decision.

Chapter 20

1. False.   A book report summarizes existing knowledge, whereas economics research creates new knowledge.

2. False.   The sources listed are secondary sources; they can be used to get ideas, but they should not be used in a literature review.

3. False.   Collecting data is just a step. Analyzing data based on a research question would be research.

4. False.   Many research questions can be answered using existing data that have already been collected.

5. True.   The different stages in the research process can take considerable amounts of time.

6. False.   A research question should be a single, answerable question.

7. False.   A published finding may be modified or challenged.

8. False.   The goal of economic research is to build the body of economic knowledge.

9. False.   It is the other way around.

10. True.   Economic research tests a hypothesis and attempts to control for changes in factors outside the factor of interest.

Answers to Final Exam

1. B.   A nation's land resource is more than just the area of the nation's territory; it also includes natural resources such as timber harvested from the land, minerals mined from below the land, and fish and shellfish that are caught from the offshore waters. Food is not one of the four economic resources (land, labor, capital, and entrepreneurship/technology).

2. A.   If Kelly studies for two hours, the opportunity cost is the most valuable thing that she gave up in order to study. She couldn't *both* work as a babysitter and work in the campus library, so the most valuable thing she gave up is 2 hours of babysitting at $10 per hour.

3. C.   A consumer must decide whether the additional (or marginal) benefit received from that activity is greater than the additional (or marginal) cost incurred from the activity. When the marginal benefit is weighed against the marginal cost, the consumer is engaged in marginal analysis.

4. D.   Macroeconomic topics are centered on the national or international economy. The Ford factory in Louisville and the Motorola product are both microeconomic topics because they discuss one producer of cars and one producer of cell phones. The market for gasoline is a microeconomic topic because it discusses the price of a single product. The nation's unemployment rate is a macroeconomic topic.

5. C.   Each soda has a price, or marginal cost, of $1.50. Since Sherman will receive $3 of marginal benefit from the third soda, he should buy it. He will not buy the fourth soda because the marginal benefit of $1 falls below the marginal cost. Adding a new column to the table and adding the marginal cost of each soda is a useful way to solve this problem.

6. A.   The equation for the budget constraint states that income (I) is equal to the total spending on good X ($P_X \times X$) plus the total spending on good Y ($P_Y \times Y$). The equation given for Josh's budget constraint, $100 = \$4 \times S + \$20 \times V$, tells us that the price of a can of soup is $4. Thus, with $100 to spend, he could buy at most 25 cans of soup.

7. D.   For a combination to lie on the budget constraint, it must add up to $100. At $4 per can, 10 cans of soup amount to $40 of Josh's income. At $20 per video game, 3 games add up to the remaining $60 of income.

8. B.   Total utility from consuming 3 slices of pizza is the sum of the marginal utility from the first slice (18 utils), the second slice (15 more utils), and the third slice (12 more utils). Adding a column of total utility and doing a running total for each row is a useful way to solve this problem.

9. C.   If there is no price paid for a slice of pizza, the consumer will stop eating pizza at the point where the marginal utility is equal to zero. Because marginal utility declines, the eighth slice of pizza will provide negative marginal utility, which would lower the consumer's total utility. Even though the seventh slice provides zero additional utility, the important point is that it will not *reduce* his utility.

10. C.   A consumer maximizes utility when the marginal utility per dollar is equal for all goods. In this case, the ratio (marginal utility$_{coffee}$)/price$_{coffee}$ must equal (marginal utility$_{bagels}$)/price$_{bagels}$. The marginal utility per dollar is equal to 5 for both goods, so Brody has already found his utility-maximizing combination of coffee and bagels.

11. C.   Cars and trucks are complementary goods with gasoline. When the price of these vehicles goes up, fewer cars and trucks are purchased. And when fewer vehicles are purchased, the demand for gasoline to power them also falls. Choice A is incorrect because a higher price of gasoline does not cause the entire demand for gasoline to fall, it causes only a decrease in quantity demanded. This would be seen in a graph as an upward movement along a fixed demand curve.

12. A.   The law of demand states that, all else equal, when the price of a good rises, fewer units of that good will be demanded. When Stan reduces his driving in the face of rising gasoline prices, he is exhibiting the law of demand.

13. B.   The price elasticity of demand is the percentage change in quantity demanded divided by the percentage change in price. We can use the following formula, with the information that we know, to solve for the component that is unknown:

$$E_d = \frac{\%\Delta Q_d}{\%\Delta P} = \frac{\%\Delta Q_d}{5\%} = 1.5$$

Multiplying 1.5 by 5 percent gives us the answer of 7.5 percent.

14. D.   The cross-price elasticity of demand for peas is equal to the percentage change in quantity of peas demanded divided by the percentage change in the price of carrots. If carrots increase in price and the quantity of peas demanded increases, they must be substitutes. Dividing 4 percent by 2 percent gives us the cross-price elasticity of 2.

15. A.   Total revenue is equal to price times quantity demanded. When the price falls, we know that quantity demanded will rise. For total revenue to rise after a price decrease, it must be the case that quantity demanded increased by a greater degree. This tells us that the demand for laptops is price-elastic.

16. D.   A fixed input is a short-run input that does not change when output changes. For example, when more pizzas are made, more tomato sauce, more labor, and more electricity are needed. However, the size of the kitchen and dining room cannot be changed to sell more pizzas in the short run.

17. B.   Total costs are the sum of fixed costs and variable costs: $TC(Q) = TFC + TVC(Q)$. The variable cost of producing 0 units, $TVC(0)$, will always equal zero, so the total fixed cost is the only cost that is paid when zero units of output are produced. Thus the total fixed cost of $100 is the same cost at zero units as it is at 36 units of output.

18. B.   Marginal cost is the change in total cost divided by the change in output. So when output rises from 8 units to 18 units, marginal cost is $50/10 = $5. But when output rises from 36 to 38 units, marginal cost is $50/2 = $25. This demonstrates that marginal cost is rising; it is an upward-sloping curve.

19. A.   This equation is correct because TVC + TFC = TC. Choice B would have been correct if total product of labor had been divided by labor. Choice C would have been correct if the change in the total product of labor had been divided by the change in labor. Choice D would have been correct if the change in total cost had been divided by the change in output.

20. D.   If the marginal product of labor is falling but is still greater than zero, it simply means that the total product of labor is rising at a slower rate. The total product of labor will be falling only if the marginal product of labor is negative.

21. C.   Raw carrots are a key input in the production of carrot cake. When the carrots become less expensive, it becomes less costly to produce each carrot cake and the supply of carrot cake increases. Remember that the higher price of carrot cake (choice B) does not shift the supply curve, it causes only an upward movement along the supply curve (an increase in the quantity of cake supplied).

22. A.   The price elasticity of supply is the percentage change in quantity supplied divided by the percentage change in price. We can use the following formula, with the information that we know, to solve for the component that is unknown:

$$E_s = \frac{\%\Delta Q_s}{\%\Delta P} = \frac{-6\%}{\%\Delta P} = 2$$

Dividing −6 percent by 2 gives us the answer of −3 percent.

23. A. While supply curves are typically less elastic (steeper) in the short run than in the long run, the law of supply still describes them as upward-sloping in both cases.

24. B. If the price has remained at $2 and more coffee is being produced, the supply curve must have shifted outward.

25. D. As farmers see the alternative crop become less lucrative (the price of cabbage has fallen), more land will be devoted to lettuce production and the supply of lettuce will increase, as shown in Figure 1.

26. B. Market equilibrium is found at the intersection of the supply and demand curves. The equilibrium price is on the vertical axis, and the equilibrium quantity is on the horizontal axis.

27. A. Producer surplus is the area above the supply curve and below the price. This is the area of a triangle that is $6 high ($6 equilibrium price minus where the supply curve intersects the vertical axis, or $0) and 16 units wide. The area of PS = $1/2 \times (\$6)(16) = \$48$. It is important to remember that producer surplus (as well as consumer surplus) is the net value ($) of the output to the producers (or the consumers).

28. D. In order for both price and quantity to increase, demand must increase by itself (recall that if both supply and demand change, then we will be able to determine only the change in either equilibrium price or equilibrium quantity). For the price to be $8 and the quantity to be 20 units, demand must shift to the right. If this good is a normal good, more income would cause demand to increase.

29. D. Price controls and excise taxes will all cause deadweight loss in a market by moving the market quantity away from the competitive equilibrium quantity.

30. C. By itself, an increase in demand will increase price and increase quantity. By itself, a decrease in supply will increase price and decrease quantity. When these two shifts are combined, the price will certainly rise, but the change in quantity is uncertain because we don't know whether the demand shift is stronger than the supply shift, or vice versa.

31. D. If price is below average total cost, losses are occurring in the short run. Losses prompt the exit of firms, and this exit causes the supply curve in the market to shift leftward. As the market price begins to rise, the firms that remain increase their output along their upward-sloping marginal cost curve.

32. A. Profit is found by multiplying the profit-maximizing output by the difference between price and average total cost. The formula for profit is $\Pi = TR - TC$. Since $TC = ATC \times Q$, $TC = 7 \times 20 = 140$. Since $P = 10$ and $Q = 20$, $TR = 10 \times 20 = 200$. Therefore $\Pi = 200 - 140$. Another way you can state this is profit $\Pi = 20 \times (\$10 - \$7)$.

33. B. The long-run outcome in perfect competition is that the price is equal to average total cost. This creates a situation in which economic profit is zero and thus there is no incentive for new firms to enter or existing firms to exit.

34. C. The competitive outcome is efficient, which means that no other outcome can increase one person's welfare without also hurting someone else's. When this outcome is achieved, deadweight loss does not exist.

35. A. The profit-maximizing choice of quantity will be where the price is equal to the marginal cost, so at a price of $7.50, we need to find where marginal cost is $7.50. Total cost (or total variable cost) increases by $7.50 from 2 units of output to 3. so the third unit would be produced *provided* the firm is above the shutdown point. The total variable cost at three units is $13.50 and the total revenue at three units is $22.50 (3 × $7.50), so the firm will not shut down. However, profits are negative: $\Pi = \$22.50 - \$33.50 = -\$11$.

36. C. The demand curve for the monopolist is downward-sloping, so in order to sell more units of output, the price must be lowered on all units. When the price is lowered, revenue is lost on the units that previously sold at a higher price, so the marginal revenue from the additional units sold is less than the price. The marginal revenue curve therefore lies below the demand curve.

37. B. The monopolist produces where MR = MC, and it's also the case that $P >$ MR because the demand curve lies above the marginal revenue curve.

38. D. Perfect price discrimination occurs when each consumer pays a price equal to her willingness to pay. Thus no consumer surplus is earned; all surplus goes to the firm.

39. C. Profit maximization occurs at the output where marginal revenue intersects marginal cost. The price, however, is found by going up to the demand curve. In Figure 4, the intersection of the marginal cost curve and the marginal revenue curve occurs at Q_1, and the $MR(Q_1) = P_5 = MC(Q_1)$. However, the demand curve indicates that the consumer is willing to pay P_1 for Q_1 units, so the price charged is P_1.

40. D. If profit is equal to zero, the price must equal average total cost, and this occurs when demand intersects the ATC curve.

41. D. Because there are short-run profits, new grocery stores will enter the market, thus decreasing the demand for Frannie's product. As her demand curve shifts inward, price falls as she reduces her output. Once profits are equal to zero, no additional firms will enter or exit.

42. A. One of the characteristics shared by monopolistic competition and perfect competition is a lack of barriers to entry. This is why firms in both market structures will break even in the long run.

43. A. A dominant strategy is one that should always be played, no matter what the rival firm is doing. If Kroger expands, Safeway will expand and earn $5 million rather than $3 million from not expanding. If Kroger does not expand, Safeway will expand and earn $10 million rather than $4 million if it did not expand. If Safeway expands, Kroger will expand because it will earn $6 million rather than $3 million by not expanding. If Safeway does not expand, Kroger will still expand to earn $3 million rather than $1 million. So both firms will always expand, no matter what the rival does.

44. B.   Kroger has a dominant strategy to expand, but Safeway does not have a dominant strategy. However, given that Kroger will always expand, Safeway will choose to not expand. This decision allows Safeway to earn $3 million rather than $2 million.

45. C.   When two firms combine to sell more than 70 percent of the product in the market, this is very much an oligopoly. In fact, because these two firms are so dominant, one might even call it a duopoly.

46. C.   The value of the marginal product of labor is the price of the output multiplied by the marginal product of that worker. The marginal product of the fourth worker is 8 units. To calculate for the fourth worker, $VMP_L = P \times MP_L = \$4 \times 8 = \$32$.

47. A.   The firm will hire where the wage is equal to the value of the marginal product. At 3 units, the marginal product of labor is 10 units, and the value of the marginal product of the third unit of labor is $30 ($VMP_L = \$3 \times MP_L = \$30$). Therefore, profit is maximized when 3 workers are hired.

48. D.   To produce her output at the lowest possible cost, Rebecca must hire where the marginal product per dollar is equal for both labor and capital (MP_L/wage = MP_K/rental rate of capital). The marginal product of labor per dollar is 48 units divided by $12, or $4 per unit. The marginal product of capital per dollar is 125 units divided by $25, or $5 per unit. Since hiring another unit of capital will provide more "bang for the buck," she should hire more capital and less labor.

49. B.   A housing boom will increase the demand for the resources, like carpenters, that are needed to build houses. If the demand for carpenters increases, both the wage and employment will increase as well.

50. C.   One of the foundations of our study of the factors of production (like labor) is that demand for a resource is a function of (derived from) the demand for the products being produced by that resource. For example, when the demand for healthcare increases, the demand for nurses increases. When the demand for autos decreases, the demand for autoworkers decreases.

51. A.   Gross domestic product (GDP) is the most widely used measure of the value of a nation's output. Gross domestic product includes all production within the geographic borders of a nation.

52. B.   The circular flow diagram shows how factor markets and output markets facilitate the exchange of production inputs and goods and services between households and firms. Households buy goods and services in output markets and sell labor in factor markets.

53. D.   Recall that using the expenditures approach, GDP = $C + I + G + (X - M)$. When an American buys an imported product made in Japan, that spending is subtracted from U.S. GDP under imports (M) because those dollars actually "leak" out of the American economy and flow into the Japanese economy. This would be counted in the exports of Japan (X), which increases Japanese GDP.

54. C.   A nation's GDP is the sum of domestic consumption spending (C), investment spending (I), government spending (G), and exports to other nations (X), minus the spending on goods imported from other nations (M).

55. C.   Consumption spending is the largest component of GDP. However, it is worth noting that, while it makes up a smaller proportion of GDP, investment spending is the most volatile.

56. D.   The unemployment rate is the ratio of those classified as unemployed (U) divided by the labor force (LF). The labor force is the sum of the employed (E) and the unemployed (U). So we calculate UR = $(U)/(E + U)$.

57. B.   If a person who is without a job is actively seeking work, she is classified as "unemployed." If that person has not been actively seeking work, she is classified as "out of the labor force."

58. D.   This theory may explain why some workers receive wages that exceed the market wage and possibly why unemployment exists. It is costly for firms to hire and train new workers, so paying a worker a higher wage may keep that worker at the firm for a longer period of time. If the higher wage induces higher productivity, and also reduces training and hiring costs, the employer may actually increase profits with this strategy.

59. B.   We need to focus only on those 1,000 citizens that are above the age of 16. Since 200 of them are out of the labor force and 600 are employed, there must be 200 unemployed (1,000 − 600 employed − 200 out of labor force = 200 unemployed). So we calculate UR = $(200)/(600 + 200) = 0.25$ or 25 percent.

60. D.   There are 1,000 citizens above the age of 16 who could be participating in the labor force. The labor force is 800 (600 employed and 200 unemployed), so the LFPR = $(LF)/(population) = 800/1,000 = 0.80$ or 80 percent.

61. B.   While any price index can be used to measure an increase in price, the most widely used is the Consumer Price Index (CPI) because it includes many goods and services that are typically purchased by households.

62. B.   In the base year, no matter what year is actually used as the base year, a price index is equal to 100. So if the CPI is 113 in 2011, it has increased 13 percent since the base year. To find the percentage change, we calculate %ΔCPI = 100 × $(113 − 100)/100 = 13$ percent.

63. D.   When a salary rises by 3 percent from 2010 to 2011, we say that nominal salary increased by this amount. Nominal salary is the salary measured in current dollars, unadjusted for inflation. If the CPI has increased by 2 percent in that time period (from 100 to 102), the increase in nominal salary is reduced by the amount of inflation, and so purchasing power has increased by only about 1 percent. Therefore, Cartman's real salary, in terms of what he can really buy with that salary, increased only 1 percent.

64. D.   Rapid, unexpected inflation hurts people receiving fixed income payments. This also means that any recipient of fixed money payments would be hurt by this unexpected inflation. But if you are a borrower, you are repaying money that was

borrowed when inflation was low and repaying it when inflation is high. Remember that the nominal interest rate is equal to the sum of the real interest rate plus expected inflation. If actual inflation exceeds expected inflation, borrowers repaying their loans will gain some purchasing power.

65. D.   In the model of the Phillips curve, the long-run equilibrium is when the economy is at full employment. This occurs when the long-run Phillips curve is vertical and intersecting the short-run Phillips curve.

66. A.   An increase in consumer wealth causes consumption spending (C) to increase. If any of the components of AD increase $(C, I, G,$ or $[X - M])$ this will shift AD to the right. An increase in interest rates would make investment (I) more expensive and decrease investment.

67. C.   All three of these effects describe why the AD curve is downward-sloping. A drop in the price level will lead to a decrease in interest rates, which would increase aggregate demand. When the price level decreases, households feel wealthier and the amount of consumption they do will increase. When the price level in the United States increases, U.S. exports are relatively cheaper for other countries, and the amount of exports will increase.

68. A.   Higher consumer optimism increases consumption spending and shifts the AD curve to the right. The short-run impact of this shift is that the price level and real output (GDP) both increase along the SRAS curve.

69. B.   Because the SRAS and AD curves intersect to the left of the LRAS, the economy is operating with a recessionary gap. This means that real GDP is currently below full-employment GDP, and thus the unemployment rate exceeds the natural rate of unemployment. The economy would be at full employment if SRAS and AD intersected on the LRAS curve.

70. B.   If the economy is allowed to self-correct, the recession would cause factor prices to fall because factors of production (like labor) are underutilized. When this occurs, the SRAS curve shifts to the right, real output increases (unemployment decreases), and the price level decreases along the AD curve.

71. D.   Fiat money is money that is declared to be legal currency by the government. It has no intrinsic value (like gold), so it cannot be used as a commodity.

72. C.   When cash is moved from one's home to a checking account, nothing happens to the quantity of money in either M1 or M2. Remember that cash is already included in M1 and M1 is included in M2.

73. A.   The money multiplier is the inverse of the reserve requirement. So if the reserve requirement is 0.05, the money multiplier MM = 1/0.05 = 20.

74. A.   The money multiplier MM = 1/0.05 = 20, so if $1,000 is deposited into a bank, this should multiply total demand deposits by a factor of 20 to $20,000.

75. D.   The theory of liquidity preference models the money market with a downward-sloping money demand curve and a vertical money supply curve. Equilibrium interest rates are found at the intersection. If the demand for money increases, the new interest rate will rise along the money supply curve.

76. A. This is one of the foundations of classical theory. The economy will self-correct in the long run at full-employment GDP because all prices are flexible in the long run.

77. C. If the economy is in a recession, fiscal policy should be aimed at increasing aggregate demand. This can happen with more government spending, lower taxes, or both. An increase in the money supply is appropriate during a recession, but this is monetary, not fiscal, policy.

78. D. With the MPC = 0.90, the government spending multiplier is equal to 1/0.90 = 10. This means that if government spending increases by $5 billion, it will multiply by a factor of 10 to ultimately increase spending by $50 billion.

79. C. Open market operations involve the buying and selling of Treasury bonds by the Federal Reserve. In a period of high inflation, the economy needs to cool off. Selling bonds decreases the money supply and increases interest rates. As interest rates rise, investment spending and consumption spending tend to fall, decreasing aggregate demand and the price level. Choice D is not correct because open market operations do not change the interest rate directly.

80. A. In the long run, we believe that a recession will self-correct. With weak aggregate demand, output is currently below full employment and factors of production are underutilized. As factor prices adjust downward, the SRAS curve shifts to the right. Output returns to full employment at a lower price level.

81. B. Suppose the nation was producing 5,000 candies, but wanted to switch to producing 1,000 cars. The gain of 1,000 cars comes at a cost of 5,000 candies, or 5 candies lost for every 1 car gained. You can also solve for this by setting 5,000 candies = 1,000 cars and solving for cars.

82. D. It costs England 1 unit of bread to make 1 unit of butter. It costs Ireland $\frac{1}{2}$ unit of bread to make 1 unit of butter. This means that Ireland can make butter at lower cost, giving Ireland a comparative advantage in butter. It costs England 1 unit of butter to make 1 unit of bread. It costs Ireland 2 units of butter to make 1 unit of bread. Thus England has a comparative advantage in bread.

83. C. Ireland has a comparative advantage in butter, and England has a comparative advantage in bread. England will export bread to Ireland, and Ireland will export butter to England. Of course this means that Ireland imports bread from England and England imports butter from Ireland.

84. C. Stronger popularity of American-made goods in other nations will translate into a stronger demand for U.S. dollars. All else equal, as the demand for the dollar increases (shifts to the right), the price of a dollar rises. Since the price of a dollar is measured in how many units of a foreign currency it takes to buy a dollar, the dollar is said to be appreciating (rising in value) in this situation.

85. A. The sale of an American-made T-shirt to Canada means that money from Canada is flowing into the United States. The current account tabulates short-term transactions like the import and export of goods and services.

86. B. Public goods are those that are nonrival and nonexcludable. A police department provides services to the entire community, not just to those adults who pay their

taxes. And one person's use of police services does not deny another person the use of police services. All of the other options are private goods because they are both rival and excludable.

87. B. The graph shows that the marginal social cost is greater than the marginal private cost. This tells us that there are additional costs to society that are not captured by the firms' production costs. At the market equilibrium quantity, MPC = MPB = MSB, but the MSC is greater, which is referred to as a negative externality.

88. C. With a negative externality, too much of the good is being produced by the market, so a per-unit tax equal to the vertical distance between MSC and MPC should remedy the market failure. A subsidy would only worsen the problem by causing the market to produce even more of this good.

89. C. A positive externality exists when production or consumption of a good causes a third party (you in this case) to receive a spillover benefit. When the beekeeper's bees pollinate your cherry trees, they provide just such a benefit to you.

90. D. The next ton of pollution emitted causes both additional cost (MSC) to society and additional benefit (MSB) because goods are produced along with the pollution. It is efficient if we can limit pollution to the level where MSB = MSC.

91. B. Now that Mr. Pham has a very good health insurance policy, he feels that he can engage in a risky endeavor like climbing Mount Everest. If he should get sick or injured, all of the financial risk falls on his health insurance company. This is an example of moral hazard.

92. A. Insurance companies require the patient to pay a deductible on any medical treatments they seek. By putting some of the financial risk on the patient (Betty), this helps to reduce the moral hazard issue.

93. C. Since 10 people (1 percent of 1,000) are expected to get sick, the insurance company expects to incur losses of $10 \times \$200,000 = \$2$ million. Dividing this by 1,000 policyholders amounts to $2,000 per person. So when each person pays the loading fee of $100, the premium charged is the loading fee plus the actuarially fair premium = $2,100.

94. C. Because healthy people figure that they won't need to use health insurance, many may opt to go without. This leaves only the sick people in the pool for health insurance.

95. B. A copayment is a fee that the patient must pay at the doctor's office for medical treatment. When the patient is required to assume some of the financial risk, the patient will be less likely to visit the doctor for small or frivolous treatments.

96. D. The literature review process allows the student to learn more about the research history of his topic so that he can discover where his research might contribute to the set of knowledge.

97. A. If we have a hypothesis about how the world works, we must gather data and rigorously test whether the hypothesis is sound or not. This allows economic research to follow the scientific method rather than just publish conclusions based on weak or anecdotal evidence.

98. D.   This is a testable hypothesis because Terrence could gather data on how many cold fountain drinks he sold on each day and the high temperature in his town that day. If he found a significantly strong positive relationship between the two variables, he might confirm his hypothesis.

99. D.   When Raquel is using the relevant data to statistically measure the relationship between her two variables, she is engaging in empirical analysis.

100. A.   Most research today involves empirical analysis of how economic variables are related to each other.

Index